FROM
MISERY TO

Mastery

A REVOLUTIONARY NEW
TREATMENT FOR ANXIETY & DEPRESSION

RICHARD SILVESTRI, PH.D.
& JILLIAN RACINE, PH.D.

Robert D. Reed Publishers • Bandon, OR

Robert D. Reed Publishers
P.O. Box 1992
Bandon, OR 97411
Phone: 541-347-9882; Fax: -9883
E-mail: 4bobreed@msn.com
Website: www.rdrpublishers.com

Editor: Carol Cartaino
Designer: Amy Cole
Cover: Chris Seelbaugh

Soft Cover ISBN: 978-1-944297-73-2
EBook ISBN: 978-1-944297-74-9

Library of Congress Control Number: 2020942957

Designed and Formatted in the United States of America

The content of this book is not intended to be a substitute for professional medical advice, diagnosis, or treatment. Always seek the advice of your physician or other qualified health provider with any questions you may have regarding any medical concerns or conditions.

DEDICATION

This book is dedicated to my wife, Susan, and daughters, Kate and Jillian. They never cease to inspire me!!

This book is dedicated to my husband, David, and our son, Logan, for their unwavering love and support.

ACKNOWLEDGMENTS

I would like to acknowledge the inspiration and support I received from my family—my wife of 48 years, Susan, and my daughters Kate and Jillian.

There are many other people who contributed in countless ways to the creation of this book, including my clients, who trusted me with the most private aspects of their lives; my colleagues, who shared their clinical expertise with me; and my relatives and friends who provided a sounding board for my thoughts and feelings about my work.

I especially would like to thank Bonnie Hawk for reviewing the manuscript in great detail and suggesting many edits and ideas. Dr. Harvey Milkman and Dr. Lloyd Sederer provided many helpful personal communications about the book and its contents. My assistant, Stacey Ford, was invaluable in helping to organize the research and case histories, and the technical advice from numerous consultants.

I am grateful as well to Kenneth Axen, Ph.D., and Kathleen Axen, Ph.D., for their contributions to the creation and design of the front cover, and Amy Cole for the handsome interior design of the book.

A very special thank-you to my editor, Carol Cartaino, for her tireless attention to the quality of the text, her help with book production, service as my literary agent, and above all for prodding me to put the best of all I know into this volume.

CONTENTS

ABOUT THE AUTHORS

RICHARD SILVESTRI, Ph.D., has been in practice as a clinical psychologist for more than forty years, specializing in the treatment of depression and anxiety-based disorders. Most clinicians do not spend a lot of time treating patients. They may do 10–15 hours a week and spend the rest of their time in administration, in meetings, supervising interns, etc. Dr. Silvestri has done far more hours of actual therapy than most—thousands and thousands. He has been called one of the top fourteen therapists in the country by *Cosmopolitan* magazine.

Dr. Silvestri has also been an assistant professor in the New Jersey state college system. Prior to this, he was the director of the Graduate Program in Psychology at William Paterson College (1973–1978), and Senior Psychologist for the Family Courts of New York City (1975–1979).

Dr. Silvestri has authored two previous books. Through his private practice and clinical consulting, Dr. Silvestri developed a method of treatment for anxiety that has become the treatment of choice within the therapeutic community for many anxiety-related problems. His first book, *CT: The Astounding New Confrontation Therapy* (William Morrow, 1978), presented that technique with great success.

How to Fall Out of Love...and Land on Your Feet (written with Bryna Taubman, St. Martin's Press, 1995) provided readers with a new and highly effective approach to the problems of letting go of an unsatisfying, abusive, or mismatched relationship. It sold well in this country and was published in Polish, Chinese, Czech Republic, and Brazilian editions.

In addition to his two earlier books, Dr. Silvestri has written articles for both popular and scholarly publications, and he has been cited as an expert source in many national magazines. He has appeared on radio and both national and local television to promote his books.

He is married with two daughters and lives in New Jersey.

JILLIAN RACINE, Ph.D., directs a private practice in Austin that specializes in the treatment of obsessive compulsive disorder (OCD), panic, anxiety, and related conditions. She utilizes evidence-based approaches such as Cognitive-Behavioral Therapy (CBT) and Exposure and Response Prevention (ERP).

She received her bachelor's, master's, and doctorate degrees in psychology from Pennsylvania State University. Dr. Racine is also a graduate of the International OCD Foundation's Behavior Therapy Training Institute (BTTI), an intensive training program for the treatment of OCD and related disorders. She has also worked with the Hill Country OCD Treatment Center, which provides intensive outpatient services to clients with severe OCD.

Dr. Racine has partnered with the University of Texas and The Pennsylvania State University on mental health research. She has published several academic articles and presented at national conferences on evidence-based approaches for mental health treatment.

INTRODUCTION

This book is the product of two well-experienced clinicians working together. I have been a clinical psychologist for more than forty years, and have now been joined in the field by my daughter Jillian. In recent years we have spent many hours discussing cases and different possible therapeutic approaches to them. We finally decided to combine our experience and knowledge and collaborate on a self-help resource.

Anxiety and depression, and the other mental states and problems that are rooted in them, are some of the biggest concerns people have about mental health here in the early 21st century. I have been treating those who struggle with these issues for half a century now. My thinking has a strong tendency to go vertical—I keep plugging away at a problem or dilemma until I get to the point where I understand it thoroughly and achieve a resolution that is so satisfying that it no longer haunts me. I don't have the time to do this with everything, but I make the time when it comes to the issues about which I give others advice.

For example, I couldn't accept the idea, as suggested by Freud, that phobias were best treated by seeking insight into a person's family and history, especially unresolved sexual issues. At first, to treat phobias, I tried using simple desensitization techniques, which seemed to work well on humans as well as my initial animal subjects. Then I realized that helping a person to confront the object or situation they feared worked even better than simply exposing them to it. Later yet, I discovered that if the person voluntarily confronted the feared object, that was even better. More recently, I determined that incorporating how the person felt about the feared object was also very helpful, as was considering their personality and predispositions. And finally, combining all of these factors, along with raising the goal from "good enough to get by" to mastery when that was called for, was ultimately the best treatment of all.

In the following chapters, the techniques and goals of treatment are designed to achieve a practical and reasonable level of improvement for the client who wants to overcome their fear or depression so that he or she can regain an acceptable level of functioning. But for those who want to achieve the greatest improvement possible, so that they can be perhaps even better than they were before they were injured or traumatized, a course of therapy is also presented aimed at enabling the person to achieve mastery.

In the seven chapters of this book on anxiety disorders, we go beyond the traditional approach to dealing with the many manifestations of this problem. There are three components to anxiety—the physiological, behavioral, and psychological.

The physiological is how your body reacts to it.

The behavioral is what you do. Do you run away, approach, or avoid the feared object or situation, or try to live with it?

The psychological is how you feel about what you fear. Do you like to swim, hike, or speak in public, despite the fact that it causes you physical distress or you tend to avoid it whenever you can? It is possible to like something despite fearing it in the sense that you admire it or find it attractive intellectually, or in some other way.

The current treatment for most anxieties, which is Exposure Therapy, focuses mainly on the physiological. In these chapters we discuss how you can significantly improve on this by focusing on not only the physiological, but also on the behavioral and psychological variables, and how this can be done.

A quick look at the history of the treatment of fear and anxiety will be helpful here. Early in the history of psychotherapy, around the turn of the nineteenth century, psychologists and psychiatrists were puzzled by clients who seemed to have irrational fears. Many different theories sprang up as to the cause of this, including those of Freud, Harry Stack Sullivan, and Alfred Adler. In the early sixties a movement started to look at fears and anxieties more from a behavioral standpoint. Wasn't it possible to just extinguish them without considering all manner of complex theories? Treat the symptoms, not the cause?

In this vein, in 1968 I published my master's thesis at Kent State, the basic point of which was that these fears could be eradicated simply by exposing the experimental animal (rat or pigeon or whatever) to the feared object repeatedly. The repeated presentation of the feared object in the absence of consequences would constitute what is known as extinction, and should eradicate the fear. In fact this seemed to happen and the studies published showed that this in fact was what was going on.

In 1978 my book *CT: The Astounding New Confrontation Therapy* came out, which advanced the theory that while desensitization using exposure was good, adding a behavioral element would be even better. I suggested that we do this by having the person confront the feared object, not just be exposed to it. By confronting it I meant face it, touch it, be in the presence of it—have some kind of behavioral involvement with it. The behavioral component would enable the person to show they had developed some confidence in dealing with the feared object. Exposure was good, but adding the behavioral component enhanced the therapeutic value of the process and had a stronger desensitizing effect.

The third component we are suggesting adding now, mastery, incorporates our own decades of clinical experience into the perspective, as well as the insights explained in Chapters One and Two. This will take care of what we refer to as the psychological component. If this is done, then the three components—physiological, behavioral, and psychological—are all addressed, which gives a person what we call mastery. It also provides an in-depth way of looking at any problem or disorder. I can assure you that when you approach the resolution of fear and anxiety from all three of these directions, you will get a far more comprehensive and effective treatment than if you focused solely on the physiological.

The chapters on anxiety in these pages will show you how to overcome anxiety in its many forms, simple and complex anxiety of all kinds—including worry, stress, phobias, post-traumatic stress disorder, obsessive-compulsive disorder, anxiety complicated by other emotions, and all the rest.

As for that other big affliction of our times, depression, about fifty percent of the depressions we see in clinical practice are based on chemical imbalances such as bipolar disorder, while the other fifty percent seem to be the result of situational and circumstantial factors. This book discusses the use of desensitization with depression and explains the modifications in the process that need to be made in order for the process to work.

> The first phase of treatment for overcoming one's fears and depressive thoughts and feelings is desensitization, or gradually blunting of these feelings—Exposure Therapy. The second stage is regaining the ability to approach and not having to avoid confronting the cause of your fears and anxieties (Confrontation Therapy). The third stage is overcoming the negative feelings associated with the feared object or situation. All three parts have to be resolved in order to achieve mastery.

The chapters on depression introduce a technique we feel enables a person to treat mild to moderate depression of a psychological nature in pretty much the same way as you would treat grief. Most grief responses are resolved in three to six months; very intense grief such as over the loss of a child, takes longer, maybe several years. But the resolution of grief is in general more effective and faster than the resolution of most psychological depressions, such as from the loss of a job or other things. We explain why this is so and offer a technique that will enable you to get the results, the speed and effectiveness, of the treatment for grief applied to depression of a mild to moderate level. This is a significant improvement in the treatment of depression, and it can be done on a self-help basis. In Chapters Ten through Twelve we break depression down in terms of whether it is based on loss, guilt, grudges, the urge for revenge, or whatever. And then we demonstrate how all of the factors that are part of mastery come together to deal with these things.

In this book designed for the treatment of psychological problems in the mild to moderate range on a self-help basis, we are not attempting to treat the severely ill. Nonetheless, in many cases even the severely ill can benefit from knowing, and working with, their traits and predispositions.

This book incorporates decades of clinical experience with a great many different problems and different people in many walks of life, as well as knowledge of the research and the literature on every issue. We have also included many case histories to help bring to life and bring home the points we are making.

When you add all of this together you have a treatment that far exceeds what is commonly available. When you look at problems and focus on them this way, problem-solving is far superior to what could be achieved with a cookie-cutter approach. And you will learn in the course of the book how this can be done relatively effortlessly after a while.

This book is meant to be another step forward in the treatment of psychological issues and dilemmas. Hopefully it will help you find a brighter and calmer tomorrow.

CHAPTER ONE

THE PILLARS OF PERSONALITY
THE HEART OF WHO WE ARE

S hortly after I graduated, with my degree and licenses all in order, I accepted a position with the New York City Family Courts as a forensic psychologist. At the time I was just looking for somewhere to enter the field. I didn't know if I would like forensic psychology, and as it turned out, I discovered later that I preferred individual therapy, and spent most of my professional life in that, except for a few years as a university professor.

Forensic psychologists use their specialized knowledge to assess and help treat prisoners and offenders, as well as victims and those who work in judicial institutions. They gauge individuals' needs and assess any risks that they may pose to themselves and other people.

Forensic psychologists play an important part in the conviction and sentencing of criminals by creating psychological profiles, giving evidence where necessary, and offering expert advice to parole boards. They may also help make therapy and rehabilitation plans for the individuals they assess.

But this was my first job, and I applied myself to it assiduously. When interviewing people I didn't have much time with them, for the most part only about a half-hour. Many were Spanish speaking, and since I knew little Spanish, I was assigned an assistant to translate. This was meant to give me some idea of the person's lifestyle and circumstances, as well as cultural issues that I wouldn't necessarily be aware of otherwise.

The interviews were difficult for other reasons. Most of the time the interviewees told me what they thought the court wanted to hear. If I asked about anything that might be considered unusual activity, or whether they might have been doing something negative like getting into debt over their heads, they would just say no—they managed everything in their lives effectively and appropriately. Most psychologists are usually in the opposite situation—people come to them looking for help and want to give them all the information they can.

Another problem was that most of my experience in school had been diagnosing people who had severe pathologies—bipolar disorder, schizophrenia, depression, high anxiety, phobias, and the like. I knew what questions to ask if someone had a serious psychological problem, but most of these people didn't have that.

Given all of this, it was difficult to diagnose them. Especially since I had to go on the stand after each evaluation and submit to Q and A, be grilled and cross-examined by the experts on the other side, who asked some tough questions. Often it was not easy to figure out how to respond to some of the things I was being asked. Such as, "Does this person seem responsible, conscientious, and reliable; is he telling the truth?" Most psychologists would find it difficult to answer such questions after a brief thirty-minute interview with a person who might well be motivated to conceal the truth.

I was pretty much on my own here, and I ended up coming up with a system that worked for me. I decided to diagnose them in terms of their characteristics, what they normally did and liked to do, their usual behavior, their tendencies. This was pretty straightforward. When I quizzed them on things like this, they would give candid answers for the most part, having no idea of what I was looking for, and since in that setting it was hardly obvious how to answer any of this.

In the decades since, I have steadily improved upon this method. My system is based on the most significant *traits* that make up a person's personality. Traits are inborn biases in our behavior, things we are inclined to do by genetic disposition. In other words, out of the whole spectrum of things we might possibly do in a given situation, what those little molecules in our genetic coding will prompt us to do. Since traits are built right into us; they can't be hidden or easily overridden— they will sooner or later show themselves. Thus if you know what a person's traits are, you will have a very dependable idea of what they are like, and what they are most likely to do in most situations.

THE TRAIT ANALYSIS SYSTEM

There has been an enormous amount of research on traits, and you can see traits in children who are only three or four years old.

After considering the entire constellation of traits that human beings can have, after trial and error, and a review of the extensive research in the field, I narrowed the list down to the five most validated traits—the ones that were the most important, in terms of understanding what makes people "tick," what most affects their relationships with others, and most influences what they actually do from day to day.

These are the big five, what I call the "pillars of personality"—the traits that have the greatest influence on personality. Along with five less important, or secondary traits that may merit paying special attention to, depending on what you are most concerned about when assessing others, these make up what I call the trait analysis system. Most traits exist as a continuum, from one pole of behavior in a particular area to another. With this system, you can identify not only which traits a person has, but approximately what level of those traits, which can make a big difference in their behavior, and in their relationships with others.

In my office, when I see a client for the first time, I build a picture of their personality from these ten traits, and even if I don't see them again for years, I will have a clear and reliable concept of their personality and inclinations. Likewise, with this system, you will be able to speedily assess others for either personal or business reasons, and narrow them down to the ones who are really worth knowing better, or with whom you could possibly build a future. You will also be able to better understand yourself—your psyche and temperament—and the ways in which your most conspicuous traits may affect any problems that surface in your life.

To develop the best, customized approach to treating a person, or for them to treat themselves successfully for anxiety, depression, PTSD, or other psychological problems, understanding personality is key. You need to understand a person's traits to know how to approach the treatment of different conditions in different people most effectively.

Also, many problems and issues that end up in therapy involve other personalities as well, and knowing how to analyze those personalities will give a lot of insight into where the problem may lie. Understanding traits makes it much easier to see how different people deal with different situations differently depending on their traits. If you know a person's traits you have an incredible advantage in dealing with them.

The first step in determining how to design a treatment approach to your problem, whether it is anxiety, depression, or something else, is determining which are your dominant traits. A careful reading of the following chapter should enable you to do this. In Chapter Two we will then consider how your traits would be expected to affect the results and success of your treatment.

Later in this book I discuss a number of cases of how different personalities and traits come together and how this can give insight into the nature of a problem and affect the nature of its resolution.

Let's take a look at the pillars now, in order of their importance.

THE FIRST PILLAR: CHARACTER

In this system character means just what it does when we use the word in everyday life: Is this a good person? Does he or she have all of those Scout qualities like truthfulness, honesty, and trustworthiness? Can you depend on them—are they sincere, genuine, and loyal? Character is the bedrock trait, because no matter what other attractions or qualities someone may have, if they lack this quality, all of the rest may well end up not mattering much. By assessing character, in personal or business relationships, you will be able to zero in on one of the first things you are looking for: truthfulness and trustworthiness. Is this person who they say they are, and will they do what they claim they will do?

Character is a complex of all the attributes that determine a person's moral and ethical actions and reactions. Adjectives commonly used to describe good character include: reliable, sincere, genuine, moral, ethical.

In the case of many of the traits described in this chapter, our opinion can change if we hear comments from friends or relatives that suggest that our perception of the person in some context was not accurate and it was based on the circumstances at the time.

There is one characteristic, however, that seems to be in a sense indelible. That characteristic is trust. For example, if you know someone for many years and have come to trust them and then one day you have an experience with them in which they prove that they are not trustworthy, you will probably change your opinion of that person overnight. You will no longer describe that person as trustworthy and tell friends that you don't think they're trustworthy. You can know a person for decades and then happen to see him reaching for your purse, or going through your drawers, and that's it. One bad experience and trust is out the window, unlikely to be regained.

The reason for all of this is that trust is so important to survival. Trust is one of the issues the brain is really concerned about. It's not difficult to change your opinion of someone as being an introvert or extrovert—there's usually no major risk in doing so. But there is a big risk in doing that with regard to issues related to whether a person is trustworthy or not. Our brain puts a high priority on trust, and has a lot of ways to judge trustworthiness. For example, the wider someone's face is, the less trustable they are seen to be. Face wideness has to do with amount of testosterone a child receives in the womb. Thus we usually trust a woman before a man. For another example, as one's mental energy rises, they may well be seen as not trustworthy. According to the brain, speed is equated with insincerity, for example, the fast-talking salesman. An agreeable person, as described later in this chapter, has a group-oriented, collaborative mentality, so they would be seen as trustworthy. A person who is very independent and self-absorbed would seem to be too selfish and therefore not trustworthy.

Even those hard to eradicate "first impressions" originate here. First impressions, we've always heard, are very important and hard to change. If you find that your first impression of someone is that they are not trustworthy, it's difficult to change that impression. First impressions determine how we will think about someone, and our first impression stays, although the second may influence it some. But contrary later examples do not necessarily change our impression or opinion.

First impressions are enduring because in nature, people didn't necessarily survive to have a chance to form a second impression.

> If you know an extrovert and call him up one day and he tells you he wants to stay home today and read a book, you don't change your view that he is an extrovert, even if this happens several times.
>
> But with trust, it only takes one instance to change your whole opinion of someone. Few other things have the profound effect that mistrust does.

In a psychological study, a group of women was asked to see how many men they could attract in a dating situation by using various behavioral techniques that professionals taught them. Another group was told to just be sincere and genuine when being approached by men in a similar situation. It was found that women who were honest and sincere attracted many more men than women who used the techniques and approaches that were shown to be very effective by professionals.

Other studies have found that if you think a person is not trustworthy and then you subsequently hear something that would suggest that the person is—for example from a friend who plays chess with that person, you may change your opinion of how trustworthy that person is when it comes to chess, but not your overall impression that the person is not trustworthy.

It's hard to sustain a relationship with someone of bad character. When a person is selfish and self-aggrandizing, doesn't play by the rules, and every so often drops a nuclear bomb of behavior on you, it is off-putting, to say the least.

Character also has a great bearing on the issue of respect. Bad character leads to contempt. Once someone expresses contempt for another person, it's hard to come back from that. When you hear this, all is probably lost.

Character always counts, and only more so when we are dealing with people online. Character is the most important issue in the often enigmatic world of online dating, for instance, the one that causes the most concern and problems, in early contacts as well as eventual relationships. People often misrepresent themselves online, either deliberately or through wishful thinking. It's been said that "computer communications of all kinds are inherently disinhibiting," and online daters prove that by often lying about their height, weight, age, income, education level, occupation, and marital and parental status, as well as what they look like.

We may persuade ourselves to look the other way, or even have an attraction to "bad boys," or "bad girls" at times. But bad character has a profound effect on interpersonal relationships—it's hard to deal with and live with, and hard or impossible to change. The most skilled psychologist doesn't even try. Trust issues are the #1 reason that women seek divorce. In second marriages and relationships, character often becomes the #1 criterion in a mate, even if it wasn't the first time around...though it should have been.

Character is very important in business and hiring, too, because bad character—what you do and how you do it—leads to bad outcomes and bad feelings, even lawsuits. When someone has bad character in a business relationship, they can't be trusted. It's very hard to turn that around, unless you can demonstrate clearly that the facts were erroneous.

People with poor character can be charming. They often tell a good story that seems to hold together, and they have an answer for everything. But they are usually self-absorbed and irresponsible, mainly concerned with meeting their own needs.

They are often very spontaneous, since they are not constricted by the rules and values of society. They flit from one thing to another, often taking the path of least resistance. People with poor character often get into awkward situations, and then just leave them and go on to the next. They think nothing of taking advantage of someone else to get out of a tight spot they have gotten themselves into. They always have an excuse, never accept responsibility for anything.

Most people do a certain amount of convenience lying, such as to take a shortcut around some complicated issue when there is nothing to be gained from going into an involved discourse on the subject. There is no harm meant. People with poor character, however, will do purposeful lying, which is designed to give them an advantage.

Low scorers here usually associate with other people of low character, which means they will also have friends you won't like, and they often have addiction problems as well.

PILLAR #2: TENDENCY TO OPTIMISM OR DEPRESSION

Optimism or hopefulness is the trait that keeps us going—when we miss the bus, when we don't get the promotion, when a boyfriend or girlfriend dumps us. Optimism tells us that this is only temporary, that things will get better, that tomorrow is a new day. We all have to face disappointments and frustrations. We may groan or vent or even host a brief pity party, but then we get up and get going again. We move on. We bounce back. We know we can't afford to let a down day turn into a down week or month.

A hopeful person is always looking ahead, looking for a way to make things work. He or she brings hope to a relationship as well. A hopeful mate is more likely to reach out, to encourage you and help you recover from difficult situations.

> Although statistically the chances of something going wrong in any undertaking are greater than of everything going well, our brain favors optimism. About eighty percent of people are optimistic. This despite the fact that if you asked a group of pessimists and optimists both to predict the result of something, the pessimists' predictions would be more likely to be accurate. Optimists may stand a good chance of failing, but they might also discover some important insight or a better way to do something that would benefit the species as a whole.

At the other end of this spectrum is depression. We can all be depressed at times for specific reasons, such as the death of a loved one, the loss of a job, the end of a relationship, or just the latest inroads of age we see in the mirror. Depressions like this are temporary, though, if the cause is something like the death of a child, that "temporary" could be years or even decades. And some people are depressed at times because of their brain chemistry, such as those with bipolar disorder.

But there is also such a thing as a depressive personality, a general tendency to be down or depressed, regardless of circumstances. Whether a person is optimistic or depressed is second in our list of pillars because few of us are eager to deal with others who are for the most part morose, negative, irritable, easily frustrated, pessimistic, and seemingly not interested in much beyond whatever they may be silently brooding about now.

A new business or personal relationship may pick them up, so that they seem more outgoing and energetic, but all of this is due to the boost of the courtship stage, and conceals the underlying depression.

Depressives tend to live in the past, and a person with a depressive tendency also often sees him or herself as a victim—they're never to blame for anything. They usually have a general feeling of hopelessness as well, so they're not too likely to change. A depressive personality is self-absorbed and tends to drain energy from others. If you have a problem, a depressive mate or partner will probably just make things worse.

A person with a depressive personality may function in jobs and other requirements of everyday life better than someone with severe depression for other reasons, but they are no fun to coexist with. It's difficult to engage them—they don't respond well to conversational gambits and are not inclined to initiate things or share their thoughts with you. In fact, they may draw you into arguments as a way of encouraging you to avoid them. There is a big burden on their mate, who not only has to live amongst all of this gloom and doom, and be deprived of the pleasure of an enthusiastic partner, but must be alert for sudden changes in the emotional climate, since depressives do have mood cycles at times.

Whether or not someone has an overall depressive tendency is a key question.

For more about depression, see Chapters Ten through Thirteen.

PILLAR #3: ENERGY LEVEL

We all know a high-energy person from a low-energy one—we have plenty of both of these among our friends, relatives, and acquaintances. What we may not know is why this trait is important enough to be number three in the list of things we need to be aware of in assessing others. Differences in energy level are one of the leading reasons for the breakup of marriages and partnerships and other relationships, because a high/low energy union is one in which both parties are sure to end up feeling cheated.

A high-energy person is always on the move, mentally and physically. She is bright, confident, optimistic, and expansive—eager to go places and do things. She talks fast, thinks fast, and has a long list of goals that she works hard to achieve. Her hobbies are usually energetic ones, and she would far rather play a sport than watch it. She is willing and able to leap obstacles at a single bound, because her can-do attitude enables her to overlook differences and overcome difficulties. This is the person who, when she comes to visit, after a long day of touring the local attractions and a full dinner, will decide this would be a great time to de-junk and reorganize your garage.

The low-energy person, as you might imagine, is much more sedentary. While the high energy person is off playing tennis or basketball or hiking through the mountains photographing wildflowers or looking for elk, he will be sitting home happily reading, playing a video game, or looking over his comic collection. When it comes to sports, pool is about his speed. He is not all that achievement oriented—usually much more interested in how he can be comfortable in and enjoy the here and now. And he tends to be more focused on himself than on others and outside activities.

When a high and low energy person get together, the person with high energy ends up feeling as if he is lugging his partner through life. He is convinced that the relationship is unfair, and that he is contributing far more than his share to it. "And my partner doesn't even appreciate or acknowledge all that I do!"

The low-energy person is not oblivious to this. He knows that his mate thinks of him as a slug—always a day late and a dollar short—and he is aware of this even when the mate is not present. He also has his own view of the situation: "Whatever I do, it's never enough. She's a dynamo; I'm not. I need to rest and decompress; she doesn't need that."

The low-energy person doesn't see any reason to feel indebted, because he thinks that whatever good the high-energy person accomplishes is more than offset by her condescending attitude, and the unrelenting pressure. The low-energy person also feels that his mate takes on many tasks and priorities that are not really necessary, and that all in all he tolerates her far more gracefully than she does him.

So we probably shouldn't be surprised that it's the low-energy person who usually initiates the breakup or divorce.

People who suffer from depression usually have a notably low energy level.

PILLAR #4: AGREEABLE VERSUS INDEPENDENT-MINDED

Another big difference between people is whether they are agreeable or independent-minded—very cooperative and easy to get along with, or entirely intent on going their own way, and living their lives by their lights alone. This trait is rooted in a person's general level of anxiety (see Chapter Seven), which makes a great deal of difference in how they are and act.

A mildly elevated level of anxiety, five or six on a scale of one to ten, produces a pretty likeable person—the agreeable man or woman. The psychologists often call these people "other-person oriented," because they are so empathetic and sympathetic with others that everyone feels good around them. Since people with high-anxiety personalities already feel a little anxious, they go all out to avoid conflict and stress in their surroundings. A very large part of those surroundings consist of other people, and high-anxious people are incredibly attuned to how those around them are thinking and feeling. This enables them to head off interpersonal problems before they happen, and to build relationships quickly and easily.

At home or at work, with family or friends, they are consummate diplomats and the perfect shoulders to cry on—they are always trying to keep the peace and understand the problems of others. In almost any situation, they would rather get along than get their way. They are good planners, too—they always have their eyes peeled and their ears to the ground, and are always looking ahead and anticipating.

Since they always want to blend in and avoid making waves, and are eager to build themselves a secure environment, their lives tend to proceed in somewhat of a straight line. They educate themselves well and develop many skills to make themselves useful. They pick a dependable job, work hard at it, and stick with it, even if it is not the best paying or most challenging. They are loyal and long-range employees and mates, and tend not to make big changes in their lives until they are forced upon them. Agreeable people act as sort of the mortar of society, helping people of all types blend and work together better.

On the negative side, agreeable-minded people are often frustrated because they see themselves as so influenced by others that they often fail to act in their own best interests. An agreeable person may mislead people into thinking she likes them when she is just trying to be nice. And once involved in a relationship, since she has trouble saying no, the agreeable person finds it hard to get out. By the time they are fifty, just about every agreeable person has gotten entangled with someone she shouldn't have, and paid the price. Screening prospective partners is extra-important for an agreeable-minded person.

The most challenging problem agreeable people face is the feelings they have toward themselves. Because of their compelling tendency to be overly concerned about others, how hard they find it to say no, and their habit of neglecting themselves, they often have a negative view of themselves and low self-esteem. It is not easy for them to overcome this, and many struggle with the problem throughout their lives.

People more inclined to be anxious think about the future. The low-anxious live in the present, and the depressed in the past.

THE OPPOSITE POLE—THE INDEPENDENTS

Those at the other end of the spectrum are almost the complete opposite. These are the independent-minded people, and one might go so far as to say that at least some of them are not anxious enough. They have a low level of anxiety—about a four on a scale of one to ten. Overall, independent people are not very threatened by either the environment around them or other people, and it shows. They are very brave (at least they always appear so), spontaneous, and self-confident, which often draws people to them. They have strong opinions that they do not hesitate to make known. They pursue their own interests aggressively (getting their way is very important to them), and usually think of themselves as winners, strong and effective. Others at times have less flattering labels for them, such as arrogant, narcissistic, or grandiose. The independent-minded person often makes a good first impression, but their follow-through is not as good.

Independent-minded people usually get an "F" in empathy because they rarely give a thought to anyone else's point of view or circumstances. They aren't much concerned about other people at all, with the exception of their spouse or immediate family, who are elevated into a different category, since the low-anxiety person thinks of them as extensions of himself. Thus he is often quite mindful of and devoted to them.

Needless to say, this cavalier attitude toward others often lands independent-minded personalities in people problems. The fact that they feel no need to consider the feelings of others just about guarantees it. When they get into a dispute they often try to resolve it by a sudden burst of aggression—they become irritated, angry, or hostile... which usually only digs them deeper.

Their lack of planning is another Achilles heel. They may do well outlining small tasks and undertakings, but they rarely look very far ahead, or at the big picture. Their disinclination to look past the end of the current rainbow and think about mundane but often important things like a stable career, child-rearing strategies, or saving for retirement, often finds them caught short. They are like the pig who built his house of straw, and now they need to find a quick fix. Thus their lives often have a zigzag pattern, as they run into unexpected problems or get a new offer, try something else, and move on.

- Independent types often say that they like rules—why? One would think just the opposite. Reason: By obeying the rules they can safely avoid having to deal with or attend to others' demands on them. In other words, this facilitates independence.

- Independent types are typically black and white thinkers. Reason: they like things clear so they can avoid being hassled by others.

- Independent types like strong people and are somewhat contemptuous of agreeable ones, but often marry agreeable mates. Reason: they clash with other strong personalities, which is stressful, whereas it is easy to get along with the agreeable folks.

PILLAR #5: INTELLIGENCE

There are plenty of differing opinions, even among the experts, as to what intelligence actually is, and there is certainly more than one kind of intelligence. But although women of an earlier generation made an art form of hiding their intelligence, and men of that same generation were often happy to ignore this particular quality when looking for a mate, intelligence really is a big issue in compatibility, enough so that I have made it our fifth key pillar of personality.

Some people have intellectual and verbal skills, and others more mechanical and physical aptitudes, but in general, people feel better about, and get along better with, people who are more or less as intelligent as they are. A like level of intelligence—preferably the same type of intelligence—does a lot for compatibility, and increases the chances of shared interests and activities. There is a big difference between someone with an IQ of 100, and someone who is 120 or higher. The average person just can't keep up with someone who has a high-speed, heavy-duty mental processor, and even subjects of conversation become limited. A bright person is often in an intellectual or professional job, and if his mate is in a blue-collar one, this is one more thing to divide them.

When there is a big difference in intelligence levels between partners, you get into the situation where one partner feels he is dragging the other along. The brighter person feels frustrated, but he can cope, since he has many interests and other outlets for them. The less bright partner, however, feels pressured and upset because he knows in his heart that it is hard for him to measure up.

When questions come up between the two, or decisions need to be made, the less bright person tends to acquiesce in everything. To avoid arguments, and because he assumes his opinion will have less weight and credibility, he will usually just go along with whatever the brighter one says or decides. After a while, the brighter one will no longer seek input or advice from the less bright one, and simply see them as a source of mundane companionship and comforts. The brighter person will also eventually get bored, and feel alone, even though he is with someone.

Creativity is another aspect of intelligence that can have a bearing on compatibility. Two people can be equally intelligent, and one creative and the other not.

Some people just take data or information and summarize it. These are often called "the summarizers," and they are usually cautious and methodical. Creative people find a way to do something new, different, and exciting with that same data. Creative people usually think faster, too, and may even be a little impulsive. Creatives also have a better than average sense of humor, although their quick repartee may sometimes offend others.

If you are creative, the reason you ideally want another creative person to spend your time with is that if you are both operating on the same sort of wavelengths, you will immediately understand where the other person is coming from.

Most of us have good antennae for assessing intelligence.

SECONDARY TRAITS, OR THE B LIST

In putting together this personality analysis system, I also reviewed the list of potential personality traits carefully for those that might not be as important as the pillars, but could have a strong effect on relationships at times, depending on the other traits each of the parties might have. I will outline each of these secondary, or "B List" traits here.

OPEN TO CHANGE VERSUS INFLEXIBLE

This can be a relatively unimportant issue, or a big yawning canyon between two people, depending on what they are otherwise like.

People who are open to change love to travel to new places and try new things. When the first monorail to the moon is announced, they'll be in the first line around the block. If there's a new restaurant in town, or a new dish on the menu of the old one, they'll be among the first to check it out. When they see a new spice or soup mix at the gourmet store, it's in their cart before they finish reading the label. The minute they hear about a book with a very different point of view on some subject close to their hearts, they'll rush to Amazon to order it. If the doctor says they need to give up coffee, they'll find a way to cheerfully switch their allegiance from Mocha Java to Earl Grey. If they lose their job, or their factory or industry is on its way out, they'll jump right into retooling themselves as necessary. They are always looking for new ways to do things, and ways to liven things up. They are not challenged or threatened by the new.

Those on the other end of this spectrum are more rigidly pat-terned and reactionary. They like routine and consistency, and prefer the predictable to the unknown. They usually stick with the same ways of doing things, and the same old favorite entertainments, destina-tions, companions, and even foods and drinks. They've probably had the same hairdo since high school. If they've always fished with worms, there's no way they would ever try flies. If they are trying to write the Great American Novel, and have never used a computer, they'll dig that ancient Royal typewriter out of the shed, or handwrite it all, rather than learn how to type it up in Microsoft Word. Those at the closed end of the open/inflexible scale are also very careful to follow all of the rules, and you will never catch *them* coloring outside the lines.

They're also not very good at dealing with surprises—if the car breaks down, they may go into the emotional equivalent of a grand mal seizure, rather than calmly giving the pertinent information to Triple A.

Their close-mindedness extends to ideas as well, so they're not too interested in other people's points of view, and certainly not in any-thing that might be construed as a criticism of them. If they lose their job or spouse or sweetheart, they're more likely to sit and reminisce about or mourn the old one, than get out and start the process of look-ing for new.

If the two ends of this particular spectrum get together, the very flexible person is likely to eventually feel stifled by his "stick in the mud" companion, and the more rigidly controlled partner will be alarmed and distraught by what she sees as the unsettling unpredictability or even fickleness of her mate. If the flexible person starts thinking of changing jobs, which he may well, his mate, who loves stability, may be faced with relocation and all of its associated big issues.

Two people very different in their degree of flexibility will find it hard to develop a full connection—in a sense, they don't really know what to do with each other. The flexible party sooner or later starts just assuming that the inflexible one will say no to whatever she has in mind, so she hates to even ask. The inflexible one, on the other hand, dreads his partner asking about or suggesting anything, because he assumes that the partner will end up embellishing the plan way beyond his comfort level. This creates a real barrier between them.

A difference in this area is not prohibitive, but when combined with other differences it can put the odds against a good relationship over the top. So be sure to assess the "flex" level of prospective mates or employees.

CONSCIENTIOUS VERSUS IRRESPONSIBLE

Someone conscientious is reliable, diligent, and persevering—they attend to things in a timely and effective way. They have all of the characteristics of the dutiful grind—at least we might think that way until we need something done, and a person with this inclination to do it.

People in the professions generally have this characteristic. Conscientiousness is almost taken for granted by professionals. This is because professional schools require you to be careful and meticulous in your work, to respond to any requests they make of you, to keep notes and keep track of things, to be on time, and be diligent.

> This trait puts mental pressure on the individual to be responsible and conscientious. It is usually easier for the conscientious person to do what he should be doing or is responsible for, than to ignore his internal signals.

People can develop this quality to a certain extent, but they usually have it early on, if they have it. Conscientious people are usually sincere, and popular because other people find it easy to deal with them. A relationship with them is usually a low-stress, smooth, even one.

Conscientiousness can be a great addition to other traits. For example if this trait accompanies the agreeable trait, the person will not only be agreeable accommodating and friendly, but also very reliable in carrying out responsibilities. As a result this is a powerful package because the person will be seen as having very strong character.

This trait can be a handicap at times when it pushes the person to fulfill responsibilities that they're not really able to carry out at a particular time. For example if a person is depressed, he may be so responsible and diligent in carrying out his work that he doesn't take the time to get the rest that he needs.

Conscientiousness acts as an inhibitor in many instances when it is combined with other characteristics or traits. For example, if a person is inclined to be impulsive, this trait will try to reduce the impulsivity. The conscientiousness trait will not overcome or counteract the impulsivity, instead it will go along with the impulsivity and modify it in a positive direction. High energy types such as executives, for instance, can be impulsive, which often leads to costly mistakes. So, they hire a conscientious administrative assistant to backstop them. The assistant can mitigate their mistakes through good recordkeeping and timely reminders. Or the executive may get and learn to use computer software that accomplishes the same thing.

The conscientious trait was probably developed through the evolutionary process because it did a lot to enhance a person's survivability. For one, it is very helpful in maintaining friendships and developing new ones. It is also very useful when it comes to structuring and planning one's life. And it has many other applications along the same lines.

Conscientiousness facilitates the development of trusting relationships and helps to build bridges that enable communication, cooperation, and collaboration among people. As a result, it helps to build strong connections and building blocks within groups, which is consistent with nature's goals.

When someone is low or lacking in conscientiousness, it is usually bad news. Irresponsible people are generally self-focused, narcissistic, impulsive, and insensitive. And like addicts and substance abusers, they are out for instant gratification. Not a promising quality, in light of the fact that many studies have shown that the ability to defer gratification is one of the most important factors in success of any kind.

In a work situation, it's difficult and frustrating to deal with people who don't show up or deliver on time, who never follow up or follow through. In a romantic situation or personal relationship, it may even be worse. None of us like to find ourselves waiting by the phone for a promised call, or sitting solo in a restaurant scanning the door for new arrivals, hoping our carefully arranged lunch date is among them. Whether or not someone is going to do what they said they'd do, or be where they said they would be, comes down to conscientiousness. The most charming character will wear thin without it.

Then, too, if we hope to build a life with someone, conscientious people have a much better chance of making a good and dependable living. And that issue that often concerns us greatly—will this person be true to me?—has a great deal to do with conscientiousness—whether or not a person is guided by conscience.

Conscientiousness is a trait well worth being mindful of.

INTROVERT VERSUS EXTROVERT

Although this is a well-known and notable difference between people, it is not one of our pillars because people often can get along even when they have marked differences in this area.

Introverts are largely focused on what is going on in their own heads, and less interested in the outside world and other people. They do well with people one on one, but are usually uncomfortable in groups or large gatherings. By and large, they prefer solitary activities, and are somewhat reserved and analytical. They are deep and independent thinkers, and always think things through before coming out with them. Above all, if they must spend time with other people, they need alone time afterward to recharge their batteries and recover.

Extroverts, on the other hand, shine in the spotlight and the company of others. They are outgoing, talkative, enthusiastic, and highly social. They love to interact with others, and spending time alone would be a sentence of boredom or despair for most of them. Solitary confinement was surely created as a punishment for extroverts.

Since extroverts outnumber introverts, and extroversion is more socially approved and generally accepted, this puts pressure on introverts. It shows in the fact that introverts are far more likely than extroverts to find themselves seeking help from psychological professionals.

Extroverts are very attractive at first because of their high energy and impressive networking. But their contacts with others are often superficial, and over time the charm of their glad-handing can fade. The often closed nature of introverts can be wearing in a different way. But the two ends of this spectrum can learn to coexist and accommodate one another.

THE MIDDLE GROUND

There is middle ground between these two extremes, and in fact most people are in it. The many people who would score at the fifty percent point on a test for extroversion versus introversion are called ambiverts. They are very flexible, and may behave like introverts or extroverts depending upon their mood or the circumstances. They enjoy reading and other quiet pursuits, but also enjoy people. But social interaction is not an intense need for them, as it is for extroverts. And they need some down time alone, too, but not as much as introverts. Interestingly, they are more successful at sales jobs than either extroverts or introverts, because they are as attentive to the customer as an introvert, and never pour on the fellowship too heavily as an extrovert might.

Two ambiverts are the best match of all in romantic relationships, and ambiverts will get along better with introverts than the average extrovert.

Introvert/extrovert pressure points

When extroverts and introverts do have relationship problems, it often has to do with the fact that extroverts want to go out and do all kinds of things with others, and introverts don't like having to tag along. They also don't care to be more social than they feel comfortable being. If there are a lot of different people involved in the event or activity they've been dragged to, this drains them. Extroverts also are usually involved with a lot of other people in different ways, and they have to cultivate and manage all of these relationships. The introvert is then forced to some extent to deal with all of this as well, and they don't like all of the drama.

An extrovert can be misled here because the extra energy everyone has in the courtship stage can make an introvert seem more outgoing, and when the relationship levels out the extrovert is left wondering what happened to that animated person they thought they had linked up with.

Clashes can result, too, from the fact that from the introvert's point of view, extroverts often seem to make their decisions on what seems like mood and impulse, rather research and reflection.

Are you an "insie" or "outsie" in the personality department?

VOLATILE VERSUS EMOTIONALLY STABLE

You don't have to peruse many online dating profiles to see how many men are dead set against hooking up with anyone who might be described as a "drama queen." Women are equally uninterested in forging a relationship with a raging bull.

These are some of the everyday terms for what psychologists call a volatile person, someone for whom every little bump in the road of life is a melodrama they are going to describe for you in far more detail than you want to know, and then somehow drag you into it too. They seem unable to leave anything alone—they are always stirring up trouble, looking for problems, or somehow creating them. They are easily stressed and overreact to almost every situation. Their negative reactions have a long life, so they are often in a bad mood. They are often anxious or depressed as well as angry.

Living with a volatile person is like living with a time bomb. The partner has to walk around on eggshells, and be very careful in both actions and conversations to avoid triggering his mate. Even so, it's only a matter of time until he crosses them and they blow up. Once provoked, a volatile person can wreak a lot of havoc, and may say and do things that are unrepairable. A volatile person is usually at the bottom of most family flare-ups.

Those inclined to volatility often point out that they are more direct and honest than most people. By not holding back their irritations and frustrations, they let others know how they feel quickly, whereas many others are false and misleading in their communications, which in the long run only makes matters worse.

Volatility is often fueled by earlier bad experiences. The more adverse experiences a person has had, the more likely he or she is to be a human minefield. This is one reason that "baggage" has a bad name in dating circles and elsewhere. Traumatic brain injuries and bipolar disorder can also cause volatility.

A volatile person usually uses his volatility to control relationships, and emotionally stable people eventually get very tired of this. And of the constant tension, 24/7.

A person with emotional control, on the other hand, even if upset, can discuss the issue in question calmly and productively, or put the discussion off to a better time. And he will not overinterpret his partner's responses.

EMOTIONALLY WARM VERSUS COLD

This is a quality that women tend to be more concerned about than men, but then, for generations men were trained and conditioned to keep themselves on the stoic side of this continuum.

A warm person has all of those qualities and habits that make us feel valued and feel good. They are affectionate, tender, sympathetic, and compassionate. They make us feel welcome, feel missed when we are gone, and are the ones who will leave little notes for us to discover in our lunchbox or suitcase. They are often huggers, snugglers, and shoulder-patters, although someone doesn't have to be a toucher to be warm. Some people would even say that warmth of this kind is the whole reason to have a relationship.

At the other side of the temperature range are the people we call cold. They may be aloof, reserved, standoffish. None of the other adjectives we might use here are appealing ones: dispassionate, detached, indifferent, unresponsive, heartless, cold-blooded. People at the cold end of this trait will also be sparing with physical contact, and may even recoil from it or avoid it when they can.

"Warm" is perhaps the most popular, positive characterization of another person, whereas "cold" is a universal turnoff. Research has shown that a positive recommendation can be undone by noting that the person is cold toward others, whereas noting that someone is warm can have the opposite effect.

RISK-TAKING VERSUS CAUTIOUS

People at the risk-taking end of this trait only feel fully alive when they are taking a risk. They are always either planning an adventure or engaged in one—mountain climbing, auto racing, snowboarding, skydiving, hang gliding, or riding the biggest beast roller coaster they can find. Nothing daunts them, from broken bones to statistics on how many people die on mountaintops each year. Risk takers are proud of their adventures, and this inspires a self-righteousness that is more powerful than objective facts. They sneer at "stupid" ordinary pastimes and jobs, and wonder how anyone can live like that.

Risk-takers love to gamble, literally as well as figuratively, and they'll take financial gambles as well, from iffy investments to the launching of untried new businesses. A risk-taker always assumes things will turn out all right, so he will never let a chance at an adventure or advantage pass him by.

Just about all of these attitudes would be unimaginable to someone at the cautious end of this scale. A cautious mate would not be suiting up to share the drama of some life-threatening sport, and would more likely be home worrying and wondering if their partner was going to return this time. A cautious person is more likely to value and protect what he already has, than take a chance of losing it in some gamble, no matter how great the possible return if it succeeds.

While the risk-taker is exhilarated by risks, his cautious partner is made anxious by them, and only more anxious as she realizes that her partner's actions could create problems for her as well. So she is always waiting for the other shoe to drop.

Many risk-takers end up in bankruptcy, and then the cautious one is dragged into a world he or she really hates: calls from credit card companies and collection agencies, lawsuits. In hopes of avoiding things like this, the cautious person ends up the "cop." But a risk-taker doesn't like to be constrained, to have anyone try to control him, so this will cause him to go subterranean, to start hiding things and lying, taking risks without letting his partner know. Risk-taking is a kind of addiction, and the risk-taker's partner can end up like the drug addict's codependent.

A risk-taker with a thoroughly cautious mate, on the other hand, suffers in a different way. As his partner is forever saying things like, "Let's not tackle that right now, let's think it over," he can't help but feel that a soundly and carefully thought out approach to just about everything is far too boring and predictable—a flat-lined way of living.

Both partners in this situation end up equally frustrated, as this difference in temperament becomes a black hole in their relationship.

Risk-taking, trying new things, and for that matter, optimism, are actually disadvantages for the individual, since
odds of a positive outcome are smaller than those of a negative one. The person is all too likely to end up with broken
bones, long hospital stays, or in bankruptcy. You are better
off for the most part staying with the tried and true.

But these traits are good for the group, because over time,
they result in new discoveries for our species. Evolution
always favors the welfare of the group as a whole.

PERFECTIONISTIC VERSUS
TOLERANT OF DISORDER

The old movie *The Odd Couple*, and the TV series that followed, gave
a good look at the sorts of problems a relationship between people at
the two ends of this spectrum can generate. Perfectionists set very high
standards for themselves, and wear themselves out trying to live up to
them. They want everything done a certain way (often even in a certain
order), and done well and thoroughly, with all of the i's dotted and t's
crossed. They want things to be neat and orderly and well organized,
too. As soon as they're done with a tool, it goes right back onto the
pegboard, in the row with all of the other hammers, please!

The folks at the other end of this scale don't worry if the clothes
in their closet aren't arranged by type and color, or for that matter, if
their shirts and jeans even make it to the closet. Empty beer cans and
pizza boxes may cover half the living room floor, but if they're having
company, they aren't going to waste half a day tidying up the place.
They'll just elbow some of the clutter aside, set down the refreshments,
and launch right into having a good time.

The perfectionists are the people with tidy desktops and up-to-date inboxes, while the disorderly have to paw through the ten-inch layer of scattered papers on their desk to find anything. Perfectionists are usually pretty hardheaded and stubborn, too, while the "slobs" are much more willing to let others have a say in how things are done.

Do you need basil for the spaghetti sauce? If you're a Felix, just look under the "B's" in your alphabetized spice rack. If you're an Oscar, it could be just about anywhere—and don't rule out the bookshelf as a possible location. Time for lunch? Felix chooses from the carefully dated leftovers in the fridge; Oscar plays Ptomaine Roulette. Tax time? Felix can find his gas receipts back to 1982; Oscar can't find his filing cabinet.

But Oscar has his strengths too. A perfectionist may make you feel like you're always doing it wrong, like you can never measure up. A non-perfectionist is more likely to make you feel accepted for who you are. He is also unlikely to sweat the small stuff, and is often much more able to look at a situation in terms of what is really important and what is not. He wouldn't be rearranging the deck chairs on the *Titanic*, but looking for a lifeboat.

Perfectionists in some cases may be motivated by the desire to create a perfect result, but more commonly, they are more interested in heading off the possibility that anyone might criticize them. They don't want to hear how this or that should be changed in anything they do. They just want to be accepted and appreciated. Trying to be perfect is a way of protecting yourself.

Where are you on the scale from perfectionism to hanging loose?

ANOTHER NOTEWORTHY TRAIT

Some characteristics aren't quite at the level of what I am calling a trait here, but they are certainly worth noting. One of these is frugality.

Frugality and cheapness are not the same. A cheap person wants the lowest price or no price—a frugal person wants the *best* price. A frugal person is always looking for a deal. If the object they are vying for is very expensive, it's not the price tag that is the issue; it's whether or not they are getting a super value. If you ask them to spend $100,000 on a piece of art they know is worth $200,000, if they have the money, they may well go for it. If it costs $100,000 and is worth just $105,000, they will almost invariably say no.

The problem frugal people have is that they conduct their finances and related affairs like a competitive event. Even when it comes to simple things like how to reciprocate the gift you gave them for Christmas, where to go out to eat, or who will pick up the check, they want to *win*. If you are with someone who is frugal, after a while you will notice that they are constantly winning.

If you go out to eat with them in a restaurant, when the basket of bread is brought, they are the first person to go after it. They'll take two or three pieces and leave one or two for everyone else. Then they'll order a lot (when everyone else is ordering minimal portions), though their share of the bill will be the same as everyone else's.

A friend of mine, an excellent mechanic, tried to trade time once with a gardening guru—landscaping help for assistance with car repairs. All the green-thumbed guy (who turned out to be frugal) ever wanted to do was talk about his problems with his three vehicles, and there was much more of that than gardening help or advice given. When he did remember to address my friend's acre of plantings of all kinds, his heart wasn't in it.

If you are with someone and notice them doing things like this, it will tick you off. They will usually deny anything of the sort—say they have no interest in taking advantage of anyone. "They just want to get the best price, like anyone would."

But it is really more than that. They need to win, to get the better of someone. If they find that they are getting 49%, they will not be happy, they want 51% or more. After a while this gets tiring. People pick this up, and they are not thrilled by it. After a while it gets to them. They may not say anything to the person's face, but who knows what they are saying behind his back.

> People usually respond to the frugal person by adopting a defensive strategy so they don't get cheated, whereas they respond in kind and then some to generous people. In the long run the frugal person, studies have shown, actually ends up losing, financially as well as in terms of his relationships.

I usually call out frugal people when I encounter them. I tell them that this is not a good way to go, because there is a lot of research that shows that frugality is a losing strategy. It makes people walk away feeling bad and annoyed. Frugality can have a very negative effect on relationships, so it is advisable to start monitoring this and changing it.

WHY ALL OF THESE DIFFERENCES IN CHARACTERISTICS AND BEHAVIOR?

All species—at least those that live in groups—are diversified by individuals with different traits. For example, there are killer bees, worker bees, and then the queen. In the case of dogs and wolves, there are alpha and beta canines. Diversity is crucial to the survival of the species. Humans are also diversified. There are extroverts, introverts, risk takers, cautious types, and so on.

Every trait has its purpose, and pros and cons. Each of these types has a role that is important to the group. Nature developed these to help the group as a whole to function and succeed. We need to bear in mind here that nature is oriented to favoring the group over the individual. Group survival is a higher priority than individual survival or achievement.

Nature realized that diversity was essential for human survival. Thus, over time, different traits emerged in different individuals. Some were dependent, agreeable, and timid, and others aggressive. Some were conscientious, others a little shifty, some hoarders, and others spend-thrifts. And so on. And then there was a need for some who could hold all of these types together—people who could communicate with aggressive people as easily as the overcautious or shy ones. Some people have the ability to interact with just about anyone effortlessly, without creating enemies. Thus they are essential for building cohesiveness in a group and for enhancing its effectiveness.

Nature also realized there was a need for people who would be independent thinkers. If most of the people in a group wanted to sleep in the forest or by the river, some of the independent ones would want to sleep elsewhere. So then if a mishap (such as an avalanche or flood) occurred, at least some would survive. Independent thinkers would also be very likely to happen upon inventions and insights that would eventually help the group as a whole survive and thrive.

Things that benefit survival are usually the bottom line.

SOME FURTHER INFORMATION ABOUT TRAITS

1. People are born with traits that are programmed into their brains. People are not always happy with the traits they are born with. Risk takers, for instance, who suffer broken bones and long hospital stays may become frustrated with their lot but often feel powerless to overcome their natural urges.

2. Some traits are obvious to the individual as well as the observer, such as introversion versus extroversion and a tendency to caution versus risk taking, to name a few, while others, such as the independence trait, are not readily recognized even by the individual who has the trait.

3. If a person is asked to show more of a certain trait than he is showing now, because it is necessitated by his job or circumstances, this is difficult. You can't modify a trait easily; it operates

on an automatic or autopilot basis. If a person attempts to conduct himself in a particular manner simply by using will power or trying to focus his attention on the need for such behavior, it usually takes a great deal of mental effort to do so. Generally it's much easier to have a behavior monitored and controlled by the brain on an autopilot basis than it is to practice and ingrain it to the point where it is consciously controlled.

4. Traits are usually on a continuum, and can usually only be modified, with considerable effort, to the middle of that continuum. For example, if a person is an introvert, with practice he can become more extroverted. If someone is not very conscientious she can move to perhaps as much so as the average person. But it is extremely difficult to move past the midline—if you're an extrovert you can't become a true introvert, or vice versa, or go from risk-taker to fully cautious.

> While animals' traits are pretty much fixed, in humans traits are somewhat flexible, there can be adjustments made. People can move from one pole of a trait toward the other, and usually get close enough to the other pole to solve a behavior problem when necessary. For instance, parents and teachers often try to encourage a child who is seen as too introverted or too much of a risk taker to move toward the midline.

However, you can get to the midline, and from the midline, you can accentuate that characteristic so that you become stronger in that area.

If, for example, you're an introvert and also have the independence trait, you're likely to have very little contact with people. You can mitigate the intensity of both with the proper program. This will greatly enhance your ability to deal with people and minimize the consequences of being overly socially avoidant.

Likewise, a risk taker who's had a lot of accidents and a lot of injuries has a family now, so he may decide to put those kinds of things on the back burner, and focus on his family. No more ice climbing or bungee jumping for now.

5. Traits can vary over time depending on circumstances. Traits tend to be more rigid as one goes down the evolutionary ladder. With humans, traits are far more flexible. For example, an introvert can become more extroverted with practice, while a risk taker can become more cautious.

6. Traits can also be encouraged to become more extreme. This often occurs when a child is allowed or encouraged to indulge his natural tendencies. Parents or teachers may have reason to do this, in some circumstances. Traits tend to become more extreme unless they are governed. For example, prodigies in a particular field take off like a rocket in that area, but their personalities are often not rounded out.

7. Traits usually last a lifetime.

8. If a person has two different traits that would seem to be in conflict with one another, they will not cancel each other out. The tendency for people who have traits that would seem to counter one another is for both to be expressed—and for the traits to mitigate each other's effect. For example, if someone is both agreeable and introverted, she may have many friends that she doesn't often socialize with. If someone is an extrovert and not open to change, he'll be with people, but want to do the same things a lot. If someone is open to change as well as cautious, they will be cautious in how they try new things.

If a person is agreeable but also low-energy or depressed, he may not be as expansive as an agreeable person usually is. Being agreeable takes a great deal of energy, as the person is constantly looking for ways to resolve conflicts and avoid disappointing others. If an agreeable person seems to be very good at saying no, he is probably depressed, or his energy level is low, causing him to look for shortcuts.

Likewise, an independent person is usually not very concerned with others or their points of view. If an independent seems surprisingly empathetic or interested in others, he may have an unusually high energy level, which enables him to do this. This is also why well-established and wealthy independents may become very philanthropic in their later years.

9. The five most studied traits are: openness to change, conscientiousness, extroversion, agreeableness, and neuroticism (a mild degree of psychological dysfunction that is usually a combination of anxiety and depression). There are many traits that have not been identified or studied.

Many people don't have peaks and valleys in their psychological profile. They score from 4 to 6 on every one of their traits. People with marked differences in their different traits and predispositions usually can determine their strengths and weaknesses and thereby have a better understanding of what they are suited to—occupationally and by way of relationships. Those in the middle have a much harder time determining what course to pursue and whom to marry or link up with.

CHAPTER TWO

HOW TRAITS AFFECT THERAPY

Over the years I have found that analyzing a person's traits is an important part of helping them overcome their issues in therapy. When you know a person's traits and predispositions (I will explain what these are later in this chapter), you are in a much better position to choose the right approach for them in therapy. Their basic temperament and other traits can make a big difference in the success of treatment strategies. With the aid of trait analysis, a therapist can fine-tune the course of treatment, customize it to assure the best results—create a personalized treatment plan, a road that will assure smoother travel.

CHARACTER AND THERAPY

Character, so important in life in general, is important in therapy as well—it determines whether a person is likely to follow instructions, or for that matter, to even show up. It's a drag to treat irresponsible people. Even when a psychologist is treating patients for mental illness, regardless of the type of mental malady they have, whether or not they have good character makes all the difference.

ENERGY LEVEL AND THERAPY

A high level of mental energy helps with therapy. High-energy types are typically optimistic, enthusiastic, productive, and upbeat, so they tend to be compliant and collaborate well with therapists and respond well to examining their behavior and their perceptions of others as well as their own intentions.

On the other hand, when a person becomes depressed, their level of mental energy goes down, which greatly lowers motivation. They can't visualize anything, don't want to do the homework, and have an instant give-up response. You keep hearing, "This doesn't work for me." Antidepressants sometimes help.

A person's anxiety level often affects their level of mental energy as well. As his anxiety level goes up, he finds he has less energy to deal with all the situations that may be at hand. As his anxiety level goes down, the person usually feels more at ease and finds it easier to think of other things, and this in turn frees up a good deal of mental energy.

INTELLIGENCE AND THERAPY

Super brightness is not necessarily an advantage in therapy. Such people use their mind almost too much, and tend to talk very abstractly: "One thing is for sure. People feed off of each other. Not much you can do about this; it's just part of life." It's hard to get them to talk about what is specifically bothering them. They can also complicate things unnecessarily.

Extremely bright people sometimes have a tendency to intellectualize their feelings and perceptions, thus they may overemphasize the logical and intellectual side of their behavior and intentions, while minimizing the more emotional basis of their values and opinions.

Less intelligent people are usually more concrete—they can even be too concrete. When they ask you about something, they may feel that they have to tell you the whole story, the entire scenario in breathtaking detail. Then you have to try to interpret this complex tale to see what their concern actually is.

OPENNESS TO CHANGE

Therapy is all about change, and being open to it. Rigid types find therapy demanding and frequently find it frustrating. People who are open-minded usually find therapy helpful and enjoyable.

There is a strong relationship and interaction between a person's anxiety level and their openness to change. High levels of anxiety tend to reduce a person's openness to change. As a person becomes more relaxed about his circumstances, he typically becomes more open to change. If a person is very cautious by nature, he still may be open to change if his anxiety level is low.

Therapy is not a threat to those open to change. For those not open to change, it's tricky. In presenting any argument or discussion, you need to start at the top where they are comfortable (ideas and concepts they are sure to agree with), and work your way down to the problem areas. For an example of this technique, if you were having a conversation with a member of the political party opposite to yours, you might start by saying, "We both want the best for this country, right? And we want laws and policies that will benefit as many people as possible, no? Well…" Etc.

EXTROVERTS AND INTROVERTS

Introverts may enjoy the therapeutic analysis and insights they gain from therapy but are often hesitant to act on them. Extroverts, on the other hand, often find the introspections of therapy tedious and frustrating, but usually enjoy implementing the behavioral recommendations.

Extroverts have lots to talk about in therapy because they interact with many people, which means many interpersonal problems and issues. They have no problem talking about all sorts of things—intimate things, embarrassing things, whatever. They love the camaraderie of therapy, and as long as they are working with someone they trust and like they can go on forever. They are usually very easy to talk to because they will carry the conversation, and I can join in or interrupt as I see fit, as often as I want.

I am somewhat of an extrovert myself, and I enjoy talking to extroverts. But I do realize there are limitations to this. For instance, they can get involved in talking about things that are not of great importance, that they haven't given a great deal of thought to. They can be impulsive, go off on tangents. They can even drift into meaningless drivel if I don't keep on top of the conversation and push it in more productive directions.

Introverts, on the other hand, have difficulty talking. They are more inclined to reflect on what they think than talk about it.

I respect this, so when working with them I keep questions to a minimum and allow them to talk about things they have reflected on. I usually have to carry the conversation and I speak in a reflective manner myself. Many of the people I see I try to mirror to an extent. I am trying to get on a compatible wavelength, to see things from their point of view as much as possible. This puts them under a lot less pressure, makes them feel more comfortable, and is something they can deal with.

Therapy with an introvert is more work—I have to push more. But I try to accommodate an introverted person as much as I can. They don't like to talk about new subjects right off, things they haven't had a chance to think through and reflect on. So I talk about things in the recent past.

I often find myself giving relationship advice here—introverts often suffer from social pressure because they usually have trouble providing enough social interaction to keep others happy.

WARM VERSUS COLD PEOPLE

Warm people are usually agreeable, high energy, extroverted, open to change—all the positive traits. They are usually on the conscientious side, and not depressive. This usually finds them very motivated in therapy.

Cold people are independent, rigid, not open to change, and their energy level is low. They are often lacking in interpersonal skills.

They are also self-absorbed, however, so therapy—which is intensely focused on them—is actually very much to their liking, since they are mainly interested in themselves.

If you have a predisposition to be compliant, and accept authority, therapy will be easy for you. For therapy, being open to change and agreeable to a degree are ideal traits.

If a person is very controlling, they will want therapy organized in such a way that they have some say in decisions regarding it—so that they will not be in the position of being totally out of control. The therapist will not just be telling them things, or asking them to do things that they can't or don't want to do. They won't just be sitting there listening to what the therapist has to say. This will give them a sense of control and make the whole process more comfortable and enjoyable.

Whether you are conscientious or not will also come into play. Being regular is very important for therapy—showing up for sessions is a big factor in how successful therapy will be.

VOLATILE PEOPLE

Volatile people can get demanding and aggressive at any time, and angry in an instant. Anger is no problem for them. They have far more ability to deal with it and handle it than most of us do. Most of us are much more inclined to be threatened by our anger and so we try to inhibit it. The average person is looking to keep things harmonious and avoid conflict.

This gives the volatile person a big advantage. The volatile person, who has a great deal of experience with conflict, contentiousness, and outbursts, doesn't really take any of this very seriously. Many of them tell me that they get over their anger as quickly as they get into it. They can turn it on and off like a faucet.

For the rest of us it is pure agony to be waiting for an explosion to go off at any time. How will we stop it, and how much damage will be done before we do?

None of these considerations are very important to the volatile person. The result is that they have a history of getting their way.

When they come into therapy, they let me know immediately that they don't want to just reflect on things—they are looking for action. They want to get to the root of things, and fast. They want to know what's going on, what I think, exactly what they should do, who's right and who's wrong. They don't want to just talk in circles.

This puts a lot of strain on therapy, which is meant to be a reflective and thoughtful process, not a kangaroo court or circus.

There are ways of accommodating them, however. The technique I tend to use is to ask them what they want. When I ask this, I'm not trying to trick them into giving me something, or give them something less than they deserve. What I am interested in doing is following their answer to that question up with, "Well, I'll give you what you want, but this is what I want in return."

Now we are getting into negotiation, which we should have been in from the beginning. They said what they want and I say what it will cost. They may want to drop their request a bit or modify it. If they do, I will drop my cost (usually not a monetary one).

In everyday life the dialogue might go something like this: "OK, We can have Christmas this year at your place, however I don't want to have another situation where you explode. It's very unpleasant and uncomfortable for me. In the future I want a promise from you that you are not going to use this technique again, not hold me hostage to some ridiculous demand so that you can get your way. If you give up your anger I'll give up the Christmas meeting place this year."

When they see that it is costing them nothing monetarily to give up their anger, they usually give in. After all, they shouldn't have been using their anger as a tool in the first place.

In general, in therapy what I want in return is for them to agree that they will not use their anger—either the threat or the expression of it—as a means of manipulating me. In other words, I don't want them to think that I will give them whatever they want just to avoid having them get angry and upset. Following up on this, whenever they get angry again and it seems like they are trying to manipulate me, I will refuse to placate them in order to avoid a problem. In short, I am not interested in rewarding them for not getting angry.

AGREEABLE AND INDEPENDENT PEOPLE

One would think that people with the agreeable trait would be very receptive to therapy. But this is not necessarily so, especially if the trait is strong. People with the agreeable trait have little experience talking about themselves, so it's hard to get them to do that. They like to question me about, bring up the problems of their daughter or mate or this one or that one, because this is where they are most comfortable. So the therapist learns about all of the people in their circle!

A very independent, self-absorbed person, on the other hand, even though he may pooh-pooh therapy intellectually, when he gets into it, since therapy is very private and confidential, he loves it, because it is intensely focused on him, and he may well use it to his benefit.

For more about the treatment of agreeable and independent people, see Chapter Seven.

A PRELIMINARY CAUTION

When using the technique called desensitization (see Chapter Four) with a client I sometimes hear, "I don't think I'm good at imagining things," "I can't imagine that," "I can't visualize that," or "It doesn't seem to be working." A host of negative reactions, all of which impact therapy.

These all essentially stem from the fact that the person's traits are not consistent with those required for successful therapy. If they don't have openness to change (therapy *is* change, for the most part), are not agreeable to a degree, and conscientious, you may want to deal with this early on, before initiating therapy.

Likewise, if you are very low in empathy or narcissistic, you may have trouble with therapy. If for the most part you only think about yourself—you don't think much about other people, and have trouble seeing others' points of view—this will be a problem if the issues you want to deal with are interpersonal ones.

WHEN TRAITS RUN INTO TROUBLE

Traits are very powerful, and they *will* be expressed. Every one you detect will be expressed in some way, although perhaps at different times and in different ways.

If you live within your traits all is usually fine. It's when you try to go outside your traits that you have problems, such as when an extrovert gets a job suited for an introvert.

When I am counseling people, I look for mismatches between a person's lifestyle and circumstances and their natural traits—things that are not consistent with a person's makeup, at odds with it. Mismatches lead to a lot of stress and problems.

In the case of relationships, I look at whether two people's traits are compatible or not. Every couple will have some differences, and they can often work them out. If one is an introvert and the other an extrovert, for instance, there will be some difficulties. They can coexist reasonably well, but it's good to be aware of this and prepared for it.

ANOTHER KEY TO INBORN CHARACTERISTICS

We all have dispositions that lead us in certain directions. In insects and other animals these dispositions are more obvious. A killer bee knows right away when he is born that he is designed to be a fighter. A worker bee knows that he is designed to hunt down pollen for the hive. Dogs are alpha or beta.

But in we humans, because of our complexity and the complexity of our lives and circumstances, these predispositions can be harder to identify.

There is one very good way to find out what they are.

I developed the following system many years ago, while working for a state Department of Vocational Rehabilitation. I'd been tasked with helping people find jobs they could succeed at, and using all of the standard tests for this, such as Kuder and Strong, I didn't have a very good success rate. Then I noticed that when people described what they liked to do, they always talked about it *visually*.

Whatever we're destined to be attracted to, predisposed to do—music, art, science, math, plumbing, whatever—is kind of programmed into our brain. For example, if you are predisposed to be an artist, and are exposed as a child to a sketchpad and set of colored pencils, you will be excited by it. And soon find that you have a natural feeling for working with these things.

For someone else this might be the first time in their young lives that they come across a musical instrument, or the first time they see a carpenter at work, or see someone working with numbers.

When the brain comes across something it is predisposed to do, when the brain sees this, it lights up, and something interesting happens. It creates an arousal response—a little adrenaline is released into the bloodstream. And this influences how this memory is stored in the brain.

Normal memories are preserved by protein chains, little chains formed with the material to be remembered coded into them. When adrenaline is involved, these chains are etched into the brain. When this happens they become long-term, permanent memories.

When arousal is going on, such as if you see something you are predisposed to, or witness some horrifying sight, or undergo a trauma—whenever adrenaline is in the blood, the memory is etched into the brain.

Other memories are saved by protein synthesis, but traumatic memories are etched on the brain. This can be seen clearly with radioactive tracing.

The reason is that this is something the brain wants to remember forever. Say you jump into a pool and end up in water over your head, and are about to drown because you can't swim, so you have to be rescued. The brain doesn't want to have to go over this incident countless times to be sure you remember it, the way we often did in school when we were trying to memorize something. This built up the chains so we did retain the information for a while, maybe a long while if we used it regularly.

This other form of memory, traumatic memory, which is also used to store things you have a predisposition to, is very important.

When we retrieve a long-term traumatic memory, we don't retrieve it in same way as ordinary memories, either. If someone asks you what you know about the Civil War, as you start remembering you will find yourself thinking out loud, as you come up with various things you remember. But etched memories are retrieved in a very different way—visually. You can actually *see* the things you remember here, see yourself when you jumped into the water, when you got out too deep in the ocean. See the accident as it unfolded, when you suffered some injuries.

So whether an image is retrieved visually or verbally is very significant. If visually, it is something very important to you or that the brain thought was very important.

You might say that permanent memories are the hard drive of the brain, short-term memories the RAM. Your visual images from the past are the things your brain thinks is important, the things it decided to take a picture of, to take up hard drive space with. The phenomenon of mental photos may well be the origin of the oft-heard remark that "Your whole life flashes before you when you are dying."

This is sort of like when you meet someone just back from vacation. If you ask to see their vacation photos, what you will see is all the things that were important to them, so they took a picture.

The brain does the same thing—takes a picture of every important thing. If we look at those mental pictures, they give an indication of what our natural tendencies are.

Suppose that you were predisposed to be a musician or a scientist or whatever. You would find that the brain has two characteristics here that it doesn't have with regard to other activities. It can do the activity endlessly without getting bored, and effortlessly without getting tired. So if you were in a position where you could practice this activity nonstop, you would never feel that you had enough.

For example, if you were predisposed to ice skating—you could do it for hours and hours without letup. And do it effortlessly. Endlessness and Effortlessness, E and E, is an enormous advantage in acquiring a skill.

> If have a predisposition for it, an activity will be effortless for you, and you will be able to do it endlessly without getting tired or bored. Mozart suffered from Tourette's syndrome, but he had E and E. So he was able to practice with musical instruments fifteen hours a day.

If you don't have this, you would have to motivate yourself externally each time. Say you wanted to be a pro baseball player and didn't have E and E. Each time you practiced you would have to give yourself some kind of incentive or reward.

But a person with E and E is internally rewarded—the activity is enjoyable for him, and he never tires of it or is bored by it.

When I described this system to one of my clients, Sara, a very bright woman, she said, "Frankly, I don't buy this." I told her to go home and ask her mother what her first visual memory was. Her mother said that when she was very young she saw a beautiful multicolored flower— "I can still see it today, with all of those pretty petals." All of her life gardening was Sara's mother's favorite pastime, and she loved to have flowers sent to her, or to get some new perennial as a gift.

Then Sara finally did this exercise herself, and it turned out that her earliest and strongest visual memories were of family gatherings and family trips—to visit relatives, to local parks and ponds, the occasional out-of-state trip, and the many other places they went together. Then we considered the fact that for the last thirty years, she had stuck with a husband she'd come to hate…for the sake of the family, so that her family would be able to stay together.

The power of the brain's predisposition to certain activities cannot be underestimated. It clearly indicates which activities and functions a person is programmed from birth to find easy and effortless, and thereby what that person is most likely to enjoy and find stimulating.

When a person I am treating mentions that they are having difficulties with their spouse or at work, I can easily check to see if these inter-actions are consistent with that person's natural predispositions. This leads to a discussion of why the person would find himself working against his cognitive grains. What were the external motivations in his life that encouraged him to deviate from what would normally come naturally for him? How aware is the person of his natural tendencies?

These and similar lines of inquiry will offer an invaluable insight into the pressures and strains in his present life as well as the other opportunities he has open to him. It is difficult to overestimate the advantage this offers in determining how to adjust the opportunities and reinforcers in a person's life as you embark on helping the per-son restructure their lifestyle and priorities. This tool is invaluable in understanding and advising a person in the selection of a suitable mate, a promising career path, and how they might rethink their relation-ships for more satisfactory outcomes. Of course, this is only one tool, though an important one, in determining the architecture of a person's life goals and plans. But it shouldn't be overlooked.

CHAPTER THREE

WHAT IS ANXIETY AND THE BEST WAY TO TREAT IT?

Anxiety could easily be called the 21st century affliction. More than forty million Americans sought professional help for it last year—but in fact there is hardly anyone today who doesn't suffer from it to some degree. We are anxious about our finances, our jobs, our appearance, our health, our children, our relationships, the environment, the world situation, and even anxious about our very anxiety.

With good reason. The Latin root of "anxiety" means to press down, throttle, or strangle. Anxiety, that nagging sense of low-grade fear or uncertainty about things, known or unknown, does indeed weigh us down, depress, and stifle us. Anxiety also makes us irritable and uncertain, and makes it hard to concentrate on the things we know we should be concentrating on. Unchecked, it can almost become a mental straitjacket.

Anxiety has physical effects, too. To name just a few, when we are anxious, our muscles tense and teeth clench, our heart rate and breathing speeds up, we may have an upset stomach and trouble sleeping. (No wonder stomach acid reducers, tranquilizers, and sleep aids are among the best-selling drugs in America.) Anxiety can also lead to addictions of various kinds, as we self-medicate with all manner of things to calm us down and try to force our minds to stop cycling through our endless circle of concerns, and brooding.

Anxiety is a sense of danger without being fully aware of the cause—the same emotion is called fear when we do know what the threat is. Thus we are fearful of bungee jumping, or of losing our job, but anxious when we feel fearful but can only guess whether it stems from not being sure if we can trust our lover, or the fact that we could use more reassurances from our employer. We fear the things threatening us right now, and are anxious about threats that lie in the future.

> The manifestations of anxiety are similar to those of fear: accelerated heartbeat, sweaty palms, trembling, and so on. If you were to experience all these symptoms and there was a snarling dog ready to leap at your throat you would call the emotion fear. If there was nothing there, you would call it anxiety.

Early in my career I decided that one of my specialties would be the treatment of anxiety, because it is a very common problem that is also very treatable. Being able to successfully help people overcome their mental issues and problems is very gratifying.

There are many different types of anxiety, which include generalized anxiety, social anxiety, phobias, panic attacks, and obsessive-compulsive disorder.

The symptoms of anxiety include fearfulness, insecurity, and feelings of inferiority and inadequacy. Anxiety inhibits action. We become tentative, indecisive; our judgment is poor.

There are three primary responses to fearful or anxiety-provoking situations. The first is to escape the situation or to avoid it. If the person does this then they may experience a significant drop in their fearfulness at first. But over time their fear and anxiety will begin to increase since their brain is aware of the fact that this avoidance response indicates that they are not able to handle the situation.

The second response is to try and hide from the fearful situation. When you do this, your brain becomes panicked by the fact that you're hiding, which indicates that you do not have the confidence to confront what you fear or the ability to escape it, therefore you're hiding rather than taking some more active approach.

The third response to an anxiety-provoking situation is to approach it or confront it. If you confront it the fear will typically become more intense at first. Over time, as you continue to confront it, your fear will go down because your brain is aware of the fact that you are confronting it and therefore you must have more confidence in yourself.

The disadvantage of confronting your fears is that at first you have an increase in the fear, which is very uncomfortable. The advantage of confronting your fear is that in the long run it will go down and you'll feel much more successful and confident. This, in fact, is what desensitization, explained here and outlined in detail in the next chapter, is based on.

Fears are forged in the way described by Pavlov long ago—any event followed by a painful consequence will cause us to be fearful of that event, because we associate it with a bad experience. The key to dealing with anxiety and fears is to recognize that they are the natural consequence of painful experiences. Some people are more predisposed than others to develop fears and anxieties, but once those feelings are formed they can be eradicated by the well-established treatment techniques described in later chapters.

HOW IS ANXIETY TREATED?

Many therapists use "insight" to determine what is bothering a person. This is essentially looking deep into a person's past to try and determine why they have a particular anxiety. Unfortunately this method can be very time-consuming and expensive, and even so may not unearth the true origin. And even if it does, simply knowing what originally caused an anxiety may not remove or relieve it—in my experience, it may not even reduce it. What most patients want far more than just "insight" is *emotional relief* from their anxiety.

In conventional therapy, clinicians often spend more time seeking the roots of an anxiety than treating it. Proceeding in the way I will describe, you can quickly try out and sift through possible reasons for an anxious feeling and move on, rather than investing a great deal of effort in issues that turn out to be the wrong ones. In conventional therapy, a clinician may eventually come upon the true cause of a person's anxiety in the course of a fishing expedition, but it takes a lot of time and can be stressful.

Clinicians can do a lot of bumbling and stumbling in the course of trying to treat someone for anxiety. They often don't know where to look, and their educational bias may lead them to pursue certain themes or subjects.

They may well explore the areas that are easiest to explore, though the most fertile ground is usually where the patient says, "I don't want to touch that," or "I don't want to talk about that anymore." When this happens, a clinician frequently just has to move on.

Likewise, if a clinician thinks the real cause of the trouble may be something different from what the client thinks, this can be problematical: the therapist wants to explore his idea and the client wants to explore hers.

In situations like this, I always explore the client's ideas first and when that fails to find a resolution, go on to mine. If I discuss mine first they will still be fixated on theirs and whether it could be right. So I put mine aside and listen to theirs. This is no problem for me, but not something a client can do easily.

Also, the very act of in-depth probing and questioning to discover the cause of anxiety can sometimes inadvertently raise concerns that didn't exist previously. This can generate and feed doubts the person didn't have to begin with.

Another common way of treating anxiety is what is called the cognitive approach, discussed later in this chapter. This is essentially using a variety of intellectual arguments to help the person see that their fears and anxieties are exaggerated and unreasonable, out of proportion to the situations they are related to. Although this can be a useful technique, and I do incorporate some such strategies along with the other and more central parts of my plan, cognitive approaches alone will not do the job either. Assuring someone that their fear, say of flying, is not rational usually has little or no effect on them. Phobics often readily acknowledge the foolishness of their fears. Cognitive strategies are usually helpful in conjunction with desensitization techniques as a means of increasing a person's receptivity to treatment.

Medications of various kinds, including tranquilizers and antidepressants, are also used to treat anxiety, as discussed later in this chapter, but some of these drugs can be addictive, and some are expensive. Some have troublesome side effects as well. And in any case many people would far prefer a chemical-free treatment plan.

The methods outlined in this book will enable people to treat themselves, in the privacy of their own homes. Clinicians across the country see a failure rate as high as forty percent in treatments for anxiety. This is primarily because of the problem of receptivity—people dropping out of treatment after getting started. My approach is designed to overcome this resistance and reluctance by giving the client himself control of his own anti-anxiety therapy. Then he can design his own self-help program and enact and administer it, being well aware of the progress he is making, every step of the way.

The advantages of this treatment plan: reliability, accuracy, privacy, and low cost. It also passes the classical tests for a superior treatment: simplicity, elegance, and reproducibility (proven repeat success).

WHAT IS THE BEST TREATMENT FOR ANXIETY?

If you ask therapists today what the best treatment is for many mental issues and problems, they are likely to say "Exposure Therapy." But in fact many of them intuitively also encourage clients to have behavioral interaction with the object of their fears, which reinforces and strengthens the effect of the treatment.

In 1975 when I published my book, *CT: The Astounding New Confrontation Therapy*, I wondered whether I should call the procedure I was advancing "Confrontation" or "Exposure" Therapy. At the time, there was a preference for Exposure Therapy on the part of researchers and clinicians. I decided to use the term Confrontation Therapy because I thought Exposure Therapy didn't convey the importance of confronting the feared object or situation behaviorally. Confrontation Therapy, on the other hand, implied not just exposure but a behavioral approach to dealing with the feared object or situation. I no longer use the term Confrontation Therapy, however, because in later years, especially the 1980's and 90s, the term was co-opted by therapists treating addicts, who used it for a highly aggressive treatment intended to make addicts realize how negatively their actions were affecting themselves and others.

I will use the term Exposure Therapy in this book since it is now generally recognized as the name of the technique, and in recent times it is also commonly assumed that Exposure Therapy includes behaviorally confronting one's fears.

HOW I CAME TO DEVELOP MY METHOD OF TREATMENT

Shortly after I arrived at Kent State University to start my graduate studies in psychology, my advisor, Dr. David Riccio, asked me what I would like to work on as a research project. I told him that I wanted to study the treatment and extinction of anxiety. For the next year I conducted countless experiments with laboratory rats (safe, homogeneous, and relatively good subjects).

The first step was to develop a standardized methodology. Following my advisor's recommendation, I organized the subjects into experimental and control groups. All of the subjects in the experimental group were placed in a black wooden box from which they could not escape. They then received random, mild electric shocks to their feet from an electric grid that formed the floor of the box. There was a guillotine door between the box and a second white box that the animals could quickly run to whenever the door was lifted. The animals were never shocked when they were in the white box.

Each day for about a week I shut the animals in the black box and administered the shocks. After a week, I left the door open and measured how long it took before they moved to the white box. All of the animals quickly moved to the white box. My goal at that point was to determine how long it would take for the animals to leave the white box and go into the black one (rodents are nocturnal and prefer dark settings). In order for the animals to reenter the black box, they would have to lose a considerable amount of their fear.

In the subsequent weeks I subjected the animals to countless techniques designed to reduce their fear of the black box. I tried putting them in the black box and not letting them escape, thinking that constant exposure to it might reduce their fear. I also had them develop a variety of other fears, in the hope that this might distract them. I also tried allowing them to move on their own from the white box to the black box. After about a year of trying every approach imaginable, I felt that I had found what I believed was the most efficient way to get rodents to reenter a fearful situation.

One day I was walking through the psychology clinic at the school and happened to pass one of the clinical professor's offices, whose door was open. He invited me in and asked me how my research was going. I told him that I had spent the past year trying to develop a technique that would extinguish an acquired fear response as quickly as possible, and had developed a cookbook procedure that would accomplish this. The approach involved placing the animal in the white box and allowing him, on his own, to gradually walk back into the black box. I found that this was the most effective technique and all the other techniques, including forcing the animal back into the black box, were not nearly as successful. The professor, who was a Freudian-oriented clinician, looked at me and said, "That is pretty much what we do in psychoanalytic therapy. We basically allow the person to examine his fears and let them extinguish."

This was hardly the case. Freudian therapy is extremely complex and involves years of analysis of the person's childhood. The person's fears are presumed to originate in childhood experiences involving the relationship between the child and his parents. The subsequent fear stems not from traumatic experiences that the child may have, but from his fear that his father will discover that he loves his mother; he views his father as a rival. Moreover, the child disguises his fear of the father and thereby develops a variety of incidental fears (fears transferred to other situations or objects). This repressed tension comes out later on— the brain converts it to a fear of snakes or whatever.

The predominant form of treatment at the time was psycho-analysis. My own theory was dismissed at first. My approach, in the opinion of the majority of the clinicians at the time, was overly sim-plistic, and contrary to accepted psychological thinking. Nevertheless, I continued to develop my approach and eventually extended it to human subjects.

At the time there were a few psychologists who came before me who shared my thinking. What these clinicians usually did was expose a client to his fears by instructing him to close his eyes and imagine them. Prior to this the client was trained to stay in a relaxed state. The assumption, which was subsequently disproved, was that the fear-ful images would become associated with the relaxed state and thereby lose their fear-provoking properties. What actually happened was that when the threatening or anxiety-producing images were presented, since nothing was going on, the anxiety was paired with nothing going on. That's why there was a reduction in fear.

Another comparable approach at the time was to have the client view the fearful images in their most intense state and allow him or her to acclimate to them. Theoretically this could work, but few people could tolerate this approach. Moreover, clients weren't allowed to approach images gradually or on their own, as they did in my approach. In addition, my approach involved overcoming fears more fully by confronting them behaviorally as well.

Counterconditioning (trying to counter conditioning that occurred earlier between a stimulus and some pain, to associate it now with relaxation) would also be of limited use, since this is also an essentially passive approach.

In my practice, I have found that the presentation of fearful images is not nearly as effective as having the client voluntarily confront them. In a typical session with my clients, I ask them to imagine a mildly fearful situation, and then ask them to try to gradually intensify the image. What usually happens is quite surprising—their fear diminishes—a process referred to as paradoxical enhancement. The reason: the act of confronting their fears seems to empower the person, which counters the fears they would otherwise expect to experience.

Passive strategies are far less effective and they don't address the client's need to gain the necessary behavioral (practical) skills. Moreover, self-initiated confrontation enhances client receptivity, whereas images presented by a professional don't seem to enhance a person's confidence even though this may reduce their fears.

THE THREE INGREDIENTS OF FEAR AND ANXIETY

I have always assumed that there are three systems involved here: the body's physiological response, behavior (what the person does in the face of what he fears), and the person's subjective (psychological) view of the feared object or situation, and that all three can be manipulated independently.

Let's take a closer look at these three different things going on at once.

1. The physiological response—this includes all of our physical responses to an anxiety situation: an increase in heart rate, faster breathing, perspiration, increase in pulse rate, increased tension in the muscles throughout the body, etc. All in all, what psychologists call arousal.

2. The behavioral response—this is what a person does in response to the fact that he is anxious. Typically, people either confront the source (approach it), avoid it, or attempt to escape from it (freeze or hide from it). Running away from something reduces anxiety temporarily, but eventually the anxiety will only be greater, because running away actually scares the person's brain by indicating they obviously can't handle the feared object. A behavioral response to something might be: staying well away from it.

3. The psychological or subjective response—this is the feeling a person has about the situation or thing that is bringing about the anxiety. It includes the reaction a person has to the physiological responses that are being generated by the anxiety.

Subjective responses to something might be: "I don't like doing this!" "I can't deal with this." "This is too much for me—it is something I could never get over!"

Again, each of these elements can be manipulated independently.

A person may learn how to deal with an anxiety behaviorally, but still not mentally. If they hate elevators but work in a building where they must be used, they may be able to manage to do so while hating it and still having the physiological responses.

The physiological response can be dealt with by desensitization or anti-anxiety medications. You can desensitize a person's physiological responses and the person still may not want to go on the elevator or roller coaster, or whatever.

Exposure is primarily aimed at extinguishing the physiological responses.

It extinguishes the physical reactions to anxiety so that if you are afraid of water, for instance, you can go into it without having a panic attack. It is designed to reduce and desensitize the degree to which our bodies react to a fear. If you are afraid of going on a plane or into the water, it will reduce your physiological responses to a level so that you are able to enjoy both activities without a fast heartbeat, panicky breathing, sweating, etc. The assumption is that once this is accomplished the other responses will be reduced naturally.

However to overcome anxiety you need more than this. You also have to develop and encourage a positive behavioral reaction. This then deals with both our physiological and behavioral responses, and gives one a sense of mastery. It can't get someone to like roller coasters, but can give them a feeling of confidence while on them.

My method of treatment is aimed at extinguishing the physical symptoms of fear or anxiety, but also developing the behavioral skills to gain confidence in the situation.

An example of the need for behavioral skills would be police officers, who face dangerous situations often. Consider a trainee policeman who wants to overcome his fears associated with the work. Exposure would help extinguish his physiological response—the person comes in and the therapist shows him photos of crimes in progress and other dangerous situations. This is not nearly enough to train a policeman. He needs to not only be exposed to, but learn *how to deal with* such situations. The only way you can become a policeman is to develop mastery, by doing role-playing, and eventually being trained in things like self-defense, handling weapons of all kinds, learning how to handle arrests, fleeing suspects, searches, use of force situations of all levels, how to enter threatening areas and situations, and other potentially life-threatening circumstances.

Overcoming stage fright, for another example, requires the performer to feel confident and in control in order to project himself well and communicate well with the audience. A highly accomplished scientist, who worked on the electrical and physiological mechanisms involved in breathing aids for paraplegics, consulted me because he was frustrated by his own anxieties when he presented his findings at conferences. I asked him if he'd ever had a bad experience while presenting, and he said "no." He said he overprepared for conferences so that wouldn't happen. I pointed out that since he had never had a difficult experience in this situation, he would probably not know how to handle one if it did occur. So we practiced handling various problems that could conceivably crop up, such as being asked a very difficult question, having his findings challenged, forgetting his outline or notes, etc. In the process, his fears vanished and he found that he had gained the confidence he was looking for.

When you approach something you fear, your anxiety goes up temporarily as you begin to approach it.

As you get into the activity, more directly involved in it, go into the water and start to learn to swim, you will find that your anxiety crests and then comes right down. This is why people waiting to start a game of basketball or football are usually more anxious while waiting to go onto the field to play than after they've been playing for a while. In a way this doesn't make sense—if we are afraid of something, why would our fear be less when we are actually doing the thing we fear, in the fray, than before we start? As we approach it, and get into it, our anxiety peaks, and in short order we are less anxious.

Assume someone is afraid of swimming in a pool as a result of almost drowning in one. If she goes to a pool and looks at the water (exposure), even if she goes in the water or floats in the deep end with a life preserver, she will only extinguish her physical response.

Behavioral interaction would facilitate her becoming confident in the water by learning how to swim, and swim well; it would give her mastery of the water. As a result she would be more likely to learn to like water, and to swim in the ocean and other bodies of water (i.e., her recovery would generalize). She would probably not think much about water once she realized she was able to handle it competently.

The brain does not accept mere passive exposure, because it is concerned with the person's ability to deal with a problem. If we avoid the feared thing, don't go in the water, decide not take the plane ride, at first our anxiety goes down. But then our anxiety gradually goes up as our brain realizes that we have no skill in regard to that activity, are unable to effectively face that activity.

Behavioral therapy forces you to face the activity you fear and practice it until you achieve mastery. This causes you to lose your fear.

> Competence leads to confidence.

With Exposure Therapy only, you still have to worry and think about the water, keep your eyes open for problems when you're in it. When you confront your fears behaviorally as well, you can swim, and swim well. Your brain no longer worries about you having an accident, because you have confidence. You can confront water easily, not just avoid it triggering anxiety.

But as noted earlier there is a third component, the psychological, and neither Exposure nor Behavioral Therapy deal directly with this variable. This is your view of an activity—do you like it or not, are you likely to be good at it? It does play a role in how we deal with that anxiety.

In treatment, if your psychological response to something you fear is very negative, you have no sense of confidence in that area, treatment will not be easy, pleasant, or successful, and you may not be compliant. The psychological variable will get in the way. Therapy without taking into account the third factor, the psychological, seriously limits the success of your treatment. Adding the psychological variable is very important, because it makes the other two come together. When all three components are aligned, therapy is extremely effective, and sets the stage to go on to desensitize and master many other areas.

How to effectively deal with the third aspect of anxiety, the psychological or subjective, is explained in Chapter Five.

OTHER TREATMENTS FOR ANXIETY

Before we leave the subject of anxiety treatment, let's take a closer look at the some of the other common ways of treating this type of mental distress.

COGNITIVE BEHAVIORAL THERAPY

This type of treatment is very popular with many therapists, and it has two components.

The cognitive, or intellectual side, delivers a lot of rational and logical information, and attempts to help a person see how this should alleviate some of his concerns. The information often includes statistics, human tendencies, trends in human evolution, and explanations of why we are the way we are.

For example, if a person's fear is unrealistic, you might show them that they have not made an accurate assessment of the risk (after researching what the likelihood is of what they fear actually happening). You would also consider mitigating circumstances, such as any factors that would suggest that the person is less susceptible to this problem or likely to encounter it because of his age, family history, or whatever. Then you might discuss how the person could deal with each scenario that might arise, if it did happen.

The behavioral side of therapy involves actions, such as desensitizing and role-playing. It can also include doing physical things with the person, such as accompanying them to confront some feared situation or object in person.

Clients almost always prefer the cognitive side, and want to stick with it. They will often want to pick your brain on aspects of it. This can sometimes be an avoidance strategy.

I treated a standup comedian once who had a lot of theories about his stress. He enjoyed our cognitive sessions, including filling me in on, and adding to, his theories. When I finally suggested moving to the behavioral side, he didn't like it.

When we eventually did so, he made progress faster with the behavioral therapy, but didn't feel good about it and thought that it was more like work.

I sometimes use cognitive approaches to tempt people into therapy. It sounds good and interesting, but in the long run may not last.

Behavioral therapy has a better effect, and is longer lasting. You learn skills you can keep, that will not vanish in a week or so.

ANTIDEPRESSSANTS AND ANTI-ANXIETY MEDICATIONS

According to *Scientific American* in 2018: 12% of American adults take antidepressants, and 8.3% take drugs from a group that includes sedatives, anti-anxiety drugs, and hypnotics.

ANTIDEPRESSANTS

Antidepressants include the drugs Prozac, Bupropion, Zoloft, Cymbalta, and Paxil. Prozac, one of the earlier ones, is so well known that it is almost a modern-day icon. Antidepressants are generally favored over anti-anxiety medications, because they are much less addictive.

The brain makes serotonin, a calming agent. These medications (called SSRI's, selective serotonin reuptake inhibitors) interfere with the brain's ability to reabsorb the serotonin it has created, and thus increase the amount of this chemical left between the brain cells. Antidepressants are very good at relieving stress, and also relieve anxiety to some extent, but are not actually so good at reducing depression. This became apparent in the nineties, so manufacturers added a bit of stimulant to them.

Antidepressants may take one to six weeks to work fully. In the long term, as noted above, they are not as addictive as anti-anxiety medications. The hope is that while using them the brain will have a chance to get reconfigured, and the person to create new habits.

ANTI-ANXIETY MEDICATIONS

Generalized anxiety is one of the most common psychological problems, and at least six percent of Americans take anti-anxiety medications. Some anti-anxiety medications include Xanax, Klonopin, Valium, Ativan, Serax, and Librium. Beta blockers are often given for social anxiety.

Use in therapy

Anti-anxiety medications can be useful in therapy when a person is extremely anxious. If a person's anxiety is too high, 7 or above on a scale of 1 to 10, they can be paralyzed by it, like the person standing on a high diving board, who won't jump no matter what the coach says— they just want to get off.

You can't desensitize someone whose anxiety is at a 10—they would be overwhelmed by the process. You couldn't even call up images.

In a case like this you would have a doctor prescribe an anti-anxiety drug to lower the person's anxiety level to 2 or 3, and then gradually reduce the medication. The medicine will lower their emotional response.

What if someone wants to be a fireman and can do everything for the fireman test except climb a fifty-foot ladder? This is not actually realistic because most fire departments are not going to have a 50-foot ladder. But the test requires it.

If you give this person anti-anxiety medication, now his fear at ten feet is going to be a 3, not a 9. At twenty feet, a 4, not a 10+. And so on. The medication makes desensitizing someone very anxious about the idea of climbing a fifty-foot ladder much faster and easier. Once the therapy has been successful with that, the therapist or doctor can then work with the person to gradually reduce the dose of their medication.

A lot of people come in for desensitization already on anti-anxiety meds, and this makes the process faster and more efficient, because they are not as reactive.

Drawbacks

The problem with these medications, aside from their addictive quality, is that they dull you across the board, including emotionally. These are sedative chemicals, the opposite of stimulants.

A trial lawyer, skyscraper ironworker, or professional driver couldn't function well on Xanax because he wouldn't be as sharp. You wouldn't want to run dangerous equipment or do anything else that requires you to be alert and focused while taking such meds. You would be more casual, wouldn't be as detailed and creative. You might fall off Mt. Everest trying to climb it, but you wouldn't be nervous.

General practitioners are the ones mainly prescribing these medications. A person comes in to see them and says he feels overwhelmed. "If I can just get through these next couple of months, I'll be OK." So the doctor writes the person a prescription and leaves. The person should be weaned off them once the crisis is past, but by then the doctor is on to other things, and once someone is on a drug like this, he feels at peace and at ease, and often stays on it.

A WORD ABOUT PSYCHIATRISTS

Before ending this chapter I'd like to say a word or two about psychiatrists, whom most people see as the very top level of knowledge about psychological matters. Many people unknowingly go to a psychiatrist instead of a psychologist for psychotherapy. This is not the place to go when you are looking for advice with life problems. Bear in mind that psychiatrists are medical doctors. Anatomy, physiology, and biology are much of what they study in college.

In the sixties and seventies they were very involved in therapy, because there weren't many psychoactive drugs then. Once these powerful tools came onto the scene, psychiatrists moved away from psychology.

They don't do psychotherapy regularly—they now mainly prescribe medication for mental conditions. They usually see five to eight thousand people a year. Someone's first session with them is often an hour, to give the psychiatrist a chance to observe symptoms, gain some insight into the person, and diagnose them. After that they usually spend ten or fifteen minutes with each person, usually adjusting medications.

If they are called into a court case and asked to examine someone, they can provide both neurological and psychological input and explanations for behavior. Thus they are often used for this when someone may have neurological damage, or there is some extreme or unusual behavior involved.

They also have an important function in medical centers, aiding in the treatment of people who have diabetes or some other medical condition as well as a psychological problem. Here, being doctors themselves, they have a better understanding of the medical situation— the course of a disease and how the disease will be treated—as well as insight into psychological issues and knowledge of meds.

For these two settings they are exceptionally well suited. They are also very good at the diagnosis and treatment of psychotics of any kind.

When it comes to psychology in general and psychotherapy, however—talking to people to try and help them with their everyday psychological problems—they are not really involved in such things much anymore. If they still wish to do this today, there are special internships and programs they can take for it in college and medical school, to learn how.

So psychotherapy has become the bailiwick of psychologists. Most psychologists have PhDs or PsyDs—it takes about eight years to get through a Clinical Psychology program and meet licensing requirements. This includes special programs and internships, and all of this time is spent on psychology.

CHAPTER FOUR

WEARING OUT YOUR WORRIES
THE DESENSITIZATION PROCESS

Desensitization is the core element of the fear reduction process. Desensitization involves the following, in brief: exposing yourself to your fears in carefully controlled doses, in a systematic way, with the exposure rate (time and place) controlled entirely by you, so that the fears eventually lose their ability to upset you. If you summon up an emotion, and do this over and over, in the absence of any adverse consequences, as would be the case during a desensitizing session in a therapist's office, or if you are at home just thinking about or imagining the situation, it is only a matter of time before your response to it lessens. This fact is so well established that it is virtually one of the laws of psychology.

But exposure to thoughts and images that make us anxious, done in an unplanned way, is a random and inefficient process. This is because focusing on distressing thoughts is something we usually avoid, so that under normal circumstances the mind actually works against itself to resist the very process that would ultimately produce maximum relief. We may be driven to summon up emotionally distressing material in an attempt to extinguish it, but then we run into a counterbalancing desire to avoid it. As a result, our mind vacillates and the healing process is drawn out. Thus over the course of many months, the actual exposure is likely to be brief and sporadic, even though we may feel as if our mind is constantly on the heart of the problem.

> Some people continually divert their attention from unpleasant thoughts by engaging in low-stress activities such as hobbies or even work—any alternative that they feel more comfortable with. Drugs and alcohol are a powerful means of diverting our attention to more pleasurable thoughts. Again, this acts to prevent the processing and discharge of emotionally laden material.
>
> Unfortunately, one can only ignore more important concerns for so long without ill effect.

With no more than twenty minutes of a day on this program, on the other hand, a person can experience as much therapeutic exposure in a week as would ordinarily be achieved in months. The course of desensitization, as detailed in this chapter, takes the process a giant step further than exposure alone. You will not only expose yourself to your fear by conjuring it up, you will call up many different scenarios involving the fear and manipulate it in various ways, and then imagine your responses to these various situations. The mental experience of visualizing these different versions of a threat, and then your responses to them, results in a more fully rounded, sounder, and more enduring form of extinction.

WHY A FEW MINUTES A DAY IS ENOUGH

People may think they've thought about an upsetting thing a lot, but my estimate is that it's more like thirty seconds before they veer off into avoidance, start thinking about going to the gym or whatever. If asked, they might think they spent five minutes on the sensitive subject, but two or three of these were probably still on the approach, not the actual point of exposure.

A total of ten minutes of actual exposure twice a day is plenty.

WHAT FIRST?

As described earlier, there are three ingredients in any fear or anxiety—behavior, a person's subjective (psychological) response to the object of dread, and the physiological, and all three can be manipulated independently. I usually ask clients which component they want to extinguish. I often suggest that they extinguish the physiological component first, since it is then easier to extinguish the others, but I will start or focus on whichever one they choose. You can do the same when self-administering a course of desensitization.

IMAGERY VERSUS REALITY

The desensitizing process is based upon the fact that our brains use the same neural pathways to process imagery as reality. Usually through imagery you can knock down a fear by at least seventy-five percent. Even the most successful desensitization process will remove at best seventy-five to ninety percent of an anxiety. That usually sets the stage for desensitizing the balance of the fear or anxiety through actual confrontation of the feared object or situation.

Whenever you desensitize a response, you actually do two things. You desensitize the emotional reaction, and you also fatigue that response. Over time, the fatigue element will wear off, and so you are left at the point where the desensitization may not have been one hundred percent complete. The rest must often be removed by direct confrontation of the anxiety-generating situation or object, when possible.

There are situations that people cannot easily experience in actuality, such as having a particular disease they fear. If your fear is of drowning in a shipwreck, going down in a plane crash, or being eaten by a shark, obviously, you can't (or don't want to!) recreate that in reality, so in that case the only way of overcoming that fear is through imagery. In those cases like this, desensitization often is the best that can be done.

THE IMPORTANT SECOND STEP

Is moving from visual exposure to active exposure (confronting the feared situation in person). It means getting out of the therapist's office and into the actual situation. It means being behaviorally involved with the thing you fear: such as approaching a snake, touching it, handling it, and so on. If you fear water (as in the example noted earlier), you would need to not just visualize yourself getting into a pool, but actually get into a real pool. Confrontation Therapy begins where Exposure Therapy ends, and will get you a long way toward mastery.

> There are simulators for pilots, car drivers, and other scenarios. These are programs that will plunge you right into getting on a plane and taking off, handling a car in heavy traffic, going to a zoo or pet shop to confront snakes, or dealing with a fear of dogs or sharks. These can provide behavioral practice, too.

When working with clients, I usually have them create a hierarchy of feared situations. The Subjective Units of Distress Scale (SUDS) can be used to rate their level of discomfort and then situations are gradually approached. I typically aim for clients to feel a distress level of 3–4 when actively confronting situations. Over time, situations rated at the top of the hierarchy (7–10) will lower in discomfort so that they can be approached. It typically takes about twenty minutes for the client's discomfort to go down after confronting a situation. During this time, their attention needs to be on the situation as opposed to avoiding it. Rating their level of discomfort during the confrontation process can help them see that their discomfort is going down.

The Subjective Units of Distress Scale (SUDS) was originated by Joseph Wolpe in 1969 as a means of measuring mental distress. It can be found online. An approximation of this scale can be found below:

0. You feel peaceful and serene, no anxiety of any kind

1. You feel basically good, with perhaps a touch of discomfort

2. Slightly troubled

3. Somewhat worried, bothered to the point that you are aware of it

4. Negative thoughts have begun to affect you

5. You are definitely upset

6. You feel bad enough that you think you need to do something about it

7. Bad feelings dominate your thinking and are hard to control

8. You've reached the point of panic

9. You feel desperate—hopeless and helpless

10. Your distress is almost unbearable—you can't function and may be on the verge of a breakdown

WHY DESENSITIZATION WORKS

As explained in detail in the Appendix, our reactions to the world around consist of two basic responses—emotional and intellectual.

For most of us the intellect functions reasonably well and rarely poses psychological problems. There are some instances of severe psychiatric disturbances—schizophrenia is an example—wherein the individual's thought processes are confused and troubled, but such maladies are rare. As a rule our intellect responds logically to events and circumstances. We put our finger on a hot stove, feel the shock of pain, determine that the one is the cause of the other, and we don't do it again. We taste a dish, experience the gratification of our senses, recognize the cause of the pleasure, and take another mouthful.

Our emotions are not so comfortably leashed, for they aren't guided by logic. They respond to a simple association of events, whether cause and effect are at work or not. For example, one of my clients ended up in an accident on the first day he was driving on his own after getting his license. The accident was a bad one, and he ended up with broken bones and casts for many months. Although he'd been eager to start driving, now he associated cars with the pain and terror of the accident. Any time he was asked to even ride in a car he experienced a strong emotional reaction and was not even able to enter a car. People were always telling him there was nothing to fear—this is a different car, the accident was a freak, the driver now will be very careful, millions of people ride in cars every day without mishaps, and so on. In short, it was pointed out time after time that logically his fear was out of proportion to the reality. He retained the fear nonetheless, and until he used desensitization and behavioral therapy to extinguish it, was unable to even be around a car without acute discomfort.

Most of us know someone who has fallen from a horse, or almost been drowned, or been mugged, and have tried to convince that person that there was no logical reason to believe there would be a repetition of the incident. Rarely are such assurances effective—he or she will, for a while at least, remain wary of horses, or water, or city streets.

Sometimes the victim has the insight to say, "I *know* there's no reason to be afraid—I *know* it's unlikely to happen again…." But the fear lingers.

This is because when a particular event is followed by a trauma, the emotions will associate the two experiences—even if the link has been forged by mere chance.

There is one simple—though ultimately harmful—way to handle situations that cause such discomfort: avoid them. Let's go back to my client's car accident. After the accident, the next time he was supposed to ride in a car he found the idea too painful, too fraught with anxiety, so he chose to walk. On other occasions, when walking was not feasible, he simply stayed home. His behavior was "rewarded," so to speak, by a reduction in his anxiety and discomfort—and this, in turn, encouraged similar behavior the next time he had to face a car ride or was asked to drive. Eventually he got to the point where his life was arranged so that cars played no part in it.

This reaction is called, in psychological jargon, an "avoidance response," or "avoidance behavior." It is often unwisely encouraged by even the most well-meaning people. In a syndicated advice column, a woman (who signed herself "Aching Heart") wrote in to say that her husband had left her two years previously, and she was unable to reconcile herself to her loss. The columnist advised her to get her mind off of him, to think of something else, take up a hobby, travel…and eventually she would forget him. It is natural to want to avoid pain, and the columnist's kindly advice would seem to be quite in order. However, such a course of action would mean that the woman would be prolonging her pain and ultimately would probably never eliminate the cause of it. She would be avoiding it, just as the victim of the car accident was avoiding cars.

Such behavior, although immediately soothing, is in the long run quite constricting. It is like a low-grade fever that lingers and lingers, a malaise that doesn't quite knock the patient out of action. But just as a low-grade fever can develop into severe illness, avoidance behavior can spread throughout one's whole attitude, so that a person will eventually be avoiding more and more experiences, and his or her life becomes painfully narrow.

The best way—the only way—to root out a negative emotion such as fear, anxiety, or depression is to confront it. Other, more evasive methods will only prolong the emotion and the attendant discomfort. Since, however, we have a natural tendency to avoid pain, confronting a negative emotion is not the simple matter it seems on the face of it. Our instinctive method of applying balm to any kind of emotional distress is to try to avoid it—switch our minds to pleasant thoughts, think of something else, get away from it. So in order to confront a negative emotion, we must also confront the avoidance behavior that usually surrounds it and sometimes masks it from our view.

Now, what happens when we put ourselves in a situation that arouses our anxiety and we experience no trauma, no disaster? What happened to the victim of the car wreck when he finally did take a ride and there was no accident? What happens to the person who almost drowned when he enters the water without trouble, to the horse rider who doesn't fall off the horse again, or the mugging victim who takes a stroll along a city street and doesn't get bashed in the head? Obviously, these people will get used to activities that at one time seemed threatening, if not downright sinister. The fear will eventually wear off.

Psychologists call this phenomenon "extinction" of an emotional reaction. Extinction occurs because the emotions connect events on a temporal rather than logical basis. If an event is followed by no real consequences, our emotions associate no real consequences with it, just as they can associate horrendous consequences with the most innocent event such as a car ride, a swim, or a walk down the street.

How can we cause extinction? How can we banish that vague anxiety, that nameless fear, that suffocating depression? With Exposure Therapy, or desensitization.

This is a process that enables a person to confront a distressing emotion through the use of imagery, while also overcoming avoidance responses that tend to preserve the emotion.

This is merely the utilization of a very natural process; given enough time, most emotions will extinguish (though frequently imperfectly) by themselves. So all that desensitization is doing is compressing and harnessing a natural resource.

THE FIVE SIMPLE STEPS OF DESENSITIZATION

This is something you can do by yourself quite easily, with a little practice. There are five basic steps:

1. Education
2. Preparation
3. Imagination
4. Repetition
5. Relaxation

Let's take each step and see how it works.

Step One—Education

I educate the patient regarding the research on Exposure Therapy. For example, in an overview of the effectiveness of exposure techniques with various anxiety-based disorders, including post-traumatic stress disorder (PSTD), Obsessive-Compulsive Disorder (OCD), Generalized Anxiety Disorder (GAD), Social Anxiety Disorder, and phobias, the research indicates that they are an effective and recommended first line of treatment. See the list of references in Appendix II.

Step Two—Preparation.

Choose a pleasant, familiar area, one in which you feel at ease, and seat yourself in a comfortable position. It is important that you be as open and receptive as possible. Relax, and close your eyes.

Step Three—Imagination.

In your mind play over the scene that has evoked the emotion you want to get rid of. Let us say that you are experiencing fear. Imagine all of the events that led up to the moment or situation that provoked the fear, all of the circumstances surrounding it, all of the details of the scene that you can come up with—right up to the point at which the actual threatening action, sighting, or exchange took place. Then stop. This can take a while. Let your mind slowly and gradually imagine all of the details of the feared object or circumstances until it provokes an uncomfortable arousal response (such as rapid heart rate, fast breathing, or a nauseous feeling). Then stop. Start from the beginning and do it again and again until it no longer provokes any physiological response. Then, let your mind wander forward, a little at a time, until you can imagine the entire incident without showing any response. This can take days, weeks, or longer, depending on the intensity of the fear. Nevertheless, as you proceed, you will eventually discover that you are making significant progress and your overall level of fear is gradually desensitizing.

> Just telling your mind to worry about the feared object or whatever thoughts it has about the feared object is OK as well. In this approach, you just let your fears sit beside you—you do nothing but let them be for five to ten minutes. You do want to monitor the situation to make sure the thoughts don't become too frightening and after a short while—those five or ten minutes—stop the process and wait a while before you do it again. This passive approach works well, but it is not as fast-acting as a more aggressive approach. But it is good to encourage control and voluntariness when it comes to desensitization.

Step Four—Repetition.

Begin again, as in Step 3, imagining the scene that caused the discomfort. Immerse yourself in it. Only this time let your brain go a little further. To use the example of fear again, go through all of the details and circumstances as in Step 3, right up to the point at which the threat or action took place, only this time let your brain go as far as it can. Go a little further, get into the experience, go through in detail what you saw and heard and felt. Then begin again and go through the whole scene. Repeat the scene until you no longer feel uncomfortable going through it. Repetition is the most important part of the process. Don't push your brain to go beyond where it is comfortable. If you need to go further, but you aren't comfortable, then get professional help.

When you get to the point that the fear is totally desensitized—you have no physiological response to it, have no difficulty interacting with it, and are psychologically comfortable with the feared object or circumstances—you are done. If your anxiety is not completely resolved at this point, regardless of the progress you have made, you can then seek professional help. Whatever degree of desensitization you have successfully accomplished is in your favor and you should be proud of it. You have probably saved yourself a lot of time in therapy, at the very least. You have also learned a new skill that will be of enormous value in the future.

In some of the cases presented in this book, I go faster and further with the client than you should attempt. In many cases I push the individual more aggressively than I would recommend others doing. This is because I have a lot of experience with these techniques. The techniques, as described in this book, are very effective and eventually you may find yourself pushing yourself to go a little faster as you become more confident with them. I caution you that slow and steady is the way to go. There is no advantage in stressing yourself.

Step Five—Relaxation.

Think of some unrelated but calming and pleasant scene, such as a still lake at dusk, or a sunrise on the desert. Put yourself in this scene as completely as you can for a minute or two.

These five steps are the nucleus of the desensitization process. They are what you need to master your emotions.

> The desensitizing process, and its practical applications, is so simple and elegant that it could easily be construed as obvious.

WHEN VISUALIZING

Since visualization is not as intense as actuality, you should desensitize yourself to more intense images than what actually occurred to take into account the greater intensity of actually going through the stages physically. If you are afraid of flying on planes, which for you could create an anxiety level of 8, 9, or 10, when you summon up this thought in imagery it may only be a 4 or 5. So you may want to up the imagery to being a passenger on a plane during severe turbulence, which will probably trigger the higher level of anxiety you are trying to generate here.

In visualization you can practice going through the stages at your own pace. You can back up the stages and analyze them, and you can imagine things you consider important that may not have actually happened—such as what would have happened if your injuries from an accident prevented you from going back to work, or if you were disfigured.

TWO EXAMPLES OF THIS PROCESS

For an example of this whole process, Sandy was so fearful of flying that she was sure she would never be able to overcome her plane phobia. She could hardly tolerate sitting on a plane, and had no idea what it was about flying that she found so anxiety-inducing. I suggested the technique outlined above.

Step 1: Education. Sandy read up on it, and discovered that flying was not as dangerous as she had thought. Then she read the research that reviewed the effectiveness of Exposure Therapy, and decided to give it a try.

Step 2: She sat down in her favorite chair and closed her eyes. She let her mind wander and within minutes she thought of driving to the airport. Just the thought of driving there put her at a level 4. She stopped and it was seven or eight days before she was able to imagine arriving at the airport. But things started to pick up after that—several more tries and she was through security. Eventually, she could imagine getting on a plane that was not taking off. Eventually—three months later—she was able to see herself going up in the air. The takeoff was very difficult. Weeks later she was able to handle flying in mild turbulence. Four months from the start she had accomplished flying in imagery without getting anxious. Ultimately, she flew in actuality.

Daniel also had a phobia about flying in planes, but unlike Sandy, he felt that his fears were justified because he was an engineer and aware of how often and easily things could go wrong. He flew all over the world on a regular basis, inspecting plants and warehouses, and overseeing construction projects. During those trips, many times he encountered turbulence and airline mishaps that could have proved fatal. So he accepted his fears as realistic and "white-knuckled it" as best he could.

To his amazement, desensitization worked to drastically lower his fears, using the same methods as Sandy, with one significant difference. Instead of passively confronting his images as he allowed his mind to wander each day, he pushed the images a little at a time. If his mind started to imagine that there was mild turbulence while he was flying, he stayed with the image a little longer or pushed into it by imagining that the shaking and bumpy feelings in the plane were a little stronger. In so doing, he felt that he speeded up the process a little, and he probably did. But use this method sparingly and very gradually. It is not necessary, and may discourage you if it makes the process too uncomfortable.

ANOTHER DESENSITIZING OPTION

When desensitizing, you basically have two choices: to allow the brain to set up and run its own desensitization program, and just watch it. Or to aid the process.

You can speed the desensitizing process up by doing it in the way described earlier, or let your brain pick the time and place.

If someone's anxiety is very intense, I let the brain run it. And wait for the brain to work it down before I join the process.

If a person's anxiety is low, I help the person speed up the process, as described in this chapter and elsewhere in this book.

The brain has a very sophisticated way of going about desensitization—it's rather ingenious, actually. It may seem somewhat disjointed because it doesn't follow a direct logical line, but the brain doesn't work in a linear fashion. It regulates the process in terms of a subject's intensity and its effect on you.

The brain will regulate the desensitization process on its own, based on your own needs, delve into at its own pace. Let the brain decide how much to do and when to do it. This is the epitome of voluntarism, and it offers great flexibility and freedom. The brain is in charge here, which calms it.

Your brain wants you to be safe. So it goes slow—touches something, goes all around and then touches something else. It knows the best thing to get into now, the intensity level it wants to hit it at, a 3 maybe, not necessarily a 10. Other times it sees what has the greatest emotional charge, and touches that. Let your brain go as far as it wants to go.

This may seem slow at first, but it picks up after a while. If you leave the brain alone, it will manage the whole process. The brain is cautious, which is why it goes slow. If you don't like the rate at which the brain is proceeding, you can speed up the process as described elsewhere in this book.

If there is material the brain doesn't want to touch, it will deal with the surrounding material and then gradually move in on the sensitive area. If you are afraid of snakes, it may start by having you walking in open fields or through forests, then places where snakes are likely to be, such as sunny, rocky areas and places where things like old boards or stumps are piled up.

What if your brain doesn't come up with the problem subject? Your mind doesn't want to go there. Perhaps the subject is not intense enough, not really relevant to your survival right now. Maybe you're not feeling well today and that is more important. Likewise, if the intensity of something is too strong, the brain may not want to go near it.

Desensitization by the brain-directed method is initiated by sitting in a quiet place, and waiting for the brain to bring up the anxiety-producing issue. For the first thirty or sixty seconds you should wait for the brain to kick in.

You can nudge the brain, push it a little at first if it seems necessary to get it started on the imagery of the issues you are concerned with, if it is not getting into them.

Or you can wait until your brain brings this up spontaneously, and wait to do the exposure until then. The brain may wait until a time when nothing else is demanding your attention, there are no distractions, you have free time, thus are available to start doing its thing.

AN EASY WAY TO AID THE CAUSE

When we are trying to cope with or banish upsetting thoughts, the remedy is essentially to assist the mind to do what it has been programmed to do. The process of desensitization described in this chapter and later in this book, employs guided imagery to do just this.

But simply taking long walks, for example, while allowing our mind freedom to think about whatever comes to mind, is a very effective means of assisting it to clear itself of negative thoughts and clutter. Just realizing how the mind processes our experiences and concerns (see the Appendix for a detailed description of this), and allowing it to proceed freely and without the burden of the countless avoidance strategies people use, will be a major asset.

I suggest walking around the neighborhood, or somewhere else you know well so that you don't have to be too focused on your surroundings. Go for at least twenty minutes, and thirty or forty-five would be even better. Allow your mind to wander into thinking about whatever it feels like thinking about. Usually within a few minutes it will wander onto something that is disturbing. The reason for this is that the mind is very concerned with your security—looking out for your interests is its top priority. The mind thinks about the issues that you're concerned about, especially the issues that you're anxious about. The mind gradually thinks about these issues as well as other subjects that are connected with them. In the process it gradually begins to desensitize them. This is a gentle desensitization process. After five or ten minutes, go on to something else—a more pleasant thought or other things you have to think about. Walking seems to provide the ideal amount of distraction to keep you from getting overwhelmed by your thoughts.

I would keep on walking like this regularly until you become extremely comfortable with it and with all the issues that your mind is bringing up. Do this three or four times a week.

> If your anxiety soars to six or more on a scale of ten when you are doing this, then you need professional help. If you are at a four or less, let your mind continue to think about the issue on its own.

At first, you probably won't notice anything. But after three or four sessions, you should start to notice some improvement. For example, you may notice that your mind wanders off the initial issues and moves on to other issues. This is because the initial issues are losing their anxiety-raising power.

You may eventually find your thoughts on the walks becoming more concentrated on the problem issues, more focused. Eventually, two or three issues may stand out as problematic, and you will find yourself thinking about how to handle them—should you do this or that? You might even find yourself role-playing them in your mind. Your brain will eventually come up with a solution to them all.

Later in the day, sit in a chair for about fifteen minutes and do exactly the same thing. The more you allow your brain to do this, the better.

You can continue these steps indefinitely until you gradually desensitize all of your issues. If you feel comfortable with the process, you can add another step: gently push into an issue that you have been working on and is now desensitized to a lower level—say level 2—and see what you would have to consider to gently raise it to level 3 or 4. You can use this technique to gradually increase the range of issues you are desensitizing and the depth that you can achieve with them.

You need to stick with this schedule, this "grinding," which is designed to fatigue the distressing issues. If you don't you may be fine for a day or two and then get hit with a really bad day. The reason for the bad day is that during your respite, the fatigue that has built up during the desensitization process has worn off and the strength of the threatening material now seems to be much greater.

POSSIBLE PITFALLS IN THE PROCESS AND HOW TO DEAL WITH THEM

The technique of desensitization is simple, certainly, but there are a few things to watch out for. Let's take a look at some of the obstacles you might run into.

- "I don't think it's really helping me." When you first use Exposure Therapy it may be a somewhat negative experience. You are dredging up a lot of emotion, and putting your nose right in it, so you probably won't feel better right at first. Avoidance does have some advantages.

What's worse, the night after using it for the first time it may be hard to sleep.

The next morning you will probably feel a little better. But this is not because you have exhausted that emotion. You have simply fatigued that emotional process on that issue.

So you do it for the first time one Monday and have trouble sleeping that night.

On Tuesday morning you feel a little better, because your mind doesn't want to think about that issue again right now. So on Tuesday you get some relief.

Then on Wednesday, voila, it regains strength, so on Wednesday you have another wave of sadness (this is where the expression that grief comes in waves comes from).

On Wednesday you feel terrible, as bad or worse than originally, and you thought this was going to work. But you keep going anyway.

On Thursday you feel better, and then on Friday worse again.

You can expect this process to happen, but things do get better.

The next Monday the relief will last until Thursday until it gets worse again.

This is the result of some desensitization as well as fatigue of the issue.

The third Monday you use the process, the relief will probably last until Friday before the grief is back again. This is what you should watch, how long you feel good before the problem comes back again. This is the first thing I ask people when they come in for a session of desensitization the next week.

They will eventually get to the point when it holds off until the next session with me. Their grief is now compartmentalized to their sessions with me. Eventually it only returns once in a great while, such as once a year on the anniversary of the tragedy.

- One of the most frequent objections to desensitization is, "It makes me uncomfortable—I don't like the stress it puts on me." This usually happens when someone is using the technique too rapidly. Take your time, for a negative emotion can color your life every moment of the day. It can seep into your attitudes and outlook and quite literally govern you. It is much better to recognize and isolate a negative emotion, and then go through a little concentrated stress to extinguish it, than to live under its unchallenged influence twenty-four hours a day indefinitely. Just the act of recognizing it, in fact, is already a big step toward its extinction.

If you find yourself stressed by the desensitization process, you can speed over the part you find stressful. If there is a patch or two you find upsetting, go over these very quickly. This is kind of like jumping over it—imagine it just for a tenth of a second or so. If you do this several times, even though you are doing this in a speeding way, before long you will see that going over it gets easier and easier, and then maybe you can extend the time you spend on it. And it will desensitize over time, maybe even fairly quickly.

- Be flexible about when you treat yourself. Some might prefer to do the exercises once in the morning and once in the evening. At times it might be preferable to do them, circumstances permitting, as soon as the negative emotion occurs or surfaces. For particularly strong emotions, you can do the exercises once, then wait a few minutes and do them again.

- If a strong emotion arises and you are not able to deal with it immediately, recognize it, and tell yourself that you will take care of it as soon as circumstances allow. This is already a big step toward controlling it and will bring a measure of relief, for you will be dealing with the emotion, and at the same time you will not suffer the guilt that is usually engendered by an avoidance response. As you begin to recognize emotions and realize that you are either going to deal with them or put them off until a later time, you will feel a certain amount of power over them. Also, once you say you will deal with an emotion later, you will not be so preoccupied with it.

- The point of closing your eyes during the exercises is to avoid distraction and permit concentration on the process. Some people have difficulty closing their eyes. Perhaps it has something to do with a feeling of vulnerability. It isn't absolutely necessary, but if you keep your eyes open, focus them on some object that will provide a point of concentration.

- People vary in their ability to conjure images: some can create them with the greatest facility, others cannot. Some people, when asked to visualize a tree, can summon the image right down to the veins in the leaves; others simply see a somewhat branched blob. When imagining a scene in Step 3, a vivid imagination is not necessary. What is important is that you think about the scene with all of the concentration at your command—that you recreate it as best you can. If you can't evoke an image, the technique will still work because you can think about the emotion that you are going to extinguish.

- As you get into Step 4, repetition, watch out for avoidance responses, for this is where they are most likely to deflect your attention from the root emotion. One of the danger signals is too strong a reaction to the scene you are imagining. If you start to sweat, or to grip the arms of the chair you are sitting in, you are probably working up an avoidance response. Go back and start again, more slowly.

- One technique to use if you can't seem to concentrate (and lack of concentration is usually an avoidance response) is to talk the situation through to yourself, very fast—as fast as you can—the first few times. For example, "I'm going to imagine walking right up to an elevator, pressing the 'up' button, and when the doors slide open, I'm going to step right in. Then I'll stand calmly in the middle of the elevator as it starts whooshing up the floors..." Etc. This will allow you to get to your goal—the root emotion—with the least possible deflection of attention. Then you can start slowing down, savoring the details more thoroughly on subsequent repetitions.

- It is very important to be aware of avoidance responses. Signals that you have to watch for are a wandering mind and rationalizations ("This issue is not really that important," or "It's not really that much of a problem," or "This is not going to work!") When avoidance responses occur, recognize them as detours your mind is trying to set up, and circumvent them by concentrating harder.

- It is also important to praise yourself when you overcome avoidance responses. Notice how you have spotted and defeated them and take credit for it—the praise will reinforce your alertness to things like this in the future.

- Once you have repeated a scene a number of times, you may start to get bored. Although this is actually a good sign, it can also be an avoidance response. But it most likely means that your brain is just fatigued with that subject right now, so back off and your brain will let you know when it is ready to start again.

- As you repeat a scene it has a tendency to expand. One of my clients, for example, was trying to extinguish anger connected to what he considered an unjustified reprimand from his boss. By the third time he had repeated the scene it had gone far beyond the reprimand and grown to include an insult that he had long forgotten, and a rudeness that had taken place when he had been dining at his boss's home. This type of wandering is beneficial, because it brings in material that is obviously related to the root emotion. It is not the same thing as if you were suddenly to find yourself speculating on what you were going to wear tomorrow, or what you're going to eat for dinner that evening.

- Don't go too fast. Later in this chapter I discuss speed desensitization, and that is the only time speed is an asset. In general when desensitizing you should be gentle, and above all do not relive an emotion so rapidly and brutally that you become anxious enough to stop the process. Gauge your speed by monitoring your feelings. Here, again, you must be wary of avoidance responses. Periodically, be sure to keep reassuring yourself that you are summoning images only, and they are in no way threatening to you.

- The fifth step, relaxation, is a healing step, a little like applying a salve. The scene that you imagine now should not be connected in any way with the root emotion. If, for example, you have been using the technique to try and extinguish your anger with someone, do not, for your relaxation, imagine yourself shaking hands with the person you are annoyed at—that would be an avoidance response.

HOW LONG WILL THE PROCESS TAKE?

The time required for the extinction of an emotion varies with what the emotion is, and its intensity. Some minor irritations can be extinguished in one session, and other, more ingrained and painful ones, will take longer. The simple act of working on the emotion, though, is already extraordinarily therapeutic, and that in itself will bring comfort.

You will know when the emotion is finally extinguished because, even though you will still be able to recognize that you have suffered from such a feeling, you will no longer experience it. The young man, for example, who was afraid of cars is now perfectly aware that he once had this fear. Furthermore, he knows that it is necessary to exercise a certain amount of caution on highways and city streets—that accidents can happen. But he is no longer paralyzed by fear as he approaches a car, and is able to enjoy driving again.

Let's assume that you have extinguished your negative feelings about someone you do not like. You will still be able to say to yourself, coolly and with detachment, that you do not like so-and-so, but you will not suffer from the dislike as you did when you were annoyed at that person. You will have the awareness without the pain. Repetition increases memory retention—as we learned in school—but at the same time it decreases our emotional response.

WHAT IS THE RELATIVE DIFFICULTY OF DESENSITIZING DIFFERENT EMOTIONS?

There are only a few basic or primary human emotions: anger, depression, fear (or anxiety), joy, and relief. Some people would add disgust to this list.

Each of these has direct physiological effects. For example, fear triggers a variety of physical responses, such as muscle tension and accelerated heart rate and peristalsis, which prepare the body to respond to danger.

Depression is accompanied by a slowdown in mental processing aimed at encouraging the person to withdraw from circumstances and activities that are unproductive and associated with losses. It may be viewed as a braking mechanism activated whenever the rate of gratification is too low. Depression is experienced as mental fatigue, the inability to concentrate, and numerous secondary signs, such as sadness and difficulty sleeping.

Joy is somewhat the polar opposite of depression, marked by increased speed of mental processing, excitement, and an expansive attitude toward taking on new challenges.

Relief is a feeling of calm and cheerfulness that follows the cessation of a stressor, while anger is an arousal reaction to the perception of injustice aimed at motivating us to take corrective action.

All of the other emotions, such as guilt and regret, as well as grudges and resentments, are actually outgrowths of one or more of the primary emotions coupled with logical overlays.

The hardest of all emotions to desensitize are anger and affection.

Anger is extremely difficult to desensitize because anger is produced by a perception of unfairness, and usually this involves a situation in which the person was subjected to a loss as a result of the actions of another person. Because scarcity was a longstanding problem throughout the evolutionary process and one that was potentially fatal, the brain is very reluctant to accept losses.

Also, if people were able to desensitize their feelings of anger at things like being enslaved, for example, they would come to accept it and that would obviously not be good.

Often people can't withhold responding to anger, because the brain can block the pathways to the frontal lobe. It has ways of cutting off the intellect when it feels it has to, and it does this so that the mind can't communicate with the brain. By secreting chemicals, it anesthetizes the nerve pathways leading to the mind, so that you basically have been decerebrated, lost your mind. Then the answer is determined by your outraged emotions, often called an irresistible impulse. This is why courts may allow a person to go to a treatment center rather than prison if they are the victim of irresistible impulses, because this can happen.

Affection doesn't desensitize easily either because affection is related to reproduction, without which the human race would cease to exist. Nature is programmed to encourage reproduction and the care of the young. If affection was readily desensitized, if it faded quickly, this could hamper those priorities. Keeping affection alive, making it difficult to extinguish, tends to cause people to stay together, which results in the creation of more children.

Relief and joy are readily desensitized because they are not associated with threats to life or reproduction.

Anxiety is moderately difficult to desensitize because it warns of danger.

Depression is also moderately difficult because it is associated with the morale and ties of the group. If we could easily forget about the loss of a loved one, then the emotional bonds that hold us together would be tenuous and thereby imperil the group's survival.

SCRIPTING YOUR STORY

You might want to write the script or scenario of a particularly traumatic incident down. The mere act of writing is very impactful and helps things to stick in our minds better. We usually organize and express our thoughts better in writing.

Writing a letter to yourself and reading it over and over is another good way to desensitize an event.

For example, "I was running across the soccer field late at night—I wanted to cross the field. Then that man seemed to appear from nowhere and jumped at me—I didn't know what hit me. He forced me to the ground, ripped my pants off, and started raping me. I kicked and struggled, but to no avail—he was much too strong." Etc.

Then read the account back to yourself, silently or out loud. When you come to the one or two lines that are the most threatening to you

("Then he grabbed my neck, and I thought I would suffocate—the really scary part was when he squeezed my neck"), skip quickly over this hot button. Any highly sensitive part, skip over at first.

You might want to have someone with you when you read your account, to bolster your courage. You could even bring it to a group and read it to them.

You also might want to alter parts of the story: "When he tried to grab me, I sped up and got away." Or some other escape strategy. Our brain's goals in all of this are prevention and escape. It is most concerned with how to prevent or avoid something like this from happening again, or how deal with it effectively if it ever happens again. Such as never walk in an isolated area after dark, and always carry a whistle or mace. Have a backup plan, too—the brain loves that.

WAYS TO USE A FRIEND OR RELATIVE TO AID DESENSITIZATION

There are a number of ways that a friend or relative can aid you in the process of desensitization, besides simply providing emotional support and perhaps discussing the nature and progress of your treatment with you. They can also provide behavioral practice (see role-playing) and offer insights and alternative views of the problems or issues you are concerned with. They can help calm you down, as well, if you are frustrated, anxious, or depressed. An additional person is always helpful, and usually adds some life and excitement to the process.

ROLE-PLAYING

I do this all the time when working with clients in my office. I act out a part, such as of a person who is angry or disappointed with them. It's a social and fun way to desensitize things without focusing so much on the anxiety itself.

For example, I used it with Samantha, a middle-aged woman who came to see me in distress. The year before, her own mother had been taken to the hospital after a heart attack, which was so severe that her survival was questionable. During the time that this happened, she herself was in a hospital battling a pulmonary embolism. Her father and other relatives decided not to tell her about her mother's condition, for fear it would negatively influence her own mental and physical health at the time. Her mother died while Samantha was still severely ill, and they didn't let her know what had happened to her mother until she was somewhat better.

When she learned this, she was very upset, since she never got to say her last goodbye. She said she knew relatives probably felt that they were doing this for her own good, but still resented it. What could she do about it?

She was still living with her father, but found it hard to tell him how she felt about all of this. It was so hard that she probably never would.

"Let's pretend that I'm you and you're your father," I said.

"I've been thinking about Mom," I started. "I do that a lot. And I think about everyone meeting to decide I shouldn't be told. I know you did it for my benefit, but I was really affected by that, and still am."

I asked her what she would want from her father if she brought this up.

"Say it to me now, I'm your father."

No reply.

Back to my role as the father: "You were in such desperate condition!"

"I still would have wanted to see Mom."

"It would have been too hard on you, and might even have adversely affected your recovery—and your sister, brother, aunt, and uncle said the same, so I took their advice."

I kept refusing to give the apology she was looking for.

After role-playing the approach to her father a number of times with me, it eventually became less of an obstacle, and she was finally able to ask him for an apology, and got one.

When you are role-playing you can switch roles with the person you are doing it with, to aid the process. You role-play all by yourself, and even do things like put yourself in the role of the person who harmed you. You can get a better perspective on almost any event when you look at it from both points of view.

SPEED DESENSITIZING

There are times when a short course in desensitizing is needed, to deactivate a specific fear in a hurry, such as when an impending vacation or business trip includes an activity that you are fearful or anxious about. The desensitizing process can be speeded up in such instances, to achieve maximum anxiety dismantling in minimum time.

The time it takes to desensitize a given emotion is a function of how strong the emotion is and how much time you can devote to exposing yourself to the thoughts, situations, and circumstances associated with that emotion in the absence of any real consequences.

The duration of the exposure required is pretty much fixed. The main issues are the time available to undergo this process and your ability to tolerate it. A quick job will be intense—you will have to imagine bad stuff, and be aggressive in imagery. Some people, such as police officers, may just want to get the desensitization process over with fast so they can get back to work.

For an example from my own life, I was afraid to go ziplining, though I wanted to be with other family members who were planning to do this on an upcoming vacation. I don't like heights, but I wanted to be with my children and enjoy this activity with them.

So I repeatedly summoned up the emotions that were associated with ziplining for me and did this over and over again until the emotional response subsided. I visualized traveling to where the zipline was located, arriving, and getting hooked up to ride the line. I went over and over and over these images until they were desensitized. But since visualization is not as powerful as reality, I also needed to consider what I was afraid of. Falling? Slamming into a tree? What would happen if

I fell? I would probably have injuries, pain, a hospital stay, perhaps a permanent injury, and expenses connected with all of this.

All of this took only a few hours, yet I got to the point where I could tolerate the activity and was able to go and even enjoy it.

> If you can do speed desensitizing, this is a sign that you are comfortable with the process and good at it. If you can't do it at this point, you may find it much easier later, after you have more practice and experience with desensitization. The process will get easier and easier.

WHEN DOING SELF-TREATMENT FOR ANXIETY

Monitor your progress. People who monitor their progress tend to do better. Try to think of ways you can measure your progress—are you thinking less about the issue, less fearful, more energetic, going out more, avoiding people less, being more assertive? Measurements will improve your motivation.

CHAPTER FIVE

WHEN MASTERY IS NEEDED

If someone goes to a therapist with a phobia of heights or some similar issue, treatment usually focuses on extinguishing the fear using desensitization techniques and perhaps behavioral approaches as well. The full ramifications of the person's fears, such as how they affect their social life, work, self-confidence, and so on, are not delved into. Sometimes, in order to fully eradicate a problem, one needs mastery. For total elimination of fear and anxiety, you want mastery.

Early in my career, I became aware of the need to discuss the level of improvement my clients were looking for before initiating therapy. For example, does a person who is suffering from a simple phobia, such as fear of flying, want to overcome their fears so that they can take an occasional flight when they go on vacation, or are they planning to return to work as a medic on a helicopter that specializes in rescue missions, which often involves extremely hazardous maneuvers? The standard level of treatment would likewise hardly be sufficient for a professional firefighter, police officer, or commercial pilot.

Regular imagery and desensitization are designed to get someone to the 75% level. Psychologists have usually looked at fear as something you want to resolve to that point. This has not been formally adopted as a principle, but in practice they have followed this rule of thumb. Most people are satisfied with a level of improvement that approximates 75% of normal. In fact, traditional disability policies specify that a 75% level is considered sufficient to return to work.

Confrontation Therapy can move this to the 100 percent level, or close to it.

Achieving mastery is going beyond that. Do we want to do this in every case? No. If a person who almost drowned comes in and wants to get his anxieties resolved so he can go back in the water, 75% would be okay for this. But if someone works on a platform out in the ocean, or on a fishing boat, or the like, where they might have to go in the water and help save someone, I would recommend the 100% resolution. If someone said they wanted to become a trainer to help others who are afraid of water, I would say that this person needed to reach 120%.

Likewise, if you liked to ski and had a bad experience skiing, ordinary desensitization and behavioral therapy would get you to the point where you were no longer afraid of being on the slopes or of being injured. But if you wanted to do ski racing, play games on skis, join search and rescue operations, or teach others to ski, you would need mastery.

A lot of psychologists don't think you can get a person to this point. I can, and in fact I believe I could get someone to 125%. This opens up a whole new set of options for treatment. Originally I myself thought a stronger than normal treatment for fear or anxiety was not recommended or possible. But then I considered the body's healing process. When a bone is broken, it heals in that spot to be much stronger than the bones in the rest of the body. Likewise, when I asked a plumber once to fix a broken pipe, he made it extra strong in that spot, because he said there must be some stress there. Now it would never break again.

In the progression of overcoming a fear, a person gets to the "functional" level where they can do laps in a pool, but not necessarily swim in the ocean or become a lifeguard. This is the first phobic recovery level.

The second level is the "recovered" level, but a recovered phobic is not as good as a normal person, or what they themselves used to be like, when confronting that particular fear. The recovered person is always monitoring the circumstances, and making modifications, to be sure he will not have to deal with that issue ever again.

A normal person is not concerned with the subject at all. Mastery gives you the full freedom and fluidity of behavior around the formerly feared object or situation that even Exposure Therapy and Confrontation Therapy will not provide

Achieving mastery takes too much time and effort to be a good goal for all. When I treat someone I first ask them what their goals are. Do they want to reduce or eliminate a fear, or master it and be on the level everyone else is with that subject?

> To illustrate this with a different example, you could get a knee replacement, and with enough physical therapy reach 75% of normal knee function. Or when stem cell research is perfected, you might grow new cartilage for your knee and reach 100%. A knee with additional strength and protection for athletes who play very vigorous sports might be developed someday for those who need to reach 125%.

WHO SHOULD CHOOSE MASTERY?

Does the typical client who has a fear of deep water expect, or even want, to achieve a level of proficiency suitable for becoming a lifeguard? Probably not. But mastery may be desired for many reasons, including even some that a clinician might question. For example, early in my career, a client who had suffered a severe neck injury in a surfing accident wanted to overcome his fears of returning to the ocean to perform advanced surfing maneuvers against his doctor's advice.

As noted earlier, once when I wanted to go on a zipline with my family during a vacation (I am afraid of heights), I spent a couple of hours in my hotel beforehand prepping myself. This did get me to the functional level. But you would need the mastery level if you wanted to be a camp counselor and help kids overcome their fear of heights, so they could do ziplining.

Mastery, like that extra layer of bone after a break has healed, increases confidence. You can even talk about the subject you used to fear, whereas otherwise you would not.

Who should choose mastery is determined mostly by need. Some need mastery for work, for play, or to improve the quality of their lives. For a professional athlete, it's important to be at the mastery level. One of my clients once told me that when his wife injured her wrist, he told her doctor that his wife was a semi-professional tennis player so that the doctor would raise his standards to the highest level of care. A homemaker might want mastery in the area of child care but in other areas not.

Mastery is not for everyone, but it is usually needed by professionals in the area where the fear resides. Professionals usually need to return to the level of functioning they had before a trauma. If you need to get back to work in a profession or a very important career, you need mastery. Overcoming a fear of public speaking is one place where mastery is called for. Fear of public speaking is bad enough in itself. Fear of questions you can't handle, or hecklers, is much worse. Even the best speakers worry about this. Comedians have no such fear—they incorporate such things right into their routine.

An anxious student might want mastery. Otherwise he might be able to take a test, but would not do well on it if he did not achieve mastery. Some people only want it on rare occasions and in rare circumstances, such as only when have to go back for their last deployment overseas. The highest level of mastery is needed by people such as police officers and firefighters. If a firefighter or a police officer comes in with anxiety issues and wants to go back to work, mastery is necessary. I explain to them at the start that reaching that level will be an intensive process, so they had better plan some training days.

Clinicians and surgeons often make their own assessments of need. When I broke my wrist, the surgeon, in repairing it, tightened one of the tendons around my knuckles. Afterward I had only 55–75% flexibility in that hand, but no pain in that wrist, or arthritis. But I couldn't play basketball anymore because the ability to flip the wrist is needed for that. The surgeon decided this without consulting me. Physicians routinely make such decisions for you. They shouldn't. And in psychological matters, you should be the one to decide if you need mastery or not.

You can determine this by discussion with your therapist. To keep the cost down it can be done on a self-help basis, if the problem is a low-level fear.

IMAGERY FOR MASTERY

In the typical session with a client, I discuss the nature and intensity of the images I will have them reviewing before the session begins and the client can abort the process whenever they feel uncomfortable. The goal of therapy is to repeatedly present the fearful images, say of the client starting to drown, until the client indicates that they are no longer fearful of them. This could take any number of sessions, depending on the nature, complexity, and intensity of the fear, the severity of the client's distress, and the degree of control over the fearful images that the client experiences.

Most clients seem to discontinue the process once they have achieved the desired result, which might be when they feel they can go back in the water, or possibly when they feel comfortable with their decision to no longer go in the water.

But those whose job (such as rescue worker) or location (they live near a large body of water) requires them to deal with the possibility of finding themselves in deep water must attain mastery of their fear of water. For them, the sessions have to be modified accordingly.

In this much more aggressive imaging, the person would imagine not just swimming in a pool, but having problems in a pool, struggling in a pool, even getting hurt or embarrassed there. The intensity of the images may even go beyond the realistic, such as imagining that they are at the beach and are hit by a rogue wave.

The intensity of the images has to be increased to include the possibility of them experiencing long-term or permanent injuries from a mishap in the water, as well as severe financial consequences, and collateral damages to their family and friends. They have to imagine and rehearse rescue operations. They have to imagine whatever events or circumstances bother them until they reach the point that they cannot generate any images that provoke a fearful response, then in the next (confrontation) stage, replicate this with actual experiences.

When I desensitize a client to a fearful image, I start by developing an image that seems closely tied to the incident. For example, I may ask the client who is fearful of going into deep water to imagine entering the water at a pool and slowly proceeding until the client is in about four feet of water. I then ask him which image is more anxiety-provoking, continuing to go deeper while holding on to a rope that is suspended across the pool, or diving into the water and swimming a few feet to the other side. Since the client is imagining him or herself wearing a life jacket at the time, both scenarios are safe. At first, the client proceeds with the safer option as she sees it. But then we gradually experiment with the more difficult one until she can imagine herself doing both of these things. In this way, we gradually desensitize progressively more difficult options, including ones that turn up by trial and error. Usually, the most frightening images involve loss or lack of control, such as swimming with less and less of a backup option. In this way we proceed to desensitize all of the possible scenarios that are remotely capable of provoking a fearful response. Then we move on to duplicating the process in reality.

Once the client is desensitized to both confronting the fearful image and then the actual event, we then explore theoretical images that may be upsetting, such as what would have happened if he were injured and hospitalized, or worse—what if he was paralyzed or even killed? At this point we are extending beyond the actual circumstances, but this is necessary for total extinction of their fear. Progressive steps may include practicing even more difficult scenarios and developing more difficult skills, such as learning to swim farther than before and how to rescue others.

The goal is to extinguish everything that might have been fear-producing in the past as well as everything that the client can conjure up beyond that. And then to follow up by duplicating this as much as possible in actuality. To attain full mastery the program would also include developing skill at CPR, and learning lifesaving skills under more hazardous conditions, such as at a lake or even at the beach.

> When I discuss what level of treatment a client wants to achieve, in the range from 75-125%, I try to go with what they want. I assure them they can change their mind at any time.

DEALING WITH THE KEY THIRD INGREDIENT OF ANXIETY

Neither Exposure Therapy nor Behavioral Therapy address the psychological component of fear—the person's subjective view of the feared object or situation. Namely, do they like it, feel neutral about it, or dislike it? Do they consider it important to overcome this fear, does it interfere with their life? These considerations are all important in the treatment of fear and anxiety. Mastery, by analyzing the person's traits and predispositions as well as circumstantial and situational factors, addresses all aspects of a person's responses to anxiety.

When I work with someone one of the first things I do is find out how they feel about the thing they are anxious about or fearful of. The course of therapy is vastly different when you go in knowing this. If they are not interested in it or predisposed to dealing with it, treatment will be slow and arduous. If you are trying to desensitize your reaction to a certain song that you associate with a trauma, for instance, it will be much harder if you are not predisposed to like music.

> Exposure and Behavioral Therapy deal with the physiological and behavioral. Add knowledge of the person's traits and predispositions, and you may well be able to deal with the psychological part of anxiety.

Are you predisposed to the activity in question? If you have no real mental attraction or connection to water, for instance, you are not psychologically well equipped to deal with the area. If you have the Endless and Effortless interest of predisposition, however, therapy involving water will go much more smoothly. If you are born with a predisposition to like water, but subsequently experience a trauma involving it—near death from drowning—this will override the predisposition. However having the predisposition of liking water will make your therapy for this problem easier and more effective even in this circumstance.

SOME KEY ISSUES IN ACHIEVING MASTERY

When I am trying to resolve a person's psychological feelings about an issue, there are some points I am particularly concerned with:

1. What are their thoughts about the feared object? I tell them that mastery involves desensitization of a number of emotions that

may be involved. Do they feel guilty about how they dealt with their fear, were they embarrassed about their behavior, were they ashamed of themselves? Such emotions often respond to group treatment, and combat veterans often use group therapy to get other vets' opinions on their issues. Do they have regrets, do they wish they could relive the moment and deal with it differently, or are they angry at someone? See the sections on anger, revenge, guilt, and regret later in this book.

2. Has the fear affected their self-image or relationship with themselves? Are they angry with themselves? Issues such as these often respond well to role playing with the therapist.

3. Do they have a need to get even? There are safe and good ways to get even—such as join or start a cause (see Chapter Twelve).

DEALING WITH DEFAULT CHANGES

How a person feels about the issue that caused the problem includes the question of whether as a result, he has changed his feelings about other things. Mastery takes into account the more complex combination of the effects of different traits on the individual. Our brain has many default settings, which took years to develop: such as what we think is a long walk, or a short walk, or a long or short conversation. These defaults also include the many manifestations of the traits discussed in Chapters One and Two.

If someone had a heart attack, for example, he might be concerned about going back to work as a teacher. Would he perhaps be preoccupied with his health now, and not have all of his former confidence? Would he still have the same passion for his subject, and motivation? If he is a gym teacher, would he perhaps be reluctant now to exert himself? If he is a drama coach, might he be afraid that some of his charisma would have eroded? Is there a change in any of the areas of his personality? Does he think any of his defaults have changed? Is he any more or less self-focused? Has his interest in socializing changed? Is he more or less serious? More or less friendly? More or less anxious? More self-reliant? More depressed? Less likely to push himself, and more likely to push things on other people? After a near-death experience, people may feel that they are living on bonus time, so they may have a more carefree, I don't give a damn attitude.

If you have been through something serious, you can assume that your defaults have changed to one extent or another.

People who have been traumatized, for instance, are no longer nonassertive. They don't just go along with things—they are always anticipating and planning. They are not just accountants, teachers, or professors any more, often they now turn to professions that are more action-oriented, much more reactive.

For another example, say a police officer comes in and wants to cope with his fears before going back on duty. He is wondering how he will deal with the usual pressures of his profession. Desensitizing and confrontation can take care of his fear and behavioral issues. To deal with the psychological part of anxiety, more attention must be paid to his traits and predispositions, because they may be a factor in his going back on the job.

One thing a cop on duty must consider for example, is his partner. He may have a lot of fears and doubts about this. Will his partner still feel comfortable relying on him? How will he react under stress now—might he overreact and be too aggressive? Or be hesitant and fearful when faced with a confrontation? I would thus do more of an analysis of his personality.

If he was involved in a shooting, if he was independent before, he might be more of a loner now, or more people oriented. I would go through his traits to see if they had been adjusted anywhere— is he not as self-contained now? He may have reset some of his defaults, and for example now be more appreciative of the value of agreeableness. He might also have changed his thinking about other people, be more or less sympathetic than he was before. Or more or less anxious, or depressive.

I would go through the major traits and look for any changes, to see if any have taken a hit. Is he taking more or less risks? How might this play out in his work? Is he more hesitant, or more active? A difference in any of these areas can be meaningful. We might spend some time imagining situations and how he would react to them. If it seemed necessary would he pull out his gun, or speed off after someone, or not?

I would ask how he was doing in general, ask questions about his day-to-day life. Is he more aggressive, does he find himself getting in fights, or more hesitant and passive? Is there any change in his anxiety level? Is he more depressive, lacking the energy to do much, refusing and avoiding things? I would check his independence or agreeable traits—more or less of one or the other of these can have a big effect on a person's personality.

I don't necessarily treat changes like this, I point out the differences and give the person insight into them. Mastery aims to restore those settings to normal, although in some cases a person may be better off with the new. My job is to call the changes to the person's attention, so they can decide whether they prefer the old or the new.

If you have one of these changes, it may take you a while to become used to your new personality. When it comes to this, I've heard people say, "I lost myself!"

The last step in treatment

My usual course near the end of treatment is to play with the emotion involved, test it to see if it still bothers the person. Just as after surgery you might test a limb that had been operated on to see if it was back to normal, see what makes it feel worse or better. I may have the person imagine extreme and unusual situations, all sorts of weird and exaggerated things, until they get to the point where they can't imagine or do anything that triggers a negative response regarding the original problem subject.

AN EXAMPLE OF MASTERY IN ACTION

Say you wanted to train someone to be a firefighter. You might start off by desensitizing them to the fear of smoke and fire, exposing them to scenes of fires, firemen running into burning buildings, and running out, working all the different ways they usually work under these conditions. This exposure would address their physiological fear by evoking physiological symptoms, which would then be desensitized. When desensitizing with the goal of mastery, you would take the extra steps in imagery outlined earlier.

Then you could get them involved in actually going on the scene of such events—going into buildings, perhaps with a supervisor, and having training experience in working with fire. You would see that they receive extra training in any areas that seemed to cause apprehension. This would take care of the behavioral aspect, desensitize them to the idea of voluntarily confronting a fire.

You would also look at the person's traits and make sure they are not too anxious or risk-taking. You would want to see that they are somewhat agreeable, conscientious, people-oriented, and not too independent (so they wouldn't be likely to go into action on their own—this is called freelancing, and can endanger the whole group). You might also examine the person's traits to see if they are consistent with profiles of successful firefighters—look up the personality profiles of same and compare.

In terms of predisposition, you would investigate whether there was reason to believe that the person really wants to be a firefighter, so that he would love the job, and put himself into it.

You would also inform him about many different aspects of fire—its peculiarities, the characteristics of different kinds, etc., along with tips and pointers older, highly experienced firemen could share. This would give him a fund of background knowledge, and round out the preparations. It would give the person mastery over the whole process, and complete the fireman's training and anxiety-proofing.

OVERTRAINING TO IMPROVE RESULTS

Overtraining is often done in sports to improve performance. If a person has trouble putting in golf, for instance, they need to overtrain in this area. Short putts cause more anxiety than long ones because no one really expects long ones to make it in. To overcome this, a person must practice three-foot putts until they are usually successful with them, almost become a specialist in them. Likewise, in tennis, if someone has a real problem with some aspect of the game, the pro will often have them work on that area over and over until it may even become their best skill.

Overtraining and simulations are an important step toward mastery. For a cop, this would mean more time out in the field, in worse neighborhoods, etc.

Overtraining could just as easily be applied to therapy. In fact, overtraining should be the standard practice, since most people do not perform as well in real situations following treatment. For example, a person who suffers from test anxiety has to overtrain in order to allow for the typical reduction in performance once they take the actual test. Mastery is often a must. Or someone in therapy to overcome anxiety in job interview situations would have to simulate the much more tense atmosphere of an actual job interview, especially a difficult one, as opposed to the more or less relaxed situation of asking yourself and answering possible interview questions at home or in a therapist's office.

If you fear speaking in public, ET would have you imagine scenes associated with that situation and then go a little further to include problems you might encounter when speaking, such as being asked difficult questions. Mastery would go beyond this and ask you what you feared most. What type of repercussions would you envision if your talk didn't go well? What are the worst-case scenarios? You would be pushed to the point where you eventually couldn't imagine any scenes that would provoke anxiety.

Then you would be asked if there was any way you could put yourself in a situation where you could deal with your fears in actuality. Perhaps you could join a speakers' club, where you could practice dealing with the dreaded scenarios. Or might ask around to see if a friend had a similar problem and ask them what they worried about most and how they dealt with it. You might also go on the internet to see if there is a chat group that deals with the problem.

MASTERY IS THE KEY TO RESOLVING COMPLEX ISSUES

Often, the highest level of care, mastery, is also necessary to solve complex and thorny problems, such as, "Should I stay with my spouse or go off with my lover?"

For another example, consider the classic question: If you have a loved one in a danger zone, and a letter comes from the government about them, is it better it should say they are dead, or missing in action? Initially, one would think that MIA is better, because then there is still a chance they are alive somewhere. But that hope eventually costs you a tremendous amount of emotional turmoil.

One loss is defined, the other undefined. An undefined loss might mean that you don't have to worry about this right now, but it's a mixed blessing. It keeps you in suspense and prevents you from resolving it. After ten years there is usually little progress on MIAs, whereas those whose loved ones were definitely lost have made a great deal of progress.

In a complex situation you need mastery to get at the inner mechanism that is driving the grief, because this is hard to get at, especially when the grief is mixed with anger.

An example of a complex problem is seen in veterans who have psychological issues regarding their injuries. For example, I saw a Vietnam vet who told me that he felt he had a need to get back at our country because of the fact that many other young people had connived to avoid being drafted—people joked that he wasn't clever enough to avoid serving. Student protesters had also hurled insults at him when he first came home, and many others seemed to feel that a lot of veterans' complaints about their psychological injuries were overblown. Nevertheless, he said he had never applied for disability coverage.

We discussed this at length. Ultimately, he decided to apply and he got 100% disability coverage due to the complexity of his injuries. He ended up getting a considerable amount of money each month, and this made up for the difference in what he made pre-enlistment as a plumber and post-enlistment as a maintenance worker. He also now felt that he had gotten even with the government. He told all of his friends who were opposed to seeking aid from the government his story and many of them decided to apply as well. He told me that many of them felt so good about getting even in this way that it restored their pride and engendered a satisfying sense of relief. Often mastery brings with it a lot of unexpected sources of relief and fulfillment.

Mastery may sometimes require group therapy, as was often the case with the vets described above. The group therapy would be in conjunction with, or before or after individual therapy. Group therapy can accomplish some things that individual therapy cannot, and vice versa.

Mastery often involves some education on the nature of psychological processes as well, such as the need for getting even found with anger. Knowing this is common when someone is angry, it is helpful to discuss constructive ways of getting even—starting a cause, organizing victims of a similar problem, consulting a lawyer regarding possible legal measures that might be taken, contributing to a cause that is similar to your own issue, or helping others with similar issues.

WHAT ARE THE ADVANTAGES OF ATTAINING MASTERY?

- No more ruminating about fearful images and thoughts that you are unable to stop or control. Those fearful thoughts won't pop up unexpectedly, and you won't have to be on guard against encountering the fearful triggers. Your preoccupation with the fearful triggers will stop, and you will no longer be sensitive to the issue.

- The brain doesn't have to keep monitoring things to make sure you are not coming in contact with the feared object or situation again. This saves a certain amount of energy and frees up the brain to focus on more important matters.

- It eliminates avoidance. At the usual level of therapeutic success, there are usually still some signs of avoidance.

- Your self-confidence will significantly improve, in part because you have overcome a major handicap that was interfering with your life, impairing your relationships, and lowering your self-esteem.

- You will feel a sense of pride because you overcame something that made you question your ability to control your life.

- You may be able to once more enjoy something—say swimming or skiing—that you previously loved but was taken away from you.

- Your friends will notice and be impressed by the new you.

- You will be much more effective in overcoming other traumas or future traumas.

- You will regain your respect for yourself.

For most people, the relief from the worry, stress, irritability and lower self-esteem are the biggest gains. People feel that they have gotten their mind back.

When I sprained my ankle once, I went through a course of treatment with a physical therapist. After about two months I found that I could run, walk, and play tennis again, so I stopped therapy then. Years later, when the knee of the same leg started to bother me, I saw an orthopedist. She told me that the ankle of this leg, the one that had been treated with physical therapy, was extremely tight, and this had contributed to my knee injury. If I had completely recovered from the ankle injury, I probably would not have had the knee problem. At a later time, I ruptured my bicep. After surgery this time, I made it a point to fully rehab my injury. As a result, I have never had another problem with my bicep. If you treat an anxiety completely—all the way to mastery—the same will be true of it.

Once you have achieved mastery, your positive feelings about what you previously feared should return. For example, if you enjoyed a sport or pastime that you have come to fear, mastery will maximize the likelihood that you can regain your initial interest in it. If you enjoyed swimming or hiking but following a traumatic incident you no longer do, then through mastery there is a good bet you can regain those feelings.

THE BASIC STEPS TO OUR PROGRAM FOR TREATING ANXIETY:

STAGE 1: EXPOSURE THERAPY. The first step following any experience that leaves a person with an anxiety or fear-based condition is to extinguish the emotional connection between the triggering agent and the emotional response. For example, if a person has a near-death experience, say they almost drown in a pool, they will find that going in a pool, or even the thought of it, will cause them to become extremely anxious. The best way to extinguish this connection is to treat them with Exposure Therapy.

Exposure Therapy involves having the person gradually and progressively imagine dealing with the feared situation, in this case going into the pool. The images are presented at a slow enough pace so that the client finds the process painless and easily tolerated. Once the person can accomplish imagining images that are mild to intense with ease, he or she is encouraged to repeat the process in actuality—in real-life situations involving the feared subject. When they are able to do this with ease and without showing any signs of discomfort (anxiety)—for example, they can go into the pool and even swim about without discomfort, their condition is assumed to be resolved. At this point their anxiety or fear would be 75% resolved. Many people discontinue treatment at this point, although there is usually is at least some residual anxiety that distinguishes them from someone who never had the condition.

STAGE 2: CONFRONTATION THERAPY. This involves building on step one by having the confront the problem situation aggressively—such as gradually practicing more advanced maneuvers in the pool, swimming in the deep end, perhaps diving in, practicing rescue exercises, swimming in larger pools, even swimming in larger bodies of water such as lakes or even the ocean. Completion of this stage will bring a person's recovery from anxiety or fear to 100%. At this point, they are at or slightly above the normal range.

STAGE 3: MASTERY. This level is for people who want or need to significantly exceed the level of improvement that is typical for the average person overcoming an anxiety. For example, a lifeguard who is returning to duty after having a near-death experience in the water. Other examples would include firemen and police officers who were traumatized on duty and now want to return to active duty without a trace of hesitation in their response to dangerous situations. This would also include overcoming their tendency to question themselves; no longer experiencing nightmares; regaining their love of their profession; restoring their confidence, and so on. Their recovery level from fear at this point would be 125%. That is, it would be considerably better than normal.

In order to achieve this level of improvement, the person would have to conjure up extreme examples in imagery before they return to active duty. If a physical injury was involved, a physical therapist or trainer will be helpful. When it comes to the confrontation part of therapy, practice is good but overtraining (see page 117) is even better.

Someone seeking mastery will probably benefit from group therapy with other professionals who have undergone similar experiences. This is commonly done with soldiers who experienced traumas in combat. Dealing with difficult issues such as shame and guilt is often a significant part of treatment.

The average person may want to accomplish varying levels of mastery depending on their condition and circumstances. For example, a promising young athlete who wants to become a pro may have very high standards; a coach or mentor may want to regain his swagger; a person who suffers from nightmares or a sleeping disorder may want to achieve relief through mastery in just that specific area of his life.

It is important to discuss the level of improvement you are looking for with your therapist. You should be on the same page. Your circumstances, including your finances, what appears to be your prospects for recovery, and your personality and psychological issues may all suggest a different level of improvement to your therapist than you think is warranted.

If you are self-treating and want to get to get to a higher level than you achieve initially, when doing imagery, you need to think of the most difficult situations you might have to ever deal with in regard to the problem issue. You might also find people who have a similar issue and share your experiences.

Keep in mind that disability programs may specify a 75% improvement as the acceptable level for return to work.

CHAPTER SIX

OVERCOMING FEAR
AND ANXIETY

THE ESSENTIAL FIRST STEP

The purpose of anxiety is to alert us to a threat to our well-being, and the first step in dealing with it is to determine where that threat, real or imagined, is coming from. The cause of anxiety is often unclear, and you can't effectively work on your anxiety until you isolate the cause… the true cause.

Most anxiety does have a definite cause burrowing around underneath all of those feelings of dread and worry cycling through our bodies and brains. The question is, just what is it? Even when we think we know, we are often wrong. Treating the wrong cause is not only a waste of time and energy, it is not going to give us the emotional relief we are so desperately seeking.

Many years ago now I began to assess clients' arousal responses during our sessions. And to my amazement, what I found was that often when a client was describing a situation that seemed to be relatively benign, they would show a surprisingly high arousal response. When I questioned them about this, the client often said, "Well, you know, I do feel uneasy about that. I'm surprised you brought that up, but it is in fact something I've been worrying about." At other times, people would tell me that they felt very concerned about something, and when my further observations and inquiries failed to confirm this, I questioned them about this, too. Their response often was, "Well, it is something that bothers me, but it doesn't really get me upset. In the past it did, but now it doesn't mean all that much to me."

It may not be the problem you think.

Often we think the problem is one thing, when something else is causing it.

When investigating or desensitizing something, don't be surprised if something else pops up that was suppressed by the original concern. Avoidance protects everything in back of it.

When I am trying to help someone pinpoint the cause of their anxiety, what I usually do is probe various scenarios with them to see which creates the strongest reaction. These are not usually physical signs, but more subtle signposts. By comparing a person's actions, as they describe them, and the issues they appear to be concerned with, to their natural traits, I usually know where the problem is coming from. I use the clues provided by trait analysis, and look at how all of a person's traits come together, as well as what their values are, and what is most likely to motivate them.

I also consider the consistency of what they say, and what makes them angry, or seem threatened, uptight. Trait analysis generally tells me what they consider important, and what they are afraid of. I also take into account whether their answers to the questions I pose seem to be consistent with their nature.

When I don't think we're making progress, I may say, "That seems to be a pretty low-key issue, I don't know why." Or, "I'm not reading that that as a real problem. Let's try some other things to see what that might show."

When people talk to me they are not usually aware of the fact that I know how all of the different emotions connect. But they like it when I investigate their minds and brains like this.

SOME EXAMPLES OF ANXIETY IDENTIFICATION BY TRAIT

Let me give you an example of how this might work. A friend called me up one day, a very well-credentialed expert witness in facility maintenance. He was being plagued by worries about losing his credibility, or his chances to testify in court for a healthy fee. Why did I think he was having this problem?

I knew that he was an independent-minded person, which meant his anxiety was low, so I said, "I wouldn't imagine that you would worry much about anything. As a result, you probably don't prepare very well for your court appearances. So you're afraid that when you are in court and not prepared you will start to freak, as you are examined and cross-examined by big-time lawyers, and they start tearing everything you've said apart."

"How did you know?" he asked. Because I know trait analysis.

For another example, this one from the headlines of 2018, consider Dr. Christine Ford, the woman who accused Judge Brett Kavanaugh of trying to rape her when they were in high school together more than three decades ago. A neuropsychologist now, she said his character was not fit for his job.

When she appeared in front of the judicial committee, she said that at a party he threw her on a bed and held his hand over her mouth as he attempted to assault her.

The committee members asked Dr. Ford what about the experience was the most distressing to her. Not that she feared she was going to be suffocated, as we might expect, but the fact that while he was doing this he and his friends were laughing uproariously.

Why did she find ridicule worse than a near-death experience? Her nature indicated that this was the most important thing to her. She is an independent type and such people are very concerned with their image, other people's and their own view of themselves. Nothing makes them angrier than when you mock them. Dr. Ford probably didn't like not being taken seriously. If I were interviewing her, I would know where to look. Her nature and traits would guide my search.

For another case from my own files, I treated a woman who told me she had been in various relationships over time, each lasting two or three years. She had just turned forty, and her present relationship had been going on for almost four years. Yet it was still unclear whether she was going to get married and have the children she wanted. Everyone told her that she needed to consider a better method of screening suitors.

Her problem, I could see, was actually an inability to get rid of unsuitable mates. This is common in people with the agreeable trait. They don't like to disappoint anyone, hurt their feelings, or tell them they are not happy with them. If the other person is persistent, they can drag the relationship out for a long time.

Instead of focusing on how to better screen people (never a perfect science in any case), she needed to start dealing with her fear of terminating relationships with men who turned out to be undesirable for some reason. She needed to just dump them and move on, without questioning herself. If she learned how to do this, she wouldn't have to worry so much about screening and could use her newfound skill to resolve her problem.

ANXIETY IDENTIFICATION IN ACTION

Let's take a look at a few more examples from my own practice to illustrate the process.

Jennifer was a young woman who was extremely uneasy about being in water. She was sure this was because as a child she'd been bitten, not seriously, by a large pike while splashing about in relatively shallow water. Ever since then she'd simply avoided swimming or wading in ponds, lakes, rivers, or any body of water. This worked fine until she met a young man who loved the ocean and the shore, and wanted them to honeymoon at a Caribbean resort. So she came to me in hopes of defusing her reluctance to even get her feet wet.

We sat down and started to explore her feelings in this area. I had her imagine stepping into a lake or the sea, going in up to her ankles, then her knees, and eventually her waist. Next diving in over her head, and swimming in deep water, by herself, and with friends. What if a barracuda or giant manta ray suddenly appeared, or a shark fin poked up on the horizon? What if she was in the water for just a few minutes, or for a long time?

As we worked our way through these images, surprisingly, none of them registered near the reaction, the degree of arousal, that either of us expected. Then, as I was having her conjure up other possible scenarios that might take place in such a setting, she moved deeper into the ocean (where she could no longer see the bottom) in her imaging and it suddenly became obvious. It was a fear of dark or murky water—where you couldn't see what might be there, or lurking in it—that was the real stressor. She was another agreeable person, and such people are very fearful of things being out of control, so they can't do whatever they feel they might have to do to circumvent some difficulty or problem. Once we had identified this, since I had already explained the desensitization process to her in detail, she was able to deal with the murky-water issue on her own. A triumphant postcard she sent me from Aruba a few months later cheerfully underscored this.

Another client, Gina, was afraid of flying. She was a buyer for an importing company, however, so there was no way around it at times. At first she took an anti-anxiety drug to deal with her problem, but this often made her feel tired, and had other undesirable side effects. So she came to me in hopes of some better means of banishing this anxiety.

We began to examine the different possible ingredients involved in her unwillingness to board an airliner. I had her imagine being in a plane in the grips of turbulence, worrying about the objects rattling around in the cabin, or even the possibility of hitting her head on the ceiling. What if she was sitting in her seat and heard noises that suggested all was not well with the engines? Or heard announcements or reports from the pilot on this problem or that? What if the plane actually started floundering, or losing altitude?

At the thought of many of these things she showed signs of anxiety, but not to the degree one might imagine. She explained that she was well aware that her actual chances of being killed or injured in most of these circumstances were pretty remote. Trying to get to the bottom of her concerns here, next I asked her to imagine how she would feel if she were in the cockpit itself—would that be worse, or better? She instantly made it clear that the answer was "better!"

As an agreeable person, her real concern was over the lack of control one felt as a passenger in a plane, belted in and knowing about a possibly threatening situation only what was spoon-fed to you, and sanitized, by the pilot or the stewards. She would be happiest of all if she were actually piloting the plane herself, she said. Once we identified a feeling of powerlessness as the real issue, we put that through the desensitization process. Before long she was flying regularly and happily without chemical assistance.

Kenneth was a man of eighty grappling with an intense medical anxiety. His doctors had been watching him closely for early signs of bladder cancer for several years now, and once, he'd been asked to undergo the further precaution of a biopsy. He got through all of that, including the more frequent testing that followed for a while, without undue difficulty—he could usually manage to distract himself through the whole process. When asked for a biopsy again one year, however, he balked. He became so anxious that he made numerous appointments for it and then failed to show up for them. He was sent to me in hopes of helping him overcome this impasse.

When I asked him what made him anxious about the test, he said he wasn't really sure. So we began to go over various aspects of the situation that might be provoking his anxiety. First, of course, came the issue of whether he was afraid of a bad result. He was, but between the age he had reached (which made him somewhat philosophical about this) and the number of times he had faced this issue, his anxiety about that issue never got beyond a "2." He was wary of environmental toxins or hazards of any kind, and the doctor's office where he was to have the test had a very high-power electrical line running right outside the door—he didn't like the idea of being exposed to the emissions from it, even for a brief period. He also felt that his doctor was not particularly warm, and he didn't feel good about that. And sure enough, he did show anxiety in these areas as well, but not to the point that would suggest he would have difficulty undergoing the test.

Next I had him visualize going through the various steps of the process as they would occur. He envisioned going to the doctor's office and putting on a robe in preparation for the procedure. He knew there would be an assistant there who would help get the samples that would be used for the biopsy, and this would only last about five or ten minutes. I asked him if he thought the procedure would be painful, and he said he knew it wouldn't be because he'd undergone it before, so he wasn't concerned about pain.

As I inquired further into various possibilities, he mentioned that the test would be conducted in a small room in the basement, and he didn't like going down into what he considered to be a dungeon-like area. I asked him how he would feel if the examining room were a little smaller. "Forget it!" he said. And with that, I knew we had the answer.

It turned out that this was the pivotal issue—he wasn't much concerned about anything else about the biopsy other than the fact that he didn't want to be confined in a small space. We went through his history and found out that in fact he did have problems with claustrophobia earlier in his life, and then proceeded to desensitize him to claustrophobic settings. This took about six weeks, during which we spent about an hour a week on it until he was fully desensitized. At that point, he arranged to have the biopsy and did so successfully. He was thrilled to not only be able to do it, but without any stress or difficulty. Even his urologist was amazed at how uneventful the procedure was. As it turned out, he didn't have cancer, and he was very happy about that, too!

Amber, who was in her fifties, also had a problem related to the "big C." She had once been discovered to have a small area of skin cancer, and though it had been treated successfully and eradicated, she was constantly anxious about it showing up again anywhere. As I questioned her and she replied to my questions, we confirmed that fear, but it somehow didn't seem to be the whole story.

True, she didn't want to lose any of the fourscore years and ten we all hope we have coming, especially since she was planning to retire soon and spend more time with her children and grandchildren. But it finally came to light that a possible side effect of her own anxieties was of even greater concern. Her husband had some health issues as well, including high blood pressure. When she noticed anything out of the ordinary in her own health or appearance, she would panic and question him intensely: "What about this little spot here—does it look like cancer?" As anxious people do, she would keep hammering away at things like this, until finally he became disgusted. Her worst fear, it turned out, was that her obsessive repetition of things like this would stress him and possibly harm his own health.

With the help of trait analysis and my assessment of her, we were able to find this out within less than half an hour, whereas a conventional clinical approach would probably take three or four sessions to do the same. This would not only be expensive, but when inquiries of this sort are broken up by days, weeks, or even months, the trail may be lost or derailed into a detour along the way.

Relationship issues often crop up among the things my clients are most anxious about. When someone is concerned about a love affair, or afraid of being rejected, what aspect of this are they really worried about?

That it might be hard to find someone new as good or better, or fear of having to plunge back into the dating scene? Social embarrassment or peer pressure, the prospect of being humiliated by others knowing about the rejection?

Or that they will simply miss the person—a grief response?

Or ten other possible reasons. With experience and the aid of trait analysis, it's easy to track down the real culprit.

Ellen, a woman in her fifties, was caught up in anxieties about her marriage. She'd been married for twenty years to a man who had many fine qualities. He was attractive, warm, kind, and generous, and had a good reputation and many friends. He'd adopted her three children from her first marriage and treated them well, which she especially appreciated after her bad experience with her first husband.

After two decades of happiness, however, came the fly in the ointment. She discovered that at one point he'd had an affair with a younger woman. She didn't want a divorce—she had no way of supporting herself, and she still cared for him. So she came to me to help her overcome the anxieties that were tearing her apart.

As we examined her emotional state, many issues I was sure would be bad ones did not register nearly as strongly as I would have thought. We ultimately discovered that she had burned many of the most obvious issues out—such as her anger and disappointment over the affair—worked them over so much in the past couple of years that she had effectively desensitized herself to them. So where was her problem coming from now, we wondered as we discussed the possible causes and imagined a wide range of scenarios.

What she was really afraid of now, it turned out, was the possible effects of his anger. After she first became aware of the affair, she started finding reasons to needle him, criticize and belittle him, in public and private, all as a way of retaliating for the affair. As she picked away at him, he became irritable and quarrelsome himself, to the point of bullying her at times. She was afraid this might spill over into his actually leaving, or starting to mistreat the children. As an agreeable person, she was very fearful of situations that might involve anger and conflict.

Once we had determined this, we started the process of desensitizing her to his anger, getting her to focus on the anger itself, rather than any specific issues that had provoked arguments. Now, when he erupted over something, she would ask him why he was so angry—"Couldn't we discuss this peacefully and reasonably?" He didn't like being identified as an angry person, a hothead, so before long he learned to become aware of and control his own anger when it arose.

I also suggested that instead of constantly trying to get back at him, put him down (since this seemed to be a passive-aggressive issue), she should do more positive things. Such as improving the life of the family—taking more trips together and arranging for more time together in other ways. This seemed a more useful and realistic response than constantly knocking him down.

After these adjustments were made, their relationship was restabilized, and her fears of being left alone disappeared.

A younger woman, Francine, was also very anxious about a relationship. She was very much in love with her boyfriend, and feared she might someday lose him. This worried her endlessly, despite the fact that he was very affectionate, and insisted that he loved her, too. True, he didn't tell her that often, and she wanted to be ever present in his thoughts. Finally in our investigations it came out that she was constantly checking on him and monitoring him, to assure herself that he really did love her. A tipoff to this was the fact that she too was the agreeable type, and thus likely to have high anxiety. Agreeable people are also somewhat insecure and lacking in self-confidence, inclined to be suspicious of things that suggest something could go wrong.

Once this was clear, we started the process that would desensitize her presently groundless fear, and enable her to stop the actions that might in fact create a problem.

But relationship issues are not the only ones that keep people on the edge of their seats, or keep them from sleeping nights. Hannah was a young woman who came to see me because she was very reluctant to travel, and when she did, she didn't enjoy it much. She seemed to spend more time worrying about how things might be at home than taking in the new sights and experiences of wherever she had gone. This took a lot of the fun out of any expedition, and she asked me to help her pin down and deal with the cause.

So we started imagining our way through all of the conceivable reasons for her unease. Was she afraid of being robbed while she was away, or of her house burning down? Did she worry that the pipes might freeze and burst, or a tree fall on the house and damage it? Was there anyone she would be leaving behind at home, who might do something to cause a problem?

Well, she did have a number of pets, it turned out. She wasn't worried about anything they might do to the furnishings or each other, but somewhere here was obviously the trouble area. Did she fear they might get sick in her absence? No. Her real anxiety, it seemed, centered on the very specific issue of whether the instructions she wrote up for the pet sitter (feeding, watering, escape prevention, attention-giving, and in some case medicating) were really adequate. An easy issue to deal with, once identified. Hannah was another agreeable type, and she was so concerned with not offending the pet sitter, she was reluctant to be authoritative and direct, or raise any possibly difficult issues. The result was not fully clear or complete instructions that didn't address every one of the animals' needs. This then rebounded back on her in the form of the anxiety she felt.

Another of my clients asserted that she was frequently anxious, but not sure why. She reported that she had a good reputation at work, a good relationship with her husband, and good health. Yet, she felt anxious.

When I met with her, I first had her imagine how she felt about her job (she was a saleswoman). In the process, she found some aspects of her job that were appealing and pleasurable, while others made her feel fearful—such as having a confrontation with the district manager. The positive areas were obviously not responsible for her fears, so I had her imagine a confrontation with the district manager.

Once again, some aspects of this were not threatening—such as perhaps his reassuring her of her job security, whereas other areas might make her fearful, say his threatening to reassign her to another area. I then directed her to imagine being assigned to another state. Some aspects of the relocation might be painless, others difficult, and I told her to imagine the difficult ones—such as having to find a new home and establish new relationships. In this manner, I systematically followed the trail laid out by her anxieties to find the source.

In our conversations it became clear that she was a perfectionist. Perfectionists have a very high success rate in their undertakings—they don't experience much failure so they are overly anxious about it. They are very sensitive to criticism and failure, and this sets them up for trouble because they are not used to failure or prepared for it. It turned out that his woman was indeed very anxious about being perceived as a failure and consequently being criticized or looked down upon by her friends and family.

Once the fear underlying her anxiety had been uncovered, I then treated it with the desensitization process as described later in this chapter.

Even though her underlying fear with regard to work was her fear of being seen as a failure and thus being rejected by her family and friends, I gradually desensitized all and any fears she had about her work life before proceeding to desensitize her fear of rejection.

I had her imagine a discussion with her manager that would make her feel slightly fearful—such as him inquiring about how she felt about her work. I went over this image repeatedly until she felt completely comfortable with it. Then, I intensified the scene—such as by having him voicing some minor disapproval—until she again felt slightly anxious. I went over this scene and had her recount it, from varying perspectives, until she was no longer aroused by it.

I proceeded in this manner to gradually desensitize her to any anxieties about her job, until we eventually came to her fears of being perceived as a failure and thus being rejected by her family and friends. I then had her imagine all aspects of this circumstance to desensitize her to whatever they might say.

In the course of desensitizing someone's fears and anxieties, the person often discovers there are steps they can take to gain control of their situation—such as, in a work situation, taking advanced courses to increase their salary and enhance their standing. Whenever possible, the person is encouraged to gain control of their circumstances and improve themselves. But often it is not possible to find situational solutions to one's fears and anxieties—such as might occur with an irrational employer—and in that case, it is best to simply desensitize them.

The essence of desensitization is that by imagining one's fear in the absence of any consequences, a fear gradually loses its ability to generate an emotional response. Stripped of its ability to trigger an emotional response, the fear loses its power over us and ceases to be of much concern. The mind attends to what it perceives as important. Priority is given to focusing on our fears because they are so closely linked to our survival. As we desensitize our fears, we lower their priority, and therefore the need for our mind to focus on them. As a result, we find that the mind does not ordinarily attend to fears that have been desensitized unless we decide to focus on them. In essence, desensitization doesn't necessarily eliminate a fear as much as it renders it harmless.

THE PRIVACY PLAN, FOR DEEPLY PRIVATE ANXIETIES

Some causes of anxiety are things that people would rather not reveal to anyone else, not even a therapist. There are also people who are very concerned about their privacy in general, who simply would not want to reveal private issues of any kind to a professional, regardless of the assurances given. The methods I have described can be used to pinpoint and treat anxieties via "silent psychotherapy," so that even the most embarrassing and deeply private of inner agitations can be effectively defused without a third party even knowing what they are. All in all, an effective plain brown wrapper for therapy!

When taking the "private" approach, I have the person imagine various things, including the thing they think is the big problem or real issue. I can tell them when what they are thinking about is causing arousal, and when not, by the movements they make—tapping something with their hand, jiggling their leg, rubbing their face, facial movements, blinking more often, and the like.

One person started off by saying that he had an issue so private he didn't want to reveal it even to me. So I told him to imagine the issue, and the minute he got on the topic I could tell it was a hot one.

Eventually he said, "This is not working—let me just tell you what I'm worrying about."

It turned out that he had been avoiding processing his paperwork and was sure this would be discovered when his company did an audit. We then went through and desensitized some of his feelings and fears about this so that he could make better judgments about how to deal with the situation. We also discussed what he could say when the time came to account for this. It worked out very well in the end.

Another person was transgender and didn't want to mention this because it might get out. So we worked on desensitizing her fears about people finding out her secret, though I didn't know what it was at the time. As her anxiety about it dropped, she eventually said that she wanted to discuss it with me. And she did.

In both of these cases, after desensitization the person got to the point where the secret was no longer so threatening to him, and he wanted to discuss it.

Generally, when I am dealing with people who have very private anxieties, I try to get them to design a hierarchy of anxiety on a ten-point scale regarding whatever it is they are anxious about. I use an example of my own to give them the idea, and then have them create their own and write it down.

If they are afraid of flying, for example, because they have irritable bowel disease, and fear embarrassment during a flight, it might be something like:

10. Take flight and have big problem—lose control on plane, mess and odor.

9. Have a problem on a flight, but come prepared well enough that they can deal with it fairly well.

8. Taking a very short flight.

7. Just talking to a reservation agent about taking a flight.

Etc.

This way they have the architecture of the problem, the structure and framework to work with. The specific content is unimportant. Then they can take this list and practice visualizing these things, step by step, and allow themselves to get exposure to them by degrees.

HOW TO DO YOUR OWN DIAGNOSIS

As you imagine your way through the possible reasons for persistent anxiety, each time you reach a fork in the road, follow the one that seems to create the strongest feelings. (This is a lot like sitting in the eye doctor's office as they are asking you, "Does this lens make the letters you are looking at clearer, or less clear?")

When you reach that fork in your anxieties, one road leading up, the other to your anxiety going down, you know that the one that leads up is the anxious path. The other way, which leads down to a calm, relaxed state, is a respite but is not the road on which you are going to desensitize much anxiety.

You can check the possible themes several times in various ways, wait a while, and then check them again, to confirm your impression.

WILL WE ALWAYS FIND THE ANSWER?

You go into the woods on a rainy day, sit near an oak tree, take out a yellow blanket, then go down by the lake. You see a rowboat on the shore and get in it, only to get bitten by a snake sunning itself on one of the seats.

After this experience, all of these things will be associated with the snakebite. If the injury is severe enough, even going into woods could be a problem in the future.

If you went through a course of desensitization on this, you would first desensitize "woods," then yellow blanket, oak tree, going down to the lake, rowboat.

As you work your way down through it all, and finally find out it's the snake that's the real issue, I might ask, "What was so bad about that?

"I had to go to the hospital," you reply.

"What was so bad about that?" I inquire.

"Could have gotten really sick or a big bill."

"What if you did get sick?"

"I might die."

"So you are afraid of dying?"

"Not really of dying, but how it would affect my family."

Etc.

Often there is a bottom line, but sometimes you just keep going on and on and there is no bottom line.

TREATMENT FOR ANXIETY

Desensitizing doesn't necessarily eliminate fear or anxieties, but it loosens their grip on us, and drastically reduces their mental priority. As explained in Chapter Four, the desensitizing process involves the following, in brief:

Developing a program of exposing yourself to the underlying fears in carefully controlled doses, in a systematic way, with the exposure rate (time, and place) controlled entirely by you, so that the fears eventually lose their ability to upset you.

THE NINE RULES OF DESENSITIZATION

Our mind reacts to fear in much the same way whether we are afraid of a bug, an elevator, riding on a plane, or being mugged. Since the strategy for overcoming fears and anxieties is essentially the same whether they are simple or complex, it is easier to first consider the treatment of a simple fear, say of elevators.

1. If you had a fear of elevators and every day on your way to your office, you avoided the elevator by taking the stairs, your fear of elevators would persist indefinitely. **Rule #1:** You have to confront or expose yourself to your fears in order to overcome them.

2. If you were wheeled into an elevator while you were asleep and wheeled out before you woke up, your fears of elevators would not decrease. **Rule #2:** You have to psychologically experience or feel your fears in order to overcome them—physical exposure is not enough.

3. If someone were to lock you in an elevator, you might well decide to discontinue treatment. **Rule #3:** The best approach is to face your fears in a gradual, progressive, systematic way, to ensure your receptivity to the process.

4. It is difficult for someone else to structure your approach to your fears, since they are not aware of your feelings. **Rule #4:** It is best to voluntarily self-direct your approach to your fears.

5. Your fear of elevators may be due to any of several possibilities. You may be afraid of being confined, or that the elevator may crash. Or you may simply not like the feeling you have as the elevator zooms up and down. It is often difficult to manipulate real circumstances. For example it may not be possible to get control of an elevator to arrange your treatment. **Rule #5**: You may not be able to confront or expose yourself to some aspects of your fears in actuality. In this case it would be best to confront them in imagery. Imagery will often be the mainstay of your approach.

6. **Rule #6**: Imagery is a fully effective way to confront your fears. Studies have shown that the same neurological pathways are used whether we experience an event or merely imagine it—the same pathways in the brain process imagery and reality. This is why during dreams it is difficult to realize that we are not actually experiencing them. Many people can attain an orgasm through imagery. Many fears (such as of an elevator crash) must be confronted in mental imagery rather than reality. This usually works just as well, or even better.

7. If you are afraid of an elevator, then as you get closer, your fear will increase. **Rule #7:** The intensity of your fear increases in direct proportion to the degree to which you confront it.

8. If you had a safety harness on when you confronted an elevator, your fear of it crashing would be considerably reduced. **Rule #8:** Your perception of control over your fears is a very important factor in determining how fearful you are likely to be.

9. Don't force the issue. **Rule #9:** Let your mind wander and come up with its own desensitization plan.

Anxiety—or any emotion, for that matter—rarely exists by itself in any individual. There are nearly always some other feelings, such as anger or depression, that are present as well, though one emotion may seem to dominate for a while. When desensitizing, it is always better to focus on one problem at a time rather than try to take on the whole welter of conflicting emotions. For that reason in the following case histories I concentrate on the salient problem, usually to the exclusion of others.

WHEN SELF-TREATING ANXIETY

As noted earlier in this book, you should not attempt to work on anxiety that is at a level of 7 or higher on a scale of 10. You should have a professional give you anti-anxiety medicine to lower it first, or wait until you see that it has reached a level of 2 or 3, or 4 at most. Until it reaches this point you may want to allow the anxiety to happen a little, tolerate it for a few minutes. You always want to do any desensitization slowly and gradually.

AN EXAMPLE OF EFFECTIVE TREATMENT OF ANXIETY

The best way to show how desensitization works on anxiety is to describe how one of my clients used the technique to extinguish his own.

Roger suffered from general as well as very specific anxiety. He was a sturdy young man with red hair and mustache, and a redhead's pale, freckled complexion. He was running with a rather wild crowd that was deeply involved in drugs, although he was not a heavy user himself.

He did, however, need tranquilizers to deal with his anxiety. One of his specific fears was that he was afraid to drive, though he was quite good at it. He was also afraid to stand up in front of a group of people and look them in the eye, and since he was a substitute teacher this was a hardship for him. He also had attacks of free-floating anxiety during which he would suffer tremors, palpitations, and sweats.

He received his substitute teaching assignments each morning when he would be telephoned and informed of where he was needed that particular day. But often he would leave the phone off the hook, even though he needed the work, because he was not able to face going out. Often, when he did accept an assignment, he would call the school later to say he was sick. Sometimes, while at work, he would become so anxious that he would go into the restroom and take a tranquilizer. He had to be heavily medicated just to cope with everyday life.

Roger and I first tackled the trouble he had looking his students in the eye. I had him imagine going to school, standing in the class-room, and staring into the eyes of each of the students. Then I had him repeat this several times. Finally I had him enter into imaginary conversations with students, telling them that he was afraid to look at them, afraid to meet their eyes. The students replied that they thought he was pretty weird. I also had him imagine that he was telling some of the principals at the various schools where he worked that there was something wrong with him, that he was incapable of meeting the eyes of students in the classroom. This was repeated many times.

After five sessions Roger felt relatively comfortable in a class and even began to enter into staring contests with some of his undoubtedly startled pupils. He proudly reported that he usually won. This might sound trivial, but remember that he had overcome a situation that only a few weeks before had made him intensely anxious.

The next problem we worked on was his fear of driving. I had him imagine driving around town, driving longer distances, stopping and starting, going through heavy traffic, and so on. These images did arouse some anxiety, but it was not until he began to imagine driving on big highways that his anxiety became oppressive. So we narrowed his images to negotiating the nearby interstate. At first he imagined entering the highway slowly, and moving immediately to the slower right-hand lane. When he was more or less comfortable with this image he started imagining driving faster, and eventually moving into the middle lane. I then had him imagine moving to the fast lane, and even passing other vehicles, and finally driving fast on a highway filled with speeding eighteen-wheelers. After three sessions and three weeks of doing the exercises on his own every day as well, he extinguished his anxiety about driving. He was able to drive all the way to Albany on the interstate, in holiday weekend traffic, without any anxiety at all.

These confrontations took place over a period of a couple of months and we were extremely successful. Roger's general anxiety, however, remained as painful as ever. We started using desensitization on it, and I stressed how important it was that he do the exercises not only in my office, but every day on his own. I suggested that he do the imagination and repetition steps while preparing for bed or while getting dressed in the morning. Once the technique is grasped, the preparation and relaxation steps are not always necessary.

First, I had him imagine getting up in the morning, feeling anxious and frustrated. Then I had him imagine that he announced to his parents that he was going to get out of the house because he couldn't stand them anymore. He imagined telling his girlfriend that he was a free agent and would no longer be dependent on her. In short, anything that was happening in his life that seemed remotely capable of causing him discomfort, he confronted. After several weeks, the general anxiety did start to recede. One of the reasons was that he was doing something about it rather than just passively letting it engulf him.

The general anxiety did not disappear entirely, however, and it still recurred more than a year after he first came to me. But it had become much more manageable and he was functioning much better. He no longer had major anxiety attacks; rather, he was occasionally beset by vague and uncomfortable feelings of foreboding. He was almost completely free of tranquilizers, using them only when he became very apprehensive. Instead of automatically taking a tranquilizer when he felt distressed, he tried to find a quiet place and desensitize the immediate problem. If he was not able, for one reason or another to use the technique right away, he said to himself, "I don't feel well now, I'm anxious. It is even possible that I might get more anxious, but I will deal with this anxiety as soon as I can." By acknowledging his anxiety he had already taken a big step toward confronting it.

Generalized anxiety is more difficult to extinguish because usually there are no specific images that can be called up to combat it. But all of the above methods of dealing with it are effective.

> One aspect of any emotional problem such as anxiety is that people often begin to associate it with their personalities. They may not learn to like it, but they are sometimes annoyed when there is a threat of taking it away. As one of my clients said, "I wouldn't recognize myself if I weren't anxious."

BANISHING A NIGHTMARE

Sometimes anxiety will express itself in the form of nightmares, even when a person's waking hours are relatively calm and free from anxiety. Another of my clients, Christopher, was suffering from a recurring nightmare. For several years before coming to me, he would wake up in sweaty terror, sometimes two or three times a night, for a period of a week or so. Then there would be a respite of about a month before the cycle would begin again.

In the nightmare he was climbing a mountain over sharp and jagged rocks and boulders. The atmosphere was dark and stormy. There were wolves howling in the background, which he heard all during the nightmare, but never actually saw. An ominous-looking flock of vultures circled the mountain, always looking down at him with red-rimmed eyes. There were even fumaroles and lava pits on one side of the mountain, belching smoke and noxious fumes.

When he reached the top of the peak he would walk toward the edge of the cliff and look down at the sharp rocks far below. At times a shadowy presence would appear and try to push him over the side. At other times he would simply fall. Then he would wake up, always acutely distressed and sometimes hysterical.

Christopher had other issues he wanted to explore, but before we started working on his other problems, I decided to focus on the nightmare. We began using desensitization to extinguish it.

I had Chris imagine walking over and around the jagged rocks, right to the top of the mountain. Then I had him walk back down again, paying particular attention to the sharp edges and points. He repeated this imaginary trip several times until the anxiety had been quelled. I had him imagine the vultures swooping down, with him first dodging them and then picking up rocks to shoo them away. Then I had him imagine the wolves, and had him do more than just hear them—actually meet them, become acquainted with the leader of the pack, inspecting their sharp teeth and salivating chops and bristling fur. I even had him walk to the edge of one of the lava pits and look down calmly at the fiery hell below.

Then we would repeat the images again and again, going through each phase of the nightmare.

I encouraged him to branch out after he had imagined the basic scenario, but there was little he could add to the nucleus of his dream. The nightmare was so vivid in his mind that he didn't need to strengthen its impact.

We worked on the nightmare for three sessions. Over a year later, there had not been a recurrence.

If he was doing this on his own, he would do so in the more gradual and conservative way described earlier for self-treatment.

PERPETUAL INDECISION/INSECURITY/DESIRE TO NEVER CHANGE ANYTHING

Fear and anxiety are reactions to a perceived threat. The threat, in one form or another, usually involves a change in the anxious person's circumstances. To minimize this, they attempt to maintain constancy in their life and resist change. Generally, people who are anxious like stable, secure circumstances. While change can be exciting and fun for some, for others it is very threatening. In time, a person who resists change becomes increasingly unable to deal with it, and progressively more rigid. All of the techniques discussed in this chapter and Chapter Four can be helpful here.

Typically, the person is encouraged to make safe changes—such as eating out at a new restaurant or trying new foods at home, or watching a different type of movie than he usually watches—and gradually introduced to more threatening changes. Most of these people eventually come to realize that their resistance to change is ironically a major threat to their welfare, and this motivates them to accept treatment. Embracing and fostering consistent changes in one's life helps to relieve anxiety, just as the reverse is also true. For an example which you may be familiar with, a dog kept in the house all the time will be more anxious, high strung, and upset by strangers than one that is free to wander about or who has a lot of variety in his daily routine.

TREATING SITUATIONAL ANXIETIES

Some of the most common anxieties people grapple with are linked with stressful everyday events like test taking, public speaking, job interviews, appearing in court, or taking a new job. Some people even become very anxious about social situations such as meeting new people, or going to family gatherings.

Situational anxiety is treated very much like phobic anxiety (see Chapter Eight), simply substituting the situation for the phobia. For example, if a person were afraid of going to court, or giving a speech at a wedding, I would approach the situation in much the same way as if the person was afraid of spiders or heights. The results would be highly successful just as they are for phobias.

Another good technique for dealing with situational anxieties is to overlearn the skill involved in whatever you are anxious about. Practice, practice, take courses, attend seminars, get coaching, and so on.

If you talk to people who are good at what you fear, you will often discover that they have tricks they use, tricks that help them do the thing in question better. For example, say you are a golfer, and know you don't putt well, even though otherwise you are good at the game. Whenever you are putting, you get tight and nervous and screw up.

Most people hit too short when they are putting, and a short ball can never go in the hole. Pro golfers are more authoritative, they take longer shots, and even an over-long shot *can* go in. So they will tell you that you always want to aim beyond the hole. And also bear in mind that putting style is somewhat individualistic, so there is no one perfect way to do it.

TREATING MULTIPLE ANXIETIES

Most people who have fears and anxieties don't have just one—they may have a score of different things that make them nervous and uptight. If they went to a therapist he or she might treat each fear individually, starting with the most important one first, and even if the therapist exposed some of the fears as unrealistic, the process would probably take weeks or months.

Instead of discussing and desensitizing all of these different fears separately, they can be dealt with in a general way. All of those anxieties funnel into one, because the brain does not have a host of different triggers, one for each. Instead of desensitizing forty different fears, why just desensitize the fear of anxiety? Focus on the symptoms of anxiety itself.

If you were trying to catch an escaped pet, you could take a general approach instead of worrying about different instructions for different small animals. Instead of trying to find specific instructions for catching every type of pet, you could just do this:

Wear gloves, and get a second person to help if possible.

Approach the animal slowly and cautiously—don't panic it. Speak to it soothingly, using its name.

Try to back it into a spot where it will be easier to catch, such as a corner. Have the second person block any route to the wide-open spaces.

Spring for it when you get close, trying for a secure hold (such as on its neck), watching for teeth and claws.

Use a landing net taped to a broomstick if necessary.

When I treat someone for multiple anxieties, I have the person imagine triggering the anxiety himself or going down the path of triggering it, gradually going in and out of scenes involving it—triggering it, confronting it a little, and then going back out and away from it, over and over again, until they reach a level of confidence.

SOME POINTERS ON USING DESENSITIZATION FOR ANXIETY

One of my clients asked me, as he was beginning to use the process, "What happens if, when I start imagining a scene that induces anxiety,

I don't stop myself, and the anxiety continues to build and becomes unbearable?"

In the first place, I told him, it is extremely unlikely that anyone would induce anxiety to that point. But if you should happen to, your body will take over. This is a situation similar to the temper tantrum thrown by the child who threatens to kill himself by holding his breath. Sometimes the child does succeed in holding his breath until he passes out—and then he begins to breathe again. In the same way your body will regulate your anxiety level so that if it should become truly unbearable, your mind will shift to another subject, much like switching channels on a television.

Even so, it is not a good idea to push yourself to see how far you can go. For one thing, it will be such an unpleasant experience that you may want to stop using the technique. I strongly recommend that you go slowly at first, particularly with anxiety. Grow completely comfortable with each stage before moving on to the next.

If you should become very uncomfortable when using Exposure Therapy, however, just say to yourself, "OK, that's it for now. I'm going to deal with this later." And then do something else for a while. This is consciously using an avoidance response, but if you recognize it as such it is not harmful, and it will give you time to recover and deal more effectively with your problem later.

Keep in mind that this is not just an abracadabra method—work is required. The amount of energy you are going to have to spend is related to the severity of your problem. If, for example, you have been bitten by a dog ten times, it is going to take a great deal more work to get over your anxiety about dogs than if you had been bitten just once.

A number of my clients have noted that if they work on desensitization while taking a brisk walk, or jogging, or swimming, that combination of physical exercise and the technique seems to speed up the release of tension.

When dealing with anxiety remember that it is probably the most widespread complaint that psychologists encounter today. So if it is a problem for you—at one time or another it is for all of us—you are by no means alone. Nor need you be helpless.

The three I's—insecurity, inadequacy, and inferiority

Feelings of insecurity, inadequacy, and inferiority are complex emotions. Each of them is essentially based on feelings of anxiety regarding different aspects of one's life, combined with rational concerns about those same aspects. For example, when we say we feel insecure, in effect, what we actually mean is that we feel anxious about our finances or other aspects of our lives that we associate with security. Likewise, when we feel inadequate, we feel anxious about our ability to handle the demands made on us. In turn, inferiority involves feeling anxious about how we stack up to others.

Overcoming the three I's calls for resolving the underlying anxiety.

REVIEW OF THE STEPS FOR OVERCOMING ANXIETY

In treating yourself for anxiety, you want to follow the five steps of the desensitization process, which are, once again, Education, Preparation, Imagination, Repetition, and Relaxation.

The preparation step is fairly straightforward: put yourself in a safe atmosphere and try to be as comfortable as possible.

In doing the other steps keep the following precautions in mind, especially when dealing with anxiety.

Go through the images completely but quickly at first in order to get a sense of what the outcome will be. In other words, think through the whole sequence you will be following in your mind in the imaging. For example, "First I will imagine myself stopping my attempts to wash away all of those germs by quitting my constant handwashing. My hands might feel dirtier then—what will I do about that? Someone might notice I wasn't doing this anymore and say something—how would I reply?" Keep following the trail of "then what?" until you have reached the end. This will give you a feeling of control and keep the anxiety from getting out of hand.

Avoid branching—digressing—your first few times through a scene because this will tend to take you away from the initial emotion. Once you feel that the initial emotion is more or less in hand, then you can start to branch out. When you do start to branch, however, follow each digression through and exhaust it before taking off on another one.

Avoid pleasurable digressions, since it's highly unlikely that anything pleasurable was responsible for your anxiety or other negative emotions. In fact, it is very likely that pleasurable digressions are avoidance responses.

Fight the tendency to say, "This won't work." A sense of futility is fairly common when dealing with negative emotions, and particularly with anxiety Remember that desensitization is a short-term technique. Give it a chance.

As you wear away the avoidance responses and come closer and closer to the root emotion, you will discover, in all likelihood, what has been the cause of the emotion. Keep in mind, though, that what you are after is the *emotion;* that is what you want to eradicate and learning the cause is not necessary to effect this.

It is a good idea to do the exercises at scheduled times, but even better to do them, if possible, as soon as the emotion arises. In fact I find that Exposure Therapy is most effective when it is applied to an emotion immediately upon its arousal. Having this action at your disposal will give you a feeling of mastery.

Work on specific problems before moving on to general and vague feelings. For example, concentrate on your specific anxieties before tackling general or free-floating anxiety.

If at all possible, try to follow up the confrontation in imagery with a real-life confrontation. After, say, confronting a fear of meeting people in images, go out into social situations and shake a few hands. Sometimes behavioral practice may involve use of a coach or a buddy to work with you. If you have employment-related anxiety, you could, for example, set up a scenario such as a job interview and then act it out and practice ways of handling it with someone.

Repetition is the most important of the steps. Go over and over the issue you are working on until you feel comfortable with it. This could take several days or even longer. If any disturbing emotion crops up during the day, particularly after you start working on it during regular sessions, confront it at once if at all possible.

Do allow all of the ramifications of the scene to come to the surface during this step. Let your imagination bring up all of the possibilities that could possibly happen. But don't create horrific or wildly unrealistic images. Such scenes will arouse unwarranted fears and furthermore they are so unpleasant that they might make you want to abandon the technique.

WHEN ANXIETY IS SEVERE

There are special strategies that can be employed for severe anxiety, including very gradual exposure and very small treatment steps, and dipping quickly in and out of the sensitive subject.

Anxious people tend to be somewhat frozen in their responses. When someone is very anxious or nervous, you don't want to put them on the spot by making them talk a lot, make decisions, or discuss their inner feelings.

They really want to retreat—back off, get away from the fray. So don't be too forward. Pushing them out to front and center is not the way to go. When they feel more comfortable, they will be more willing, and you can go from there.

Frequently people who are anxious, such as those who have experienced a trauma, prefer that someone else talk for them.

Often we see on the nightly news a host or reporter who puts a mike in front of someone who has just lost his house or his spouse and says, "How do you feel about this?" They seem to get a kick out of putting people in the position of revealing raw emotion. "They just found the killer of your loved ones. How do you feel about that?"

Putting someone on the spot like this is totally inappropriate. If you are ever in such a situation I would just say something like, "I'd rather not discuss that at this time." Don't give in to their gambit by trying to address the issues they want to hear about. They are just interested in you as a hook for a news story—they don't have your best interests at heart, or at least that is certainly not a priority.

It's reasonable to back off when someone is anxious, a time when their judgment is likely to be clouded by their fears. So when dealing with such a person don't ask too many questions—adjust your communications to more of a camaraderie mode, talk to them in a low-key way. Don't ask them to make decisions or talk about how they feel about whatever they are anxious about right now.

In therapy I do this too. When people come out with something gracefully and voluntarily, when they are able to do this, we are much better off than if I tried to drag it out of them.

HOW HIGH IS TOO HIGH?

When the reading on our inner anxiety meter is too high, when it is reaching the "red zone" of the continuum, 7 or higher out of a possible 10, self-treatment is out of the question. Someone at this level is practically paralyzed, like the person up on a high diving board, who is so scared they can neither listen to the swimming coach's encouragements to jump, nor work up the courage to retreat. Before further treatment can be attempted, a professional will usually prescribe medication to bring the patient's level down much lower.

Often, when a person's anxiety level is very high they have difficulty even imagining the situation that is provoking it. For example, clients who have had a panic attack often have difficulty reproducing, in imagery, the circumstances that led up to it. They have a great deal of resistance to conjuring up the stressful event, and freely admit that they feel blocked by the intensity of the situation.

Another sign of ultra-high anxiety is that once a person touches upon an incident, verbally or in imagery, they quickly recoil and can't proceed. Some just say, "I don't want to talk about it." The intensity of an anxiety you wish to self-treat should be relatively mild, such that it is only moderately arousing or uncomfortable. Otherwise, let a professional handle it. They will gently and calmly let you proceed at your own pace until you desensitize the material to the point that the two of you can proceed more aggressively.

DEALING WITH FEARS

You can only talk and reason anxiety down so far—some things are not anxieties but genuine fears.

Fears are mostly learned. There are not many naturally occurring fears. There are a few fears—such as of high places, strange faces, odd tastes, bloody body parts, and witnessing someone get hurt or expose himself to danger—that have been shown to be universal and are apparently ingrained in us. But in most cases, we learn to be fearful from our experiences or from observing others.

Fears are forged through the associative process first described by Pavlov. Any event that is quickly followed by a painful consequence will ultimately cause us to be fearful of that event. In this manner, Pavlov trained dogs to be fearful of a buzzer, by first presenting the buzzer and then following it with a painful electrical shock. As a result, most of our fears, such as of vicious animals or bullies, are either directly learned from our experiences or through observation and an objective assessment of circumstances. Others, which are not necessarily rational, can be readily learned through accidents or news about them—such as fear of driving, swimming, flying, or using power tools. Moreover, even less obvious or rational fears, such as of rejection or disapproval, can readily develop from observing and watching other people.

People vary in their likelihood of developing fears. Some are more predisposed to this than others. Some people—such as shy people—may acquire a fear of rejection, for example, more readily than extroverts. The key to dealing with fears and anxiety is to recognize that they are the natural consequence of painful experiences, and that once formed they can be eradicated by well-established treatments. In short, these involve gradually exposing the person to the fearful or anxiety-provoking experience, repetitiously, until it is desensitized. The nature of the fear—whether it seems logical or not—is not a major factor in overcoming it, nor is insight into its origin. Treatment is essentially the same for all fears, although it should be pointed out that some people, such as those who suffer from a neurological impairment, require some modification to the treatment regimen, which may include medication.

> Anxiety and actual fears can both be desensitized. Firemen and police learn to desensitize their fears, which are realistic and not just worries that anyone might have.

IDENTIFYING AND DEFUSING RESPONSE-BASED FEARS

Not all anxiety is created in a more or less straightforward way, by the sudden appearance of—or our mental images of—something that frightens us. Stimulus-based fears are the most common: we see or encounter something that scares us—a barking dog with its teeth bared, or the view over the guardrail at the edge of the Grand Canyon. But over the years I have discovered that many people have what I call response-based anxieties, as well. These are cases where our dread and anxiety has been transferred from the original cause—the stimulus—to some aspect of our own response to it.

In this type of fear it is not the original stimulus, but our response to it, that now brings back the traumatic experience. This is a kind of superstitious reaction that is an attempt to give us a feeling of control over things we seem to have no control over.

Say a person runs up a stairs quickly. His heart will beat faster, pulse rate increase, and he'll find himself breathing faster. These are also many of the signs of the anxiety he felt when he heard that his daughter had been injured. Now the simple act of getting a little exercise can cause him to again conjure up how he felt when he sat in the hospital waiting room awaiting the doctor's grim report.

For another example, you might be practicing gymnastics, and suddenly certain movements—jumping up and down, flailing your arms—reminds you all too vividly of the time earlier this summer when you almost drowned.

Classic examples of response-based fear are often seen in people suffering from obsessive-compulsive disorder. Someone is afraid of contracting a dangerous disease, and her response is to wash her hands, because by reducing germs she may ward off this prospect. But after a while the constant washing itself becomes the problem. In a case like this you can't get at the fear of the disease without first stopping the response. This is crucial to overcoming the problem. But the person is afraid to stop the response because this may increase the likelihood of what they dread coming true.

> The treatment is to desensitize the situation slowly and gradually, by having the person imagine different responses, such as just wiping their hands instead of washing them, or imagining not washing them right away, then imagining waiting a little longer before washing them, and so on, allowing the anxiety to come through a little each time and gradually working toward eliminating the response. For more about OCD, see Chapter Nine.

These kinds of anxieties need a different kind of treatment.

Since the most common response-based fear occurs when someone exercises too hard and this generates arousal responses that the person then associates with the extreme anxiety that last stimulated such responses, the first thing I do is tell them to moderate their exercise, do it gradually, work their way to the more strenuous exercises slowly.

They can also master the response by imagining making the response over and over. I tell them to imagine exercising to the point that they get progressively more and more sweaty and out of breath, as well as the other symptoms that accompany such exertion. This is very similar to how I would treat a stimulus-based response.

MAKING EVEN REALISTIC FEARS MORE MANAGEABLE

Some fears and anxieties are not unreasonable at all, such as the fears that firefighters, police officers, and lion tamers must live and manage to function with. Rational fears, interestingly, are often easier to desensitize than irrational ones, because the latter often have some subterranean additional component in them, such as OCD (see Chapter Nine) that is harder to deal with.

Police officers and firefighters have to deal with truly rational fears. How do they do it? These people can overcome anxiety about the very real dangers that they face daily with a two-step program.

First is the gradual desensitization of the fear by repeated exposure to it, as described earlier, and the second is the development of confidence and competency in terms of the actual handling of the fearful situation. This is developed through training and practice that shows the person they can be successful in the situation in question. Desensitization, in many cases, is even more important, because otherwise our fears may prevent us from gaining the competency to successfully deal with dangerous situations.

In step two, the training, first they discuss the nature of the fearful situation, such as entering a building where an alarm has recently gone off. What are the appropriate steps to take before going in?—such as calling for backup, turning on the lights, announcing their presence, and/or bringing in the K-9 unit, for example. Once they have learned what they need to do, then they practice doing it, first in imagery or perhaps on a simulator, and then in a mock demonstration using confederates (in this case, people who act out roles to aid the therapy). Ultimately, they enter the actual situation with a fellow officer or firefighter. Eventually, they practice alone on simple situations and gradually advance to more difficult ones. This is how therapists learn as well.

"If it's a real fear, there's nothing I can do." Not true. The people running out of a burning building are usually more anxious than the firefighters who are running into that same building. The same is true of a police officer going down a dark alley: because he's been trained, he is usually aroused, alert, and focused, but not highly anxious.

What if a person becomes desensitized and develops mastery of the physical skills involved in something, but then something negative happens and they are re-traumatized? In this case they have to go back to square one. They have to undergo desensitization again, and try to develop additional skills to increase their mastery. When people are re-traumatized and have to return to the treatment program, however, each time the procedure goes faster and faster. Learning to get back on track by reprogramming themselves with desensitization removes the fear of relapse, and reduces it to a mundane experience that occasionally must be dealt with.

CHAPTER SEVEN

WHAT'S YOUR ANXIETY LEVEL?

OUR GENERAL LEVEL OF ANXIETY AND HOW IT AFFECTS US

A bnormal anxiety issues aside, we all have an inborn level of overall anxiety and it has a big effect on our lives. In this chapter we will look at people's different levels of habitual anxiety, the consequences of them, and the different treatment measures each level calls for, when these levels cause a problem.

LIFE IN THE HIGH ANXIETY ZONE

Kristin's life was a challenge. Though she'd never stopped to think about it, her every day was an almost unbroken landscape of anxiety. When she got up in the morning, her first thought was of whether her favorite cat had somehow finally managed to slip out the door he was always eyeing, and was now at risk somewhere off in the woods or fields. Not until his cheerful, chubby face burst into the kitchen was she able to release her breath. When she went to fetch a frozen waffle, she had to suppress a secret fear that one of the younger cats might have jumped into the giant freezer unbeknownst to her, and his or her rigid little body would now be greeting her amidst the frosty bags of peas and blackberries. As the sun began to peek over the horizon, and that strong orange glare hit her eyes, she couldn't help but notice her greater sensitivity to the light than in earlier years, and wonder what this might mean in terms of retinal deterioration.

As she took the morning's first glance into a mirror, she noticed a new wrinkle on her cheek, and wondered how much longer it would be before the smile lines had progressed to the point of nothing to smile about. As she brushed her teeth (which had spent the night in an annoying tooth guard to minimize the effects of nighttime tooth grinding), she hit a sore spot on her upper gums. Was this going to plunge her into more expensive in-depth tooth cleaning? She was torn out of this reverie by the sudden thought that her son had never called last night from college—could something nasty have happened to him on the way back to the campus from his visit home?

As she stepped out onto the back porch, her foot hit that soft board, the one that made her try to remember how long it had been since the house's last termite treatment. Walking up the driveway, she saw that the iris bed was showing signs of that disfiguring disease again. When she reached the mailbox, there was one envelope she never wanted to open, and was that new client actually ever going to send a check?

When she finally slipped into the car to head off to town, the little whistling sound she heard as the car started up kept her occupied all the way in, wondering if this might be early warning of a sudden breakdown.

Dianna, who was twenty years older than Kristin, had a life that was not a great deal different. She had a grown daughter with three children, but couldn't see her grandchildren as often as she liked because her son-in-law was too controlling and difficult. She anguished endlessly over this. She had another daughter as well, married to a man who was verbally and sometimes physically abusive. Dianna's own marriage had its problems, too—her husband was an amputee as a result of his service in Vietnam. At times he would threaten to kill himself, or to kill his son-in-law for hitting his daughter. When she wasn't worrying about her children or grandchildren, she worried about her husband's health, and his inability to keep a job. She worried constantly, but felt she had no control over anything.

Sam was older yet—seventy-eight. He worried nonstop about his wife, who might soon have to go a nursing home. He worried about finances, too, though he had plenty of money, and a son and daughter entirely willing to support him. He worried about his own health as well, and his home, and the repairs it seemed to constantly require. He went from one worry to the next; when I told him this was hard on both his mind and body, then he worried about that, too.

All of these people are suffering from a high degree of generalized anxiety, but every one of us has some built-in level of anxiety, and we are born with it.

THE ANXIETY SCALE, FROM TOP TO BOTTOM

A more positive-sounding term for our anxiety level might be something like sensitivity—how aware we are of possible threats to us from the environment or other people. Levels vary from very high to very low, and everywhere in between. People with high levels tend to be very sensitive to the feelings of others, and they are endlessly anticipating and trying to plan for adverse circumstances. People at the other end of the continuum, those with very low levels of anxiety, tend to be focused mainly on themselves and their own undertakings, and are such poor planners we might call them oblivious...often until it is too late.

There are plenty of people whose anxiety level is in the mid-range, too, and as we might guess, they are overall more flexible, and better balanced.

No matter where we are on the anxiety scale, that reading will have a strong effect on our lives. Though we all pride ourselves on being objective, and usually strive to be, whatever our mind thinks is filtered through our brain, and the anxiety meter built into our brain will color our every thought and action.

There are pros and cons to each side of this knuckle-chewing continuum, as we shall see later in this chapter, and also other personality factors that can affect how a given person's anxiety profile plays out. Our anxiety level may be counterbalanced or lowered by other factors. If a highly anxious person is depressed, for example, she may be assertive or candid, because she doesn't have enough energy to hold everything back.

And though our basic level of anxiety comes to us at birth with all the rest of our genetic programming, we can alter it, and learn to make adaptations, such as setting up a lifestyle that is more consistent with our nature. There are also techniques we can use to reduce and regulate it—the desensitization and imagery described elsewhere in this book. We can also learn how to lower it at a given time, such as during a job interview or important meeting, for example.

Even without treatment, our anxiety level can change a little over the course of our lives. If fortune smiles on us and we have a pretty easy ride, lots of good things happening to us, it can go down a little. And if the opposite is true, if we have a hard road full of traumas and stresses, not surprisingly, our overall everyday level of anxiety will go up some.

WELCOME TO WORRYWART CENTRAL

Let's take a closer look at the half of the population with higher levels of anxiety. If the anxiety scale is thought of as ranging from 1 to 10, these are the folks whose score would be 5 1/2 to 10. Those with a level of 5 1/2 to 6 are only moderately anxious, scores of 6-7 would begin to show some problems developing, and levels of 8 or above amount to a moderate to severe Generalized Anxiety Disorder, as the psychologists call it. People with anxiety this high are in trouble. They worry about absolutely everything, and how likely a given thing they are worrying about is to actually happen—to them—is scarcely an issue. Their non-stop anxieties make it hard for them to concentrate on anything else, so they have difficulty working, or for that matter, enjoying themselves.

They are tense, restless and fidgety, and as their mental state takes a toll on their bodies, they may have symptoms like fatigue, headaches, nausea, numbness in their hands and feet, muscle aches, difficulty in swallowing or breathing, sweating, insomnia, hot flashes, or rashes. People with anxiety this high should not attempt self-treatment, but seek help from a psychological professional, who will often prescribe medication to lower the person's anxiety level some before he or she attempts to lower it further by other means.

PORTRAIT OF A HIGH-ANXIETY PERSON

A mildly elevated level of anxiety, interestingly enough, produces a pretty likeable person. The psychologists often call these people "other-person oriented," because they are so empathetic and sympathetic with others that everyone feels good around them. Since people with high-anxiety personalities (let's call them HAPs for short) already feel a little anxious, they go all out to avoid conflict and stress in their surroundings. A very large part of those surroundings consist of other people, and HAPs have large invisible antennae that are incredibly attuned to how those around them are thinking and feeling. This enables them to head off interpersonal problems before they happen, and to build relationships quickly and easily.

At home or at work, with family or friends, they are consummate diplomats and the perfect shoulders to cry on—they are always trying to keep the peace and understand the problems of others. If their mom and their sister haven't spoken in years, they will be the ones to scheme up something to reunite the two. If everyone at work hates the new hire, they will be the ones to find a way to ease them into the company family. In general, they would rather get along than get their way. If the gang goes out for pizza and insists on ordering mushroom and anchovy, the HAP will quietly slip the anchovies under the edge of her plate rather than register a dissenting vote at the ordering counter. If they all decide to go to a movie and choose one he would never pick, he will suffer through it, popcorn in hand, in silence.

Since HAPs always want to blend in and avoid making waves, and are eager to build themselves a secure environment, their lives tend to proceed in somewhat of a straight line. They educate themselves well and develop many skills to make themselves useful. They pick a dependable job, work hard at it, and stick with it, even if it is not the best-paying or most challenging. They are loyal to the things they choose, and tend not to make big changes in their lives until they are forced upon them.

LET A HAP PACK YOUR PARACHUTE

The HAP's constant efforts to avoid trouble extend also to the nonhuman parts of the world around them. They always have their eyes peeled and their ears to the ground, are always looking ahead and planning and anticipating. When you are planning your ascent of Everest or a ten-day hiking trip far from roads and stores, these are the kind of people you would want orchestrating it.

When trouble does come, it often doesn't unhinge them—after all, they've spent their whole lives preparing for it.

Other-oriented people are such perfect models of what most people have been hoping and waiting for by way of a fellow human that a HAP is soundly reinforced in such behavior, often causing him or her to intensify it.

What's the catch?

HAPs are so thoroughly attuned to the thoughts and feelings of others that they have trouble focusing on themselves. They are so focused on peacemaking and being liked that they can shortchange themselves. In the course of a lifetime, they may discover that they have always put themselves second...or last.

They are more concerned with maintaining the peace than having their needs met; and over time, the relationship they have with themselves deteriorates and they come to have a poor view of themselves. Their friends often like them more than they like themselves.

Another troublesome side effect of the high-anxiety profile is that such people, while almost universally beloved elsewhere, are not quite so charming at home. Having spent much more time with their nearest and dearest than with outsiders, they are not nearly so worried about what their spouse or children or roommates may think of them. So here they feel free to express those hard feelings and differences of opinion they have stifled elsewhere, in the interests of harmony. As well as any frustration or grumpiness their constant kowtowing in the outside world has stored up in their soul.

High-anxiety profile people worry a lot; and tend to live in the future. They think that once they are totally secure, which they constantly strive for, they will be happy, but that day never comes, because there is always some uncertainty, and never enough reassurance to satisfy them.

Typical high-anxiety characteristics

Positives:

- Seen as the perfect friend

- Good listeners

- Unlikely to create or worsen conflicts

- Peacemakers

- Build large network of positive relationships, at work and in their personal lives

- Loyal and long-range employees and mates

- Conscientious

- Good at anticipating and planning

Negatives:

- Difficulty saying "no"

- May not be respected by others, who see them as obsequious, timid, or insecure

- Others may question their sincerity

- At times, others feel they can't count on them if the situation calls for a candid, assertive response

- Tend to have a negative self-image

- Likely to be less pleasant and accommodating on the home front

- Sometimes, their loved ones resent their numerous attachments to others

SOME REAL-LIFE EXAMPLES OF LIFE IN THE HIGH-ANXIETY LANE

The story of a firefighter who came to me for treatment demonstrates many of the points made above. Joseph was involved in perhaps the highest-risk form of his profession, smoke-jumping. He threw himself into his work wholeheartedly, and loved being a member of a team all working together to an important end. On the job he was always agreeable and upbeat, incredibly supportive of his fellow firefighters. In fact, he was the most popular member of his unit.

His wife had a different view of him. She was not pleased that he never worried about his relatively modest pay (they had little saved, and a far from luxurious lifestyle), or prepared himself for a hopefully more profitable post-retirement career. And once the afterglow of his popularity with his coworkers faded away at the end of each day, Joe was angry with himself as well. He saw himself as a loser who'd done little, either for himself or to meet the needs of his family. But still he found himself doing all kinds of things for others, for reasons he didn't really understand—such as driving colleagues to the airport, or helping them to fix or remodel their homes on his days off. They rarely or never reciprocated. His family had to listen to all of his complaints about this as well.

By the time he came to see me in counseling, he was furious. He felt his life had been wasted—he'd let it go by. Later in this chapter you will learn how we turned all of this around.

Elaine, another of my clients, was a very attractive woman in her early thirties who also suffered as a result of her other-person orientation. She was dating a very alpha man who was totally self-absorbed. He arranged their relationship entirely around his own needs and took full advantage of her. He traveled a lot, and called her when he could, but he often forgot to call or would just beg off from dates they had made. He was so caught up in getting his business off the ground that their relationship was only a side issue for him. But like a good HAP, Elaine took it all in good spirits, and sat hopefully by the phone. She was a real estate appraiser, and a good one, but this love affair meant more to her than her profession. Her parents, meanwhile, were aghast to see their lovely daughter tying herself in knots for someone they felt would never deserve her.

In the end, ironically, her very good-naturedness was what caused him to break up with her. Alpha types do like to be in control, and they like to win, but they also like to have a partner who is into winning. They may like someone to be very flexible and accommodating toward them, but they are not too happy to see this extended to others. When they see someone who is nice to everyone at every turn, they begin to see that person as failing to stand up for themselves, too dependent and needy. This eventually turns to criticism and disdain.

Another example of the HAP's strong drive to keep the peace, get along, and get by was Gisele, a middle-aged woman who consulted me. She'd been married for many years to a loud, aggressive, domineering man. Not the least of his demands was for daily sex. Between her growing emotional distance from him, and the onset of menopause, she was less than enthusiastic about this. In fact, she hated it. But she put up with it with it as best she could. HAPs have a hard time saying no to anything.

But in her heart she was just waiting until their four children finished growing up and left home, so she could divorce him. When they finally did head off to college and careers, she finally, with my help, started a dialogue with him that eventually did end in divorce. Even in this, however, her HAP tendency reared its head, as she found herself willing to give him the lion's share of their assets, just so she could end the marriage peaceably and keep their vacation cottage as part of the deal.

THE OTHER SIDE OF THE COIN

Those at the other end of the spectrum, who have anxiety levels of 4 1/2 and lower, are almost the complete opposite of the high anxiety profile. One might go so far as to say that at least some of these folks are not anxious enough.

People with the independence trait usually have low levels of generalized anxiety, and as a result they tend to be inclined to try new things, to live in the present, and to be more likely to do what they want rather than be concerned with what anyone else is doing. The fact that their anxiety is low has a significant effect on their behavior across the board.

Overall, people with low generalized anxiety are not very threatened by either the environment around them or other people, and it shows. Let's give them an acronym of their own, and call these low-anxiety personalities LAPs. LAP's are very brave (at least they always appear so), spontaneous, and self-confident, which often draws people to them. They have strong opinions that they do not hesitate to make known. They pursue their own interests aggressively (getting their way is very important to them), and usually think of themselves as winners, strong and effective. Others at times have less flattering labels for them, such as arrogant, self-righteous, narcissistic, or grandiose.

People who have the independence trait pride themselves on how self-reliant and self-contained they are. They often boast about how they virtually raised themselves and think other people should do the same. They feel that other people are simply not sufficiently independent and they tend not to respect them. They are also aware of the fact that they do not have the same level of anxiety that the average person has, and are often inclined to advise other people that they should be less concerned with possible negative consequences, with what could go wrong. They should be more positive and targeted to how they can attain their goals. People are often envious of those with the independence trait because they seem very confident and accomplished. They are not aware of the fact that this trait also brings with it a number of undesirable characteristics.

People with the independence trait are not usually very good at following other people's instructions. They are not good at dealing with authority figures or complying with the directions of authority figures. They may adjust to this by recognizing the importance of following the directions of authority figures such as the police, but nevertheless it runs against their nature.

People with the independence trait are very goal-oriented. They are usually very concerned with achieving their goals and creating new ones as time goes on. They often pride themselves on the tendency to set goals and to work very hard to attain them.

Some people may work at a job that has only minimal interest for them because it meets their needs. A person with the independence trait, on the other hand, is much more inclined to strive to find a job he truly wants and be very reluctant to settle for anything else. He is likely to view people who don't do this as slackers and not sufficiently motivated.

Simple tasks or jobs are rarely challenging enough for LAPs—but difficult problems rivet their attention and bring out their best. Thus they often seek high-stress occupations such as performer or conductor. They want to do what they want to do, and so mundane, practical advice about little things such as whether or not they will be able to support themselves decently in a given line of work has little interest for them.

During their early years, people with the independence trait are very inclined to focus on what they like, what they're good at, what their interests are, and what they can become better at. This is so they can develop into the person they feel they are meant to be. They see themselves as a unique creation, something that they are willing to spend a great deal of time developing. Most people are much more group oriented. They spend a great deal of time determining how they can fit into the group, and how they can develop skills and attributes that would be of value to the group. They are not as focused on who they are and what their natural tendencies and talents are as people who have the independence trait. They are much more concerned with avoiding hardships and developing plans in accord with what their circumstances are. People with the independence trait are inclined to be somewhat condescending to people who are mainly trying to fit in and get by, and this is reflected in their cynical tendencies.

The independent rarely give much thought to anyone else's point of view or circumstances—this might inhibit their ability to ignore any such issues. They are not particularly compassionate, and basically feel that everyone should deal with their own problems. People often see them as rather cold-hearted and lacking in compassion, callous when it comes to other people's concerns—difficult to deal with. LAPs aren't much concerned about other people at all, with the exception of their spouse or immediate family, who are elevated into a different category, since the low-anxiety person thinks of them as extensions of himself. Thus he is usually quite mindful of and devoted to them.

Needless to say, this cavalier attitude toward others often lands low-anxiety personalities in people problems. The fact that they feel no need to consider the feelings of others just about guarantees it. When they get into a dispute they often try to resolve it by a sudden burst of aggression—they become irritated, angry, or hostile...which usually only digs them deeper.

People with the independence trait do not rely on other people for reinforcement—they depend on themselves for that. They pride themselves on having their own standards and their own code of morality, and as a result they are not very interested in other people's opinions regarding these areas. They are not inclined to value the opinions of others. They will occasionally know some people who are very similar perhaps in outlook to themselves, and these people they may consider or consult in determining their own behavior.

The independent are not very group oriented—they are not inclined to join groups. How can you have a group of independent people? Their independence causes them to continually strive to be outside the group, to try to follow their own way, to find new paths and so on. As a result they may spend a great deal of time following unproductive leads, as opposed to those more accepting of the achievements of others and more inclined to try to benefit from them, rather than constantly strive to do everything on their own.

On the other hand, if the independent do feel a need to join a group because they need the support, they eventually come to see the group as an extension of themselves.

Their lack of planning is another Achilles heel. They may do well outlining small tasks and undertakings, but they rarely look very far ahead, or at the big picture. They often underestimate difficulties and overestimate their ability to deal with them. They have a tendency not to anticipate problems and as a result not to plan for them. This is not so evident in short-range situations such as going on a vacation or perhaps a day trip. It is usually more obvious in their lack of planning and preparation with regard to long-term goals such as retirement, health care, or even starting a new business.

Their disinclination to look past the end of the current rainbow and think about mundane but often important things like a stable career, child-rearing strategies, or saving for retirement, often finds them caught short. They are like the pig who built his house of straw, and now they need to find a quick fix. Thus their lives often have a zigzag pattern, as they run into the unexpected, or get a new offer, try something else, and move on.

TYPICAL LOW-ANXIETY CHARACTERISTICS

LAPs have varied interests and points of view. For example, some consider work highly desirable, or view a particular form of work, such as musician, small business owner, doctor, or lawyer, as the best form of work. But others may view work negatively, and prefer staying home and raising children, or just staying home. They all feel differently about things, but whatever their point of view, they are adamant about it; they don't care much about what other people think.

Typical low-anxiety characteristics

Pros:

- Not very threatened by the people or the environment around them

- Behavior and views are based mostly on their interests and intellectual considerations

- Spontaneous—when I ask LAPs if they would like to make plans in advance—say, on Monday, for the weekend—they generally prefer making plans on the same day as they plan on going out. They often say that planning makes them feel trapped and restricted. HAPs, on the other hand, like plans because they feel that the decision is nailed down and they can look forward to it.

- Pursue their own interests aggressively

- Independent—but this does not necessarily mean oblivious to others. It means resistant to peer pressure and therefore inclined to follow their own lead. Some LAPs like accommodating others, and may have other characteristics of HAPs, but if they do, it is because this is what *they* want to do. They are not driven by anxiety, as are HAPs.

- Usually very devoted to spouse/close family

- Often do very well on difficult, challenging work assignments

Cons:

- Candid and insensitive, which often leads to people problems

- Overconfident—they don't concern themselves with backups—they assume their first attempt will work.

- Often come across as having to be right all of the time.

- Unlikely to anticipate things, or plan ahead, which may lead to crises

- Life often follows zigzag pattern

LOW ANXIETY IN ACTION

One of my clients, Martha, showed the drawbacks of the low-anxiety profile in high relief. She was the head engineer for a highway construction company, and every report and assessment that left her office was as precise and painstakingly accurate as it could be. She'd been working there for years, and probably knew the state, federal, and local requirements for their work better than anyone else in the company.

This truth, alas, was not kept to herself, as a source of secret inner pride. She let everyone know it, and then some. She had no tolerance for anyone with lesser gifts, or who didn't do their job as well as she did. She was very outspoken at meetings, completely willing to get into arguments when she felt she was right, and always seemed to get her way. (More likely, people were yessing her to death to mask their frustration with her.) She was so candid and insensitive in her remarks—she was only telling the truth, after all—that many left her presence crushed or cringing.

Finally, she was forced out after she took on the owner of the company. Martha was not only very dependent on the income from her work, she was just plain stunned. She came to me to find out how she might modify her behavior to deal with this, and you will learn exactly what we did later in this chapter.

Sally was another case of the self-absorption so typical of the lower end of the anxiety scale. She'd had MS since her mid-thirties, which forced her to be a stay-at-home wife, which she liked better than working in the outside world, anyway, since it prevented her from having to be under anyone's thumb. It also enabled her to give full attention to her illness.

Sally was married to a very understanding man, and she ran the relationship, which seemed to be focused almost entirely upon her and her needs. Her husband spent a great deal of time delivering her to doctors, discussing and researching her problems, taking her to see her parents, taking her shopping, and so on. As time passed her medical problems intensified, as did her demands and his job of caretaking her. This only seemed to make her more self-centered. The cherry on the top of this unappetizing situation was the fact that she eventually became angry at him for being so accommodating.

Things had gone too far. Her husband began to challenge all of this, and become more assertive. He told her he was so turned off by the weight she had gained over the years that he no longer looked forward to sex with her. She was shocked at his candor—normally he would phrase his criticisms much more delicately, such as, "When you were young you had the body of a stripper" (which in fact is what he used to say to her). She suddenly became eager to please him. Though with her medical issues it was difficult to lose weight, she managed to lose thirty pounds by virtually starving herself. She also treated him better and with more respect.

Kyle is an even more dramatic example of the limitations of the low-anxiety lifestyle. He was so fearless that he got involved in a lot of activities that many people would steer clear of. He dabbled in drugs, from acid to coke, and tried everything from hang gliding to bungee jumping, cliff hanging to skydiving. He liked hockey, too, and was a demon on the ice, diving for the puck with no regard for flying fists or sticks. He felt most alive when he was doing something risky. He was such a daredevil he was exciting to watch, but he paid for it over time with broken bones and some long hospital stays. He told me once that he only planned to live until he was thirty, because life was pretty much downhill after that.

He focused mostly on his adventurous hobbies and having fun with his friends. He didn't ever intend to slow down and do all of the silly typical things like get a boring regular job, or raise a family.

Nonetheless, when he reached that unimaginable age of thirty, he did in fact get married and eventually have three children. At this point hustling for odd jobs and living from day to day began to lose its charm. He had nothing saved or put aside, and minimal insurance of any kind, and all of this was now a strain on both him and his marriage. His level of anxiety, originally about a 2, began to move closer to the mid-range, and he began to think in terms of more secure employment and all of the other things that higher anxiety people thought of long ago.

WHY DO WE DUST AND MOP WHEN AGITATED?

Different anxiety levels at work

Our anxiety level often shows itself in our approach to work. When we are feeling deeply anxious, challenging and difficult work, especially mental work, is hard to deal with. We can't get our minds off our problems well enough to do major or serious brainwork. If you asked a mother in a hospital waiting room about to hear the verdict on her seriously injured child to write a grant proposal or walk a tightrope, you might as well not have bothered.

But when we are seriously agitated, hand us an ax, shovel, or vacuum cleaner, and we will shine! For the highly anxious person there is a lot of relaxation and even comfort in simple tasks.

1. On easy tasks, LAPs do poorly, whereas HAPs do well.

2. On challenging tasks, LAPs do well, while HAPs do poorly.

On easy tasks, HAPs' high level of anxiety focuses their attention on the task and also distracts them from their anxieties, which acts as a pleasant relief. On challenging tasks, their naturally high level of anxiety is exacerbated by the difficulty of the task or its importance, and they become too anxious to concentrate or perform well.

In contrast, LAPs have a low level of anxiety that is only lowered further by a task they see as boring and unchallenging, so they have difficulty concentrating on it. On challenging tasks, their anxiety is raised to the point that they can focus better.

PEOPLE IN THE MIDDLE

Over the years, I've seen a number of people in my practice who score in the "goldilocks" range of the anxiety scale, level 5: not too much and not too little—just right. These people can be assertive when necessary, and accommodating when appropriate. Similarly, they keep their focus on themselves yet are sensitive to others as well. They anticipate unexpected problems and thereby deal with them better than LAPs, and they have more respect for themselves than HAPs. But there are drawbacks here, too. The main one is that LAPs and HAPs typically play to their strengths; they become specialists at getting along with others (HAPs) or doggedly pursuing their interests to the point of becoming very good at them (LAPs). In contrast, the 5's are often generalists who have difficulty competing against the specialists in the areas of their strengths.

Justine, whose anxiety level was normally a 5, sought therapy after her brother died. They had been very close throughout their lives. When her brother was nineteen it was suddenly discovered that he had severe type one diabetes. For the next thirty years, until he died, Justine was devoted to him, although she had her own career (she was a librarian) and was married as well. Her brother relied on Justine to keep an eye on him and help him out whenever he had insulin or sugar- level problems, and to stand up for him whenever he had a problem with a doctor or hospital. She also helped him around his home with things he had difficulty doing. And all of this was no problem for her. Over the years, Justine maintained a remarkably healthy balance between her emotional and practical support for her brother and pursuing her own goals.

Up until her brother's death, Justine never felt there was a problem with her life. Now she suddenly realized that it was hard to find something else she could so readily excel at. She had no children (in large part, because of the need to watch out for her brother) and she had recently retired. She never developed a specialty in an age when everyone wants a specialist. The transition to a new phase was therefore very difficult for her, especially since there seemed to be nothing in her life that now required a "jack of all trades." In time, she turned to charitable work with homeless people who had a multitude of needs, where she could excel. People in the middle of the anxiety scale often do better than LAPs and HAPs on tasks that require a variety of skills and interests.

TREATMENT FOR GENERALIZED ANXIETY: TOO LOW OR TOO HIGH

When people come to me with problems from either end of the anxiety scale, I use a combination of cognitive and behavioral therapy to help them, including desensitization. You can do the same in the privacy of your own home.

Let's start with measures to prevent or ease the difficulties the low-anxious may find themselves in.

WORKING WITH THE INDEPENDENT

People with the independent trait are a fairly large group—thirty percent or more of the population. They often don't realize that they have this trait (to a lesser extent this is true of agreeable people, too). Extroverts, conscientious people, risk takers, and others with other traits know that they have these tendencies. But independents tend to take their characteristics personally, as if by their own selves they decided to be that way, strong and self-contained. They don't realize this comes from a trait they were born with. This is like thinking that because you are intelligent you somehow earned it or achieved it by virtue of your own efforts. The reality is that intelligence, like most traits, is a gift of the gene pool.

> Many people don't realize they have a trait, and attribute their behavior to their own personal greatness. The best example of this is the independent type of person. They pulled themselves up by their bootstraps, forged their own career, and feel that being self-absorbed is the way to go. They feel that being strong is the highest state of human development, and think the whole world should be like them. They are chauvinistic when it comes to their characteristics, and contemptuous of others. Their mentality is THE mentality.

Since they don't see that how they are is the result of a trait, independents are contemptuous of people who are not as strong and self-confident. They see them as weak, and don't have much respect for them.

When they have the independence trait, people like to get through therapy as quickly as possible. They feel uncomfortable in a situation in which they are dependent, insecure, and lacking in confidence. They tend to be abstract when describing problems because they don't want to put themselves in the position of asking for help. On the other hand, because their general anxiety is low they can proceed rather quickly with treatment measures because they're not likely to have problems with the desensitization techniques.

Receptivity is especially important in the treatment of people with the independence trait. If they are not receptive to treatment, they do not do well, and lack of compliance becomes an ongoing problem. This is often seen when people who are referred to treatment after perhaps being charged with a DUI. One way to deal with this problem is to start by discussing the need for treatment and to try to arrange for their cooperation. It may be also helpful to point out that their cooperation is especially important given the nature of their trait. Very little has been written about this trait and most of the people I've treated, as noted above, are not at all aware of the fact that they have it.

Independents do like to talk about themselves, so that aspect of therapy comes very easy for them. They don't have many friends, so it's not easy for them to find people to talk to or to listen to them. They're not very good listeners themselves, so others are not as inclined to be as good a listener for them as they would like. Therapy can be very helpful for them, as it provides a unique opportunity to get an objective point of view, and a good listener, someone who really cares.

> Low-anxiety people are so focused on themselves that when they come in for therapy, as the joke goes, they often in essence say, "I've talked enough about myself—now what would you like to say about me?"

Independent-minded people want to be in control and are very reluctant to yield control to other people. The issue of who is in control is often an important factor in reducing their resistance to treatment. The more in control they feel, the more open to change and receptive they are. So I tend to give them a lot of control in the treatment process.

The independent do best when they see a new idea as coming from themselves rather than from other people. They are inclined to absorb opinions that they feel are good and justified and to ultimately internalize them as if those opinions were initiated by themselves. I try to take advantage of this in therapy by letting the independent-minded take credit for as much as possible: "It's encouraging to see how much of this you've together on your own, and come up with some excellent ideas for changing your life for the better."

I also always need to start from the top (with comments and statements they are sure to agree with) in my discussions with them, and work my way down from that to the sensitive issues. For example, when discussing the aftermath of a DUI:

"I realize you feel that you were wrongly convicted, but the immediate concern is how you can put aside your anger to focus on getting your license back."

WHEN BEING RIGHT IS NOT ENOUGH

Another key area of self-help for people suffering from the side effects of low anxiety is coming to terms with the LAP's obsession with always being right. When people like this come in to me for treatment, they spend a lot of time describing scenarios from their lives to me, and then asking, "Who was right?" I wouldn't have to be a psychologist to realize that what they are really asking for is affirmation of their certainty that *they* were right. Were you to suggest that this was not the case, you would get an aggressive, hostile response.

So instead I try to steer them away from the issue of who is right to the more important one of "What is the most effective way to handle this situation?" What if you are a tree lover and your neighbor insists that the state fencing law says he is entitled to cut down trees up to five feet over onto your property when he is redoing the fence. You look it up and in fact the law says four feet. Is it more important to make it clear to him, in a huff, that you are right, or to be nice enough to him that he decides there may be a way to redo the fence that manages to skirt around and preserve most of the trees on that fence line?

Or consider the LAP client of mine who was driving to the bank when he encountered a police car blocking the way. The police officer

183

was in his car talking on the phone and showed no sign of noticing him. My client was in a hurry, and annoyed at the officer's disregard for others, decided to pass him in the left-hand lane. After doing so, he noticed there was an empty parking space in front of the patrol car, close to the bank. He backed up into the spot, and then headed across the street to the bank. As he passed in front of the police car, the officer signaled him to come to his window, but he ignored him. The policeman then beeped his horn, but he kept on walking. When he exited the bank, the officer was standing outside and proceeded to give him five tickets for various violations—including driving on the wrong side of the street, eluding a police officer, and having a dirty license plate. He was furious and told the officer that he would report him to his chief, which he did the next day. When he recounted the story to me, he asked if I agreed he was right. Yes, he was, I said, but was this really the most effective way to handle the situation?

Finding the most effective, productive way to resolve a right/wrong question or situation is usually the truly right way to go. In the case of the story above, after my client adopted a less militant attitude, the police chief dismissed all of the tickets, and he and the officer apologized to each other.

OVERCOMING RESISTANCE TO ADVICE

People with low anxiety often have another problem when it comes to treatment. When a person is shy, she can usually see the difference between her shyness and herself. She might want to be less shy, to be able to make public presentations, for instance. But she sees the issue as something separate from herself.

For LAPs that distinction is blurred. They are bound up in their own identity and take pride in their traits. This makes them hard to treat, because they are stubbornly resistant to advice and suggestions. So you have to find ways to help them circumvent their own independence.

This is how I treated a low-anxiety management consultant who was totally absorbed with productivity. Aside from all of the clients he advised and did trouble-shooting for, he also wrote books and a blog. Thus he had little time for his family, or even for his own needs—not even to relax, or eat. His brain was intensely focused on the idea of accomplishment, and viewed just about anything else as unproductive. He realized he was endangering his health and family relationships, but found it very hard to change this.

So I told him that if he could relabel some of these nonworking activities, his brain might see them differently, and go along with them, rather than think of them as wasting time. If he was planning to get together with a friend, he would now think of that as not just a pleasant lunch, but a way to get feedback on one of his ideas from a professional colleague. If he was going to a show with his wife, this was an important refreshing of his outlook and recharging of his batteries. This did work for him.

For this same reason, when treating young people with addictions, getting them out of the problem neighborhood and into an interesting activity such as sports is easier than just telling them to ditch their drugs. You have to move things in the direction of something the brain wants.

MISTAKEN IDEAS ABOUT DAMAGE CONTROL

Since they don't have strong empathy, the independent often end up in arguments and problems with other people.

A mistake they often make then is to think that they can use damage control to take care of this. No sooner do they alienate someone than they assume they can turn it around by being super nice the next time they get together. They pride themselves on damage control, and are not aware of how difficult it is to actually do this. Most people don't spring back that quickly or easily.

UPPING INTERPERSONAL AWARENESS

If one has spent a lifetime largely oblivious to the fact that others have those volatile, unpredictable, but deeply rooted things called feelings, becoming more aware of this is easy to say, and harder to do. And if it isn't done right, it will only worsen the problem, since nothing is more off-putting than fake sensitivity.

But it's well worth the effort to try, since in life the personal game is often the most important one. And the majority of what we do today has to be done, at some point, through the medium of other human beings. Learning to be more in tune with the feelings of others is one big way to prevent future hassles and anxiety.

The independent need to be aware that they can accomplish this by staying alert for things like those little signals from our brain that might prompt us to laugh, say, at something another person might feel is not funny at all. LAPs are inclined to feel that poor people are lazy, sick people are malingerers, and losers are their own worst enemy. They are often shocked and humbled when the tables are turned. I advise LAPs to ask themselves how they would feel if their own child was struck by the misfortunes they see in others. Since LAPs closely identify with their family members, they can use this as a good guide for responding to others.

A technique I often use with people who tend to disregard the feelings of others is to have them imagine themselves in the position of the person whose feelings they are ignoring.

For example, if they have a very demanding boss, one who is very hard to deal with, I have them try to imagine themselves being on the receiving end of what the boss must face every day. What would they say and feel in different situations? Or I have them ask themselves why the person who hit them with her car never swerved or braked. What kinds of questions would they ask her?

Independents often have a hard time doing this exercise. And they should *not* do it when they are angry, such as when someone just stole the parking space they had their eye on.

The comedy show "Curb Your Enthusiasm" is a program I sometimes recommend to LAPs. The main character, Larry, is an LAP who continually runs into trouble because of his insensitivity.

It also helps, I often explain, when ranting to ourselves about "How could so and so have ever done such and such," to stop for a minute and think: well, why *might* he or she have done it? Try to imagine or outline the actual reasons, from their point of view.

If necessary to help up their awareness, I suggest that the low-anxious watch how people everyone loves act around others. Watch how they pick up on interpersonal cues, and make the other person always feel valued and respected.

I talked these kinds of techniques through with Martha, the engineer who had trouble supervising her underlings in a way that was not negative and demoralizing. She told me that it made her angry when things weren't done right: it made her job much harder, and put extra burdens on her, as well as posing significant safety risks for the public. Even so, I pointed out, saying things like "I hate stupid people" out loud was sure to embarrass the other person, or raise hackles. "But they're idiots," she said, "so they shouldn't take it personally. What's wrong with being direct?"

There were better ways to go about it, I insisted. When someone was asking her what she thought of the job they just finished, even if she didn't really like what they did, there were ways to say it that would leave the person with their pride intact and a desire to please. She also needed to be aware that sometimes other-person-oriented people (about half of the population) weren't necessarily agreeing with her, but just avoiding conflict, or distancing themselves from her.

I often point out to independent people that others will eventually mirror them. If they treat people a certain way, they eventually will do the same. They will adopt defensive strategies to get back at them. They will not continue to let themselves be victimized without responding in some way. They will retaliate in one form or another. If someone is cheap, for instance, leaving a scanty tip and forcing others to make up the difference, they may no longer want to go out with that person anywhere.

Independent people have a tendency to feel superior to others, and this, which is a definite turnoff, comes across. It is one of the reasons they have trouble keeping friends. I often discuss with independent people why they keep changing friends. Their friends usually last two or three years, then something negative happens and the relationship is over.

RAISING ANXIETY TO IMPROVE EMPATHY

If someone says to me that they are living with an independent person and want to improve their relationship, one of the things I suggest is that they take a stronger stance. If they raise the person's anxiety somewhat, as that person's anxiety goes up his empathy also goes up. Raising the independent person's anxiety a little, putting him on notice that you are not going to tolerate certain things, will make him more sensitive to the feelings of others, and other people's points of view.

This doesn't mean raising the person's anxiety greatly, with malicious intent, but doing things that are reasonable, such as being a little more assertive.

WHEN THE INDEPENDENT FEEL ANXIOUS

Between his obliviousness to others and his failure to look ahead, the LAP is often blindsided. His anxiety level has been running along at a nice constant low of 3 or 4, and now suddenly he's hit a crisis and his level ramps up to 8 or 9. He's really worried, and his anxiety is off the charts. Lone eagle that he is, he hasn't done much networking, and has few close friends to talk all of this over with in detail. So he often comes charging in for therapy. He is so upset that, ironically, he thinks his real problem is high anxiety.

Since their general level of anxiety is low, when independent people do become anxious they are inclined to try to bear it as much as possible. They often see other people as not willing to force themselves to deal with their anxieties, too inclined to give in to or be controlled by them.

People with the independence trait have a lot of difficulty if and when they ever do finally have to admit to anxiety because it is not consistent with their view of themselves. They see themselves as self-controlled, independent, strong-willed, dominant and so on, and so being anxious makes no sense to them. (Even though they are probably anxious now as the result of some backfire of their habitual lack of planning and anticipation.)

Getting over their anxiety is very important so they can continue to be independent, self-reliant, and confident. Therefore they respond very well to therapy in terms of doing what they have to do to get rid of their anxiety issues as quickly as possible. Since their anxiety level is fairly low compared to others, even when they are anxious, I can be much more aggressive in my treatment measures.

FINDING THE HOT BUTTON

When low-anxiety people come in for treatment, they're usually very uptight about something. They're sure they know what it is, but I want to be sure we have identified the issue that is stressing them the most, so that we can go to work to desensitize it.

One memorable example of this was Richard, who came to me with irritable bowel syndrome, also called irritable bowel disease. This is a fairly common ailment that even gastroenterologists are hard put to figure out how to deal with. When a person has IBD (which may have some genetic element), their small and large intestines are easily inflamed, and the result is periods of constipation alternating with diarrhea, especially the latter. The sufferer is told to eat more roughage and drink a lot of water, but they are often afraid to leave home, since they are never sure when they may have an attack. Since much of the cause is supposed to be stress, they feel that all of this is somehow their fault, that they are somehow being held responsible for it.

Richard was thirty-two, and had just gotten engaged to the love of his life when the IBD suddenly appeared. He didn't see how it could be caused by stress, since right now he felt better than he ever had. He did have some hardship in his life, but it was pretty far in the past. His younger sister, when she was still a toddler, was diagnosed with a progressive neurological disorder that was going to shorten her life drastically. He was very close to her and fond of her, and since their parents fought a lot, the two youngsters often had to huddle together for comfort. Everyone in the household, including him, had to keep a close watch on the little girl, and as time went on, and she moved in and out of doctors' offices and hospitals, and finally into a wheelchair, she needed more and more attention, including the assistance of hired nurses.

He loved his sister, and was happy to assist her in whatever way he could, even if it meant things like leaving his own class at school when necessary to help her go to the bathroom. His sister died when he was fifteen. "I had so much stress back then," he said, "that if this IBD was caused by stress it surely would have happened then."

We then started to investigate all of the possible stressors, starting with all the different things he'd had to do to help his sister, and then her death. He never had fully grieved over it, caught up as he was at the time in his parent's marital difficulties. None of these things registered much of an emotional response—maybe he had desensitized himself to them over time.

When I finally brought up the subject of his parents, however, I hit pay dirt. Especially when he revealed the fact that in the later years of his sister's life, he'd come to feel that his parents were so caught up in her care that they had just about completely forgotten about him. More distressing yet was the fact that after his sister died, her mother suddenly showered him with attention—a natural reaction to the loss of her other child. She was still doing so today, and this turned out to be the real hot button. Richard was a very independent young man, and his mother's intense interest in him now was actually more of a psychic burden and intrusion than his parents' earlier "abandonment" of him. Now we could concentrate on defusing all of this.

WHEN THE INDEPENDENT ARE DEPRESSED

When talking about depression or depressive issues, the independent don't like to appear weak, so they have to express these things in strong terms. If they lost their job, they don't say that they may not be able to find another one, but "I can't wait to get back to work—I'm going to show them."

Rooting for them and congratulating them on not being weak is very important. They like to suppress any negative thoughts they have and appear strong and powerful—they don't like to go around moping and whining.

> If an independent person is depressed, it is often because his goal has been thwarted, or he doesn't have a goal—almost unimaginable for an independent person.

Since they have low empathy, they often see themselves as victims. This produces a lot of anger, which makes their depression worse. They are easily angered, and not threatened by their own anger or anyone else's. So rather than trying to separate their anger and depressive feelings, they combine them. This makes a toxic brew that perpetuates the depression and makes it resistant to remediation.

Because of their anger they don't have many friends, which leads to loneliness, and loneliness leads to more depression. Their social withdrawal makes it hard to get them back into the social scene.

A lot of independents don't like desensitization strategies, because they see them as too passive. They prefer active strategies such as getting back at people, or getting even. They usually see their depression as the result of other people mistreating them or treating them unfairly, so they have a lot of get-back fantasies.

I saw a man in his mid-seventies who had been angry and depressed all his life. His depression was probably genetically based, but it was exacerbated by the fact that he had no friends. He only talked to his wife, and she was tired of listening to him, so she didn't always respond as he would like. Talking to me, he was able to go over and deal with his issues, and get realistic and objective feedback on them.

And there was no collateral damage. If he got in a bad mood and got nasty, it was not a problem. I didn't take it personally. Left to himself, he might say things that would alienate family or friends, and they might stop talking to him. In therapy he was able to discuss and vent all of this with no worries about consequences. He liked talking about himself; it was one of his favorite topics. Therapy offered him this as well.

Independents tend to be easily motivated by something that promises to improve their situation. If aroused in this way, they can be motivated to be more resilient, because they have a lot of pride. They like to see themselves as strong, fighting back, getting back, so this is an easy way to motivate them.

PANIC ATTACKS AND THE INDEPENDENT

The independent are subject to panic attacks because panic attacks are not usually the result of a specific problem or situation. Panic attacks very often are just a function of general stress; there may also be a genetic component. People with the independence trait can have panic attacks because they won't be protected by their general low level of anxiety. Typically, they have to be reassured that these are not coming from a lack of personal strength or attributable to a weakness of any sort on their part, before treating them as described in Chapter Eight.

ONE LAST NOTE ON THE TREATMENT OF LAPS

The people who show the very lowest level of anxiety are hopefully people we meet only in the pages of crime novels or the scenes of thriller movies—the psychopaths, whose concern for other people is so nonexistent that they enjoy scamming them, laughing at them, or worse. Psychopaths will cheat, lie, distort, whatever it takes to get what they want, regardless of the means or justification. In fact, if they cheat on their taxes or take advantage of their family or friends, they are inclined to brag about it, certainly to themselves, and perhaps to others as well. These people really do need professional treatment, and they often get it, but they are all too likely to turn therapy into a game in which they are essentially manipulating and abusing the therapist.

> Psychopaths have close to zero anxiety, and enjoy talking about themselves. If they see a therapist, they will pick his brain to further their psychopathic goals. Because of this, therapists in many states are not allowed to treat psychopaths now.

PROBLEMS OF THE AGREEABLE

People with the agreeable trait often don't show especially high levels of anxiety toward non-interpersonal threats, such as earthquakes, storms, and the like. But they are very sensitive to disruptions in their interpersonal relationships. They are especially fearful of dealing with people who are angry. Whenever they are confronted with someone who is angry at them, they go to great lengths to diffuse the situation, often by being overly accommodating. They are also very sensitive to rejection, even by those they don't like.

People who are born with this predisposition worry about everything, but especially the other people in their lives. While they have a tendency to have a higher level of generalized anxiety than the average person, much of this is directly related to interpersonal situations. Outside of interpersonal relationships their general anxiety may be within the normal range.

People with the agreeable trait don't like focusing on themselves and this becomes a problem when they are in therapy or if they decide to treat themselves. They often feel uncomfortable in the therapeutic situation. Since they focus on other people, during a session they have a tendency to bring up other people's problems and issues. When they go to a therapist, they're inclined to talk about everyone and anything but themselves—as a joke in the psychological community puts it, when an other-person-oriented person is dying, the lives of everyone else he knows pass before his eyes.

They don't like to disappoint a therapist, so they also describe their own fears and concerns in a way that makes them appear more positive and creates the impression that they are doing better than perhaps is the case.

Sometimes they have a defeatist attitude because they have so much trouble overriding the agreeable trait when it seems desirable to do so. This is especially frustrating when they are approached by someone they don't really want to be involved with—someone lacking moral character, greedy, or otherwise unpleasant, who attempts to establish a relationship with them. Putting such a person off—or breaking off with them if they are already involved—is very hard for them. In this situation we have to work hard on developing the skill of self-assertion.

The high-anxious don't respond well to criticism but they don't mention that at first—typically this issue comes up later on. This has to do with their tendency not to want to focus on themselves. Agreeable people are averse to conflict, and criticism always brings conflict.

Those with the agreeable trait are usually cooperative and compliant with all that is asked of them in therapy. As a result they tend to do well from the standpoint of following the instructions they have been given.

If they have panic attacks their high level of generalized anxiety will make it all the more difficult for them to overcome the condition. Many people who have the agreeable trait as well as panic attacks often find that it takes a long time for them to overcome the attacks. Much of the problem has to do with the fact that their general level of anxiety interacts with the panic attacks and makes the panic attacks as well as their general anxiety worse.

GETTING IN TOO DEEP

People with the agreeable trait can be either extroverts or introverts. If they happen to be introverted they will develop deep relationships with a few people and limit their interpersonal relationships to that group.

If they happen to be extroverted, they interact with many people and have a lot of friends because they tend to treat people very well—they get along with and accommodate others.

The two traits of extroversion and agreeableness will interact and enhance one another. This can have undesirable results at times. If an agreeable person interacts with a lot of people, they may encourage too many people to be their friend. Since agreeable people tend to have high levels of anxiety, they also tend to be very responsible and con- scientious in their dealings with other people. As a result the person takes on too much and soon finds that he's overwhelmed by all of the responsibilities and commitments he's made.

Moreover, the person finds that reducing the number of these obligations is extremely difficult and often he relies on circumstances to extract him from the situation. This is one of the times when people with the agreeable trait are very inclined to use magical thinking. They somehow assume that the people who are making demands upon them will suddenly stop.

TREATING THE AGREEABLE FOR DEPRESSION

When the agreeable become depressed they often suffer in silence, since they hate to be a burden on others. And even when they feel depressed they still tend to focus on others.

People with the agreeable trait, as noted earlier, have a high general level of anxiety. Their resilience is undermined by this. They tend to be intimidated by depression, are not good at going against it when they are down. They don't fight depression—if anything, they go along with it. They use it as another way of denigrating themselves—"I'm not good at this, or that." They see depression as a vindication of their own negativity toward themselves. "Yes, I won that award, and everyone clapped, but deep down I knew that I didn't deserve it." If they get depressed they allow it to combine with their own negativity toward themselves to deepen their depression.

In therapy, they often cancel sessions, which they may claim is for medical problems. They don't like to admit that their cancellations are because they are getting anxious or down.

They need a good listener, someone to counter their negativity. This is difficult to do, and if their depression deepens they need to be in therapy, because only a therapist is trained to work in this way.

What they respond best to over time is continuous positive reinforcement that is not unrealistic or Pollyannaish. There are areas about them that can be pointed out, real things like the fact that everyone likes them, that they are genuine and sincere, of good character, and always out to help others. These are all things that you can use to reinforce them.

One of the best things you can do is encourage them to be their own best friend, begin to establish a better relationship with themselves, or with yourself if the problem agreeable person is you.

Many agreeable people do not treat themselves very well, without even realizing it. If a friend asks if I would like to go out to dinner with him and his wife on Saturday at seven, and I say yes, running it past my wife just secondarily, she may go along with this three or four times. But eventually she will get annoyed and point out that I should stop making all of these arrangements without including her in the decision, to see if she is in a position to, or would like to do whatever has been proposed. I better start including her or she may not participate.

Agreeable people do the same thing to themselves. Someone says, "Can I borrow your car?" and they say yes without stopping to think of whether they need it themselves. Someone else asks, "Can you drive me to the airport?" they say yes without thinking of the gas, tolls, or even the time it will take to do this. They are always putting themselves second.

The brain senses this and at some point they are well aware that they are shortchanging themselves. They have a certain amount of anger at themselves for letting others use them.

BECOMING MORE ASSERTIVE

Agreeable people often have difficulty being assertive. Assertiveness takes a certain degree of confidence and strength, and people who are very anxious are not inclined to have high levels of these characteristics. Therefore, when they find themselves overwhelmed by responsibilities and duties to others, they have to take a step back and think about developing assertiveness skills.

Saying no is a big problem for people with the agreeable trait. On the other hand, they often have many friends and a very well-developed support system. Often the best remedy for them when it comes to situations involving assertiveness is to utilize their support system to help them at these times. Discussing how they might go about becoming more assertive and practicing it with other people is often a good first step to becoming more assertive.

Often, they need to also learn how to desensitize the anxieties they have about situations where assertiveness is called for. They can desensitize these in much the same way that they would desensitize any other fear or anxiety.

Helping these people to learn to assert themselves involves overcoming their anxieties as well as making allowances for their predispositions. Assertiveness training, role-playing, and learning to deal with people who are angry are all effective means of liberating them from their attachments to others. Most of them are very receptive to treatment, since as noted earlier they often find themselves overburdened by their need to help others.

A highly agreeable person may not only be reluctant to speak up, she may not know what to say when she does. The answer to both of these things is to imagine herself advising her child to be more assertive—whatever she tells him will usually be better advice than she gives herself, so she should follow it.

For example, if her son has been stuck in his job for ten years without a raise, and is so frustrated he has thought of quitting, what would she advise him to do?

Or a young teen can't understand her teacher, who mumbles, so the teen can't hear what she is saying, even though she usually sits in a seat near the front. Should she leave an anonymous note "from a concerned student," or talk to the principal? Or practice going up to that teacher and actually telling her what the problem is?

IF YOU SELF-TREAT

For the person with high but not cripplingly high anxiety, here is the way to make life easier. First, since any highly anxious person has an entire hornet's nest worth of anxieties buzzing around in his brain, we want to reduce the number. While it is possible to identify the most troublesome issue or issues, for starters you want to pick one or two of the simpler ones. Once these have been desensitized, you will have more confidence in approaching the bigger and thornier issues.

For each subject you are trying to desensitize, you will be lowering the emotional impact of that issue by repeated exposure to it, and by imagining, and working through in your mind, ways in which you might deal with every possible ramification of that particular threat. Are you afraid of losing your job? High-anxious people are usually good at preparing for a rainy day by building in alternative possibilities for handling a crisis if needed. If you haven't done this, say by having multiple sources of income (i.e., diversifying your skills), you should consider developing some options now. This will make your life more worry-free even in good times. Also, your probably excellent network of friends and associates could be of help. Think of preparation and planning as being a big part of dealing with your anxieties. Since your anxiety is already elevated, don't rush into desensitizing dreadful possibilities right away—catastrophizing. Work on building up your confidence, break big problems down into small pieces, and work on resolving the small pieces first. Use the desensitization techniques during any crises to allay your fears of interviewing, calling people, asking for help, or saying "no" to false promises, building your confidence by tackling one small piece at a time.

DO IT BY DEGREES

To return to a diving board example, let's assume that an anxious person was on a ten-foot-high diving board—their anxiety level would be very high (8 or 9 out of 10) and they wouldn't be able to jump. However, if I had the person practice on a one-foot board, moving up gradually through a three-foot and then five-foot one, until they got to a ten–foot board, they most likely would be successful. Or, a doctor could prescribe medication to quiet their anxieties, and they could then go through the progressive steps. Once they could overcome their fears of jumping, they could ask the doctor to gradually lower their medication. This is a process professionals use and you should let a professional handle a case like this.

I could also desensitize their fears in imagery until they could do it in reality. Any gradual approach would work, so long as it reduced the level of their anxiety to the point where confronting their fears was not so stressful that it prevented them from doing so.

The point is this—the best way to desensitize anxiety is progressively and gradually, starting with the least threatening aspect of the situation. In the case of the ten-foot diving board, this would be a reduced height—the one-foot board. In the case of someone anticipating a poor employee review, I would start by first having them imagine getting a good one, then a good one with a minor criticism, and so on. Eventually, we would move up to imagining a very negative review and what might result from that.

PRACTICAL MEASURES THAT CAN HELP

There are also some very mundane and practical things that can help make life easier for a person with elevated anxiety, such as living at a lower stress level, not pushing the edge, living below your means, and getting a house with a low mortgage. You can also try to avoid aggressive and disagreeable people, and start systematically taking steps to actually do something about some of the things on your worry list, the things that are really bugging you, starting with the simpler things that can be knocked off easily once you get over your inclination to avoid them, and moving to the more complex.

IF YOUR FEARS AND WORRIES ARE UNREALISTIC

In the course of therapy, a professional would normally help you to see this by assessing, with you, what the actual likelihood of a given hovering black thought actually coming to roost in your life might be. You can duplicate this yourself by, for example, doing a little research on the computer or elsewhere to determine the realistic chances of an avalanche burying you, being eaten by a Bengal tiger, being engulfed by a tsunami, or whatever your particular fear(s) might be. You would also, of course, want to factor in anything that makes the threat in question more or less likely to materialize: your age, location, family background, hobbies, profession, whatever. For example, only 15% of prostate biopsies turn out badly. You have a better chance of being in the right 85% if you have no family history of prostate cancer and eat a healthy diet that includes lots of fruits and vegetables. And if you have regular checkups, even if the news is bad, you have a much better chance of surviving the condition because it will be caught in the early stages. Etc.

Are you worried about being attacked by one of those coyotes that are now found in every state, town, and city? Though people have been attacked, your own chances of being munched on by one are less than your chances of being struck by lightning or attacked by a human predator, and infinitesimally less than being bitten by one of the pet dogs that bite more than 5 million people in this country every year.

AN IMPORTANT ASSIGNMENT FOR THE HIGH-ANXIOUS: MAKING YOUR *SELF* A PRIORITY

As noted earlier, HAPs are so exquisitely attuned to the feelings of other people, the currents, ripples, sandbars, shoals, and upcoming rocks and boulders in the stream of human interaction around them, that their own feelings are often ignored, or unexamined. Yet if they continue to disregard them, year in and year out, they are very likely to find themselves ending up in positions they regret, or have no real interest in. The only way to remedy this is to start making an effort, unnatural as it may feel at first, to start paying attention to, and striking out for, the things you want, even as you continue to try and be as pleasant and nonabrasive as possible to all of those others you deal with every day in one way or another.

Think of how you feel when someone blatantly disregards you. Perhaps they overlook your comments in a discussion; invite your spouse to something and just assume that you will tag along; or they discuss a problem they have and show no interest in any of your suggestions. This is essentially what you're doing to yourself. Imagine interacting with others without having a voice. If you're a woman, imagine living in a country where women have no voice. As a man, imagine being a private in the Marines where you're constantly ordered about.

Another way to do this, to jolt yourself out of your usual self-subjugating frame of mind, is to imagine a given situation as if it were happening to someone else you care about, especially, as noted earlier, a child. How would you feel about it, or what would you do then? Patricia, one of my clients, said to me once, "Though I made a lot of mistakes in my own life, when it came to my son, the love of my life, my only child, and activities and objectives that involved him, I always managed to rise above my own bad habits and see, and do, the very best things for him." This is a standard we should aspire to live up to for ourselves as well.

To make HAPs more aware of themselves, I often phrase questions in terms of their children. "What would they do if their child told them that their boss never acknowledged their hard work or long hours?" What would they recommend that their child do? What if their child's boss made critical comments, like "You don't seem to try very hard when something doesn't work out." The advice they would give to their child is often the advice they should tell themselves—e.g., speaking up about such things in a polite, yet firm way, offering an appropriate correction.

Joseph, the HAP firefighter we became acquainted with earlier in this chapter, eventually became all too aware of how much he had torqued his life to others who were not necessarily the most important people in his world. He started a conscious effort to be more assertive— he knew he could be, because he was no wimp during his workdays. Now he was going to manage to do the same at his unit's headquarters, and anywhere the firefighters got together and were all too likely to ask good ol' Joe for a few more little favors. He started focusing more on his family as well, repairing his relationship with his wife and becoming closer to his daughter, for whom he started a college fund. He also started training himself for a job after his retirement that would not only bring in more money, to help his family realize some of their other dreams, but would give him more personal satisfaction in every way.

It can also help to choose partners and associates that are less likely to take advantage of you. Gisele, the woman described earlier in this chapter, was an experienced doormat long married to a very domineering spouse. After she got her divorce, she eventually started dating again. HAPs don't like to be alone; they usually have a strong need to be with someone. She went out with a number of different men, most of whom seemed to have a lot of demands and didn't put much into the relationship. (HAPs also tend to seek out strong personalities who may exploit them.) As she voiced her dissatisfaction with all of this to me, I finally suggested that she look for, not an alpha type, but someone more like herself. She finally did meet such a man, and is much happier, as they nearly trip over one another in their mutual efforts to be nice.

The issue of intelligent mate selection comes up a lot in therapy. Many HAPs go onto websites like match.com, then ask me to help screen prospective mates. So many do, in fact, that I've become somewhat of an expert on this. The profiles on those sites all look a lot alike—the guys (and women) on there all describe themselves as pretty wonderful. But I pointed out to one woman, for example, that the fellow she had in mind used eight "I's "in one paragraph, describing what he liked, and so on—a red flag for self-absorption.

HAPs are very into the whole idea of screening. It does help to screen, but this is not infallible. Some bad apples will slip through. So do two things: screen to reduce jokers, and the many clever fakers, and also focus on learning how to say "no" and exit a relationship quickly when you see things are going south.

An important part of the screening process is understanding the differences between HAPs and LAPs, as described earlier in this chapter.

ANXIETY LEVEL AND MASTERY

Agreeable people are usually not so concerned about mastery. They tend to just want low-level improvement. They worry all the time, so their anxieties don't spike often. They are somewhat desensitized across the board, because they think about worrisome things so much.

Independent people are more concerned with their limitations, so they are more inclined to go for mastery. The independent for the most part have a low level of anxiety, so when they do get anxious they tend to spike. Something comes up and bingo, they have anxiety at a high level. If you ask them what would they do if a particular emergency happened, they are dumbstruck. They tend to say that they never thought about that. The worriers have usually given such things much thought.

Low anxious types—who are normally brazen, impulsive, and goal-oriented—can suddenly have a higher level of anxiety after a near-death experience. They may feel very differently about many aspects of their lives. They may no longer in push themselves so much to get things done, have a more relaxed attitude about things. A low-anxiety person, if their anxiety is now higher, may be more cooperative, less type A, more depressive. Now he is not going to risk himself as much—he may see someone on the side of the road with a flat tire and not stop to help now, in general say "NO" more.

I saw a woman who was a very outgoing and bubbly agreeable type. She got breast cancer and now had to have tests far more often. She was also much more anxious. She was very cavalier and upbeat before, and now much more cautious. She went from low to high anxiety.

Different personalities have different needs. If you are agreeable you may want to master confrontation, or what to do when someone argues with you. An independent person is not usually much concerned with others. He may want to work on his empathy level, and his ability to read others.

People can live a long time with anxiety at a mildly elevated level, such as 6, and then a horrific experience like a heart attack makes it go even higher. A head injury or severe shock such as a serious loss or threat can also cause this. The person was a worrier before, and now they are a hyper worrier. High anxiety types have to evaluate whether they can live with the yet higher level now, or try to change. They might decide they can't afford to be as high-anxious any more.

If I know what the person's general level of anxiety was before, I will acquaint them with the changes that seem to have taken place, and they can decide whether to live with them or try to alter them.

CHAPTER EIGHT

OTHER ANXIETY-BASED ISSUES AND PROBLEMS

Anxiety has many faces. It can be the constant gnawing of worry, or a sensation of intense dread, as in a panic attack. It can flex itself in the horrifying flashbacks of PTSD, or the terror and recoil of phobias. It can be so strong that we feel a need to find some way of lowering its intensity, as in the superstition-like behaviors of OCD. It can bring on feelings of insecurity and inadequacy, affecting how we feel about ourselves. It can even inspire hoarding impulses.

It is the root cause of many behaviors that are all tentacles of the same underlying problem.

WORRY

Most people, if asked, would put worry at the top of their list of mental weights. But worry itself is not the problem—worry is an essentially constructive process that helps us anticipate the future and prepare for it.

Worry focuses the mind's attention to issues that are threatening, and therefore central to our survival. Without the automatic tendency to think about what might go wrong, we would be ill prepared for the myriad misfortunes that have befallen people throughout history. Worry is a remarkably adaptive process, and the point is not to eliminate worry but to harness it and enhance its effectiveness. Most aspects of worry are advantageous. It motivates us to prepare for potential threats, it may foster a solution to our problems, and it organizes our thinking toward important issues. But worry can be troublesome as well—as when our thoughts form an endless loop that yields no discernable advantages. And worry can be time-consuming, unproductive, and frustrating, as well as undermining our confidence and self-esteem.

For the most part, the disadvantages of worry can be overcome by learning to do it correctly—how to maximize its benefits and minimize its unpleasantness. There are also techniques to increase its effectiveness, such as guided imagery and role-playing, discussed in other parts of this book. Attempts to avoid, minimize, or dispense with worry simply violate the mind's programming and ultimately endanger the individual.

> Worry is our intellectual response to anxiety. It encourages us to anticipate and plan, analyze our circumstances.

Briefly, there are several steps involved in constructive worry. The person allows his mind to focus on what it deems important. The emotional intensity of the issue the mind settles on may be so painful that it is best to restrict the focus to frequent, but short intervals. Once the material has been sufficiently desensitized in this manner, the person may choose to increase the duration of exposure to speed up the desensitization, or perhaps the attainment of some insight that may resolve the matter. If the process seems circular and unproductive, guided imagery is often effective in directing the worry to deeper issues. Mentally rehearsing different scenarios through role-playing is often very effective.

In this manner, a person comes to view worry as a natural process that can be modified to suit his needs either by speeding it up, intensifying it, postponing it, or compartmentalizing it to fit his schedule and priorities. With practice, it is relatively easy to develop a facility with regulating your worries that enables you to process worries quickly and effectively so as to minimize any unnecessary mental clutter.

As noted earlier, worry probably evolved as a means of motivating us to anticipate and prepare for future events—especially potential hazards and problems. So, we worry about what may go wrong at a wedding, even while eagerly awaiting it. We worry continually about all aspects of our lives, because we are naturally more averse to negative consequences than we are desirous of positive ones. For example, we justify the purchase of insurance as money well spent to ensure our future, while gambling as a means of acquiring pleasure from our winnings is commonly seen as irresponsible.

As outlined in Appendix I, the mind prioritizes our thoughts primarily according to their survival value, by associating varying levels of emotional intensity with them. Then, our attention is drawn to those thoughts with the highest priority or emotional intensity. In the process, the emotional intensity associated with these thoughts undergoes two changes.

First, it is temporarily diminished by simple fatigue with that line of thinking. In time, if attention is focused elsewhere, the fatigue will subside and the original intensity will be restored.

Second, it is desensitized because by merely focusing on a thought, it gradually loses its emotional intensity, as it is associated with no real consequences. The gradual chipping away at the emotional intensity of our thoughts in this manner eventually renders them unable to command our attention. Desensitization thus eventually brings about permanent reduction in the emotional intensity associated with those thoughts.

Unregulated thinking appears to proceed as follows: our attention is drawn to those thoughts with the greatest emotional intensity; their intensity is then diminished by a combination of fatigue and desensitization; which then causes our attention to shift to the next highest priority. In this manner, our attention shifts from those thoughts with the highest priorities to those with lower priorities. By the time we get to the lower priority thoughts, the thoughts that originally had the highest priority have begun to rebound, as the fatigue that depressed them wears off. The cycle repeats itself until each of these thoughts has been permanently desensitized, paving the way for new concerns to emerge with higher priorities.

When we allow our minds to wander, that is, to think about whatever naturally comes to us, we in essence invite our minds to worry, which as discussed is both adaptive and advantageous to us. Moreover, it is possible to control the way we worry to intensify its benefits. For example, to permanently reduce the emotional intensity of a particularly bothersome concern, and thereby reduce the likelihood of it popping up in your thoughts, simply focus on it repeatedly. The thought will quickly become fatigued and your attention will be drawn from it. But continuing to focus on it will enable you to further desensitize it. In this way, you will speed up the desensitization and rid your mind of the concern.

On the other hand, by refusing to think about a nettlesome concern, you inadvertently maintain its emotional intensity and thus its priority, causing it to pop up whenever you let your guard down.

By adjusting the duration and intensity of exposure to our concerns, we can effectively control how and what we worry about. Moreover, since the overall amount of exposure needed to desensitize a particular concern is roughly the same whether we focus on it in a few intense sessions or distribute it over a longer period, the benefits we derive, in the form of anticipation and planning, are likewise about the same.

There are countless ways to adjust our thinking to suit our needs without undermining our welfare by refusing to allow our mind to worry. Worry can be postponed until a more suitable time, but not indefinitely. It can be massed to achieve quick results or distributed to allow us to process it gradually with less anguish.

PUT IT IN A BOX!

A helpful technique for managing a fear or anxiety is to learn how to compartmentalize it. Otherwise, as most of us know all too well, it will contaminate your entire day. Compartmentalizing frees up the mind to do other—usually more useful and positive—things.

To do this you need to establish clear-cut periods when you will think about the subject or subjects in question, and periods when you absolutely will not.

First choose two, or at most, say, three times during the day when you are willing to concentrate on the worrisome subject. Then say to yourself: "This is important, but I am only going to think about it twice today—at 5:00, after I finish my work for the day (or at lunchtime or break time or whenever), and then at 8:00 p.m., when I take my walk."

When the appointed time comes, sit down in a comfortable spot for five or ten minutes, and think about it. Imagine the issue, and the different possibilities involved in, or surrounding it. Don't push yourself. Give your mind free rein, let the brain lead.

If the subject is a relationship concern, for example, you may be troubled by something the person said the last time you spoke to him. There was something bothersome about it. What was it? What do you think caused him to say that? What will you say to him when he calls next? Or do if he doesn't call again soon? Etc.

The next session or next day, go into it a little more. Get a little deeper each time, and see how you react to it. If does not cause too much of a stir, keep going. Eventually the subject will become less and less stressful, as you in effect desensitize yourself.

If the subject comes up at other times, or before or after your scheduled worry time, firmly remind yourself that you will worry about that at 5:00, or on your break, or whenever you have decided to do so. This *will* work, once you have established the pattern that you are going to address it later. You will be able to postpone the brooding, banish it for now, and put it off.

THE COGNITIVE COOLDOWN

There is also a cognitive approach to reducing worry, which involves trying to determine how likely the thing you are worrying about is to actually happen, how realistic your worries are.

This can take some serious thought, so it is good to have someone objective, such as a trusted friend or therapist, to help you get a realistic idea of how likely the worried-about thing is to happen.

Whether it's a spot somewhere on your skin that you fear might be cancerous, a job that you might gain or lose, or your worries about your lover leaving you, it can be important to have an outside opinion or opinions, to help come up with some reasonable expectations.

The nice thing about the cognitive approach is that it is something clear-cut you can do to deal with your worries.

The whole basis of this approach is finding information, especially if the worry involves whether you should make one decision or another. Most decisions are not difficult in and of themselves. What makes them difficult is not having enough information to inform the decision.

Once you find or solicit all the information you need, your worry will usually go down considerably. Often you will find that the likelihood of the thing you are worrying about actually happening is very low.

If the likelihood of what you fear happening is high, you can use this as a prod to make sure that you take all the steps necessary, do what you have to do to prevent the problem from actually happening, or to mitigate its effects.

THE NEGATIVE KIND OF WORRY

The second type of worry is pathological in nature. It is characterized by a tendency to cycle over the same thoughts repeatedly, without showing signs of fatigue or desensitization. Nonstop worries that never wear down with time as most worries do, but just seem to be an endless and demoralizing loop, are bad news.

This type of worry is commonly seen in people who have obsessive disorders. For example, a person may repeatedly worry about an intruder attacking them in their home while they are asleep. In this case, the person may also have a need to check that the doors and windows are locked before they retire—over and over and over again. When the obsessive thoughts are linked to compulsive behaviors the person suffers from an obsessive-compulsive disorder (see Chapter Nine).

The same methods suggested for regulating the normal process of worry can also be used, with minor adjustments, to relieve obsessive thinking. You may be able to derail mild or beginning obsessional thinking, stop it in its tracks. But full-blown obsessive thinking should be treated by a professional such as a psychologist or psychiatrist.

> You don't want to worry in a circle, which clinicians call "looping." For example, "I should ask the boss for a raise, but I could end up worse off if I did that. If he fired me, I have no backup. I don't make enough to have a backup. If I was fired, my wife would be unhappy and I could end up with a divorce. On the other hand, if I ask for a raise...." Worrying like this is all horizontal, has no depth.

> When you worry, you want to go vertical, not just horizontal. Bring up things separately, and then think about what to do to solve each one. This will give you some comfort before you go on to the next worry.

STRESS

Stress is a form of strain on a person—an emotional strain. Stress is the presence of anything that taxes your system and increases your mental load.

A certain amount of stress is desirable, as when giving a speech. It helps you focus and gives you the intensity to do your best. Exercise, sports, and striving for goals all create arousal. But too much arousal is unhealthy, physically and mentally.

An example would be if a person is very agreeable. This means they have a tendency to overcommit to things so as not to disappoint others. This could cause stress. If the person is independent, on the other hand, he may have a tendency to be selfish and to ignore other people's point of view.

Stress is treated by analyzing the person's personality as well as the situation they are in, and seeing what it is between the two that is causing the person to feel emotionally strained. I would examine the situation to determine where there was an imbalance between the person's traits and the nature of the demands put upon them.

If you are an extrovert and decide to be a party or event planner, for example, that is probably fine. For an introvert it might be a recipe for high anxiety.

Likewise, if you are an extrovert, and have to do highly detailed work such as accounting, for the most part by yourself, you will probably be unhappy.

Things like conscientiousness are important in some jobs, and they will be stressful for you if you do not have that gene.

Having a personality style consistent with the demands of your profession is extremely important. Just about every field has various fields or areas of concentration within it. Look for a match between your natural traits and the tasks at hand/job requirements.

If you are a doctor and don't have the conscientious gene, so you have a hard time keeping track of all of the things so important in the medical profession, you might transfer to some other aspect of medicine that does not call for as much detail. You could sell medical equipment, for example, a job where extroversion is more important than conscientiousness. Or become a researcher of medical issues, where creativity is the most important quality. Or you could teach, or write textbooks. These things may not call as much for conscientiousness as for other traits.

Finding the aspect of that field that suits you is a natural use of your traits.

There can be a mismatch of traits and situation on the home front, too, and this can cause stress. Someone may be an enthusiastic extrovert, for example, who would love to be with people all the time, but be stuck in a situation where they are home alone most of the time.

Unreasonable expectations ("I've gotta manage to do it" clutter)

Unreasonable expectations are a frequent cause of disappointment, resentments, and stress our minds and lives would be better off without. Whether these are things we expect of ourselves or things we believe others expect of us, we often carry these inside like an unwritten command or agenda. And then spend our lives trying to live up to them. We do this despite the fact that we may never have fully articulated these goals or objectives for ourselves, or decided we really want to go where they would lead us. Or they may be things we think we *do* want, but would be impossible for us to ever achieve.

"Agenda overload" is a very common if not universal problem today. Habitual patterns of overloading our agendas often reflect psychological needs to manipulate our attention to meet our emotional needs.

Those who have a high level of generalized anxiety often overbook themselves as a way of diverting their attention from their fears to mundane chores.

They always tend to take on too much—they try to do all that they can, and end up exhausted. They need to be aware of this, because the added load will just exacerbate their worry, and precipitate more of a depressive reaction if they happen to be depressed as well.

Those with high energy levels overbook to increase their rate of gratification; otherwise life seems too slow for them. Low-anxious people are very goal-oriented, and are constantly generating new goals. They can make too many goals and start too many projects, because they get addicted to the higher levels of gratification that come from meeting goals and seeing them come to fruition.

If you are suffering from unreasonable expectations, with the help of a good friend or therapist, write out and review every one of your goals, objectives, and to-do's. Then examine the list carefully and see where some pruning might be done to make your life more manageable and lower its stress level.

REDUCE THE DISSONANCE

Sometimes people act in one way and think in another, and this in essence is the formula for developing dissonance, a disturbing difference between your thoughts and actions. If there is a sizable difference between the two it will create mental pressure, and the pressure here will be to either change your behavior to be consistent with your thinking, or change your thinking to become consistent with your behavior.

A client of mine named Agnes, who was living with a man she didn't love and felt was very abusive, on the one hand knew that she

215

was living a lie. She was living with him, she was his wife, and she functioned as his wife, and yet at the same time she felt quite differently about him. When she realized that he was starting to become abusive with their children, this gave her the necessary push to finally make a change. At this point, she wanted to reduce the dissonance in her life. Since she didn't love her husband, she felt there was no sense in acting as if she did, and so she filed for divorce. The divorce resulted in greater confidence in herself and also the recognition that she had to deal with her own issues and pursue her own life.

People can live with a certain level of stress for a long time, but when other forms of stress and pressure accumulate, the dam breaks and the person must then stop juggling contradictory opinions, or all of the balls may drop. What laypeople call a nervous breakdown is often the result—the inability to hold on to stressors the person is no longer able to bear.

PRESSURE

A variation of stress is what we usually call "pressure."

Stress usually refers to something specific, some specific thing in the future causing you some difficulty. You may have an exam coming up and be stressed by the prospect of not doing well on it, or even a positive event such as a wedding or a speech you plan to or need to make. Stress can go on for a long time, but it is usually related to something that once dealt with, will no longer be an issue.

Pressure is more subtle, something sort of underlying. For example, if your boss thinks you are a goofball, incompetent, he may not say anything to you directly, but every day when you go in to work you feel it. You never feel comfortable. You know that if you make a mistake your boss will call you on it, and his negative opinion of you will affect the outcome—you probably won't be able to persuade him that your actions were well-intentioned, or that you did the right thing and it just didn't work out.

Pressure is hard to get at as well. You can't usually say to your boss, "Why do you have such a negative attitude toward me? What can we do to deal with it?"

Even if you do, the person may just sidestep it, and say, "Don't worry, I don't have any negative feelings toward you," and yet the pressure continues. In subtle ways it is clear that he does harbor a negative view of you.

For an example from marital therapy: A man came in to see me who did all of the work to support his household, and the family's lifestyle, working as hard as he could and often overtime. But his wife, who didn't work outside the home, did little or no domestic work either. She sat around the house not doing much (I wondered if she might be depressed), so he had to do most of the laundry, cooking, cleaning, and so on, as well.

He felt that he was lugging her through life, that she wasn't doing her share, and he was tired of it. He asked me if I would speak to her about this, with the idea of perhaps getting her up to speed. So I did.

First she immediately said that many of his allegations were true. She agreed that she did little around the house, often had trouble getting started on the day, and she did have a problem with depression. She wasn't able to work outside the home—she'd tried this on several occasions, and it just didn't work out. She had done some volunteer work, which she felt good about, but this was low pressure and unpaid, so it was questionable how much it contributed to their relationship.

But then she said, "One thing he does do, which I don't do to him, is put a lot of pressure on me. It comes across clearly that he thinks of me as always a day late and a dollar short, that I have nothing to offer, that I'm just a parasite on him. Everything is accomplished through his efforts. He walks around with a very self-righteous attitude. I can't stand it anymore and have reached the point that I want to leave."

I went back to the guy and told him that she agreed with what he said, and didn't think she had the wherewithal to do much more than she was doing. But because she felt that he was always pressuring her, she was thinking of getting a divorce.

He flipped. "She wants a divorce! I'm going through all of this and doing everything and she's the one who's unsatisfied? It's ridiculous!"

This is not uncommon. It's often the person on the receiving end of pressure who files for divorce. Pressure has a subtle way of getting to people. It's unrelenting—they can't live with it, they have to get away from it. They feel it 24/7, even when the person is not present. They feel it at home, when the person is at work, when he talks to his friends, and so on. Even if the person doesn't realize he is doing it, his snide comments and overall attitude come through.

The stress of doing housework and other jobs around the house and yard is not such a big deal. You can always put some of it off if necessary, get someone else to do it, or pay someone else to do it. Or even decide just not to do some of it. There are options and possibilities here and this will not render you as out of control as nonstop pressure of other kinds does.

Pressure is at the heart of many serious marital problems. For the most part I deal with this in therapy by trying to unearth the source and then seeing if I can help the person eliminate it. When this is possible, the situation is improved and the person is often able to function at a higher level. Whether it improves the situation enough is another matter.

PHOBIAS

FREEING YOURSELF FROM PHOBIAS

From fear of spiders or snakes to unwillingness to enter an elevator or step onto a plane, phobias are simple fears that do not have a fully rational basis. Phobias can be very intense, but fortunately they are easy to desensitize. Research suggests that phobias are formed by the association of an object or situation with a bad outcome, and that the two have been bonded together in a person's mind. When the association between the phobia and the situation or object is broken through the desensitization process, the phobia disappears. I have found that to be true in my practice, and there is also an enormous body of research to support it.

A phobia is an exaggerated or irrational fear. Take, for example, loud noises. Most people dislike sudden loud noises, and most will be startled by them. But someone who has a phobia about them will react to them with intense fear—may break out into a sweat, tremble, have difficulty breathing—may, in short, have all of the symptoms of extreme anxiety.

People have developed phobias about everything imaginable: dogs, rats, taking a bath, blue teacups, appliances. Some phobias are so common that they have been given a special name, such as claustrophobia (fear of closed spaces). Phobias and anxiety can be confused, but generally you are correct to call a fear a phobia when it is directed toward some very specific object or situation, such as a fear of spiders or heights.

If you are suffering from a phobia that is extremely intense; if it has invaded many areas of your life, making you, say, afraid to leave your home, or even afraid to leave your bedroom, and if symptoms have been acute for some time, then it is all the more important to approach the fear gradually and systematically. Most phobias can be easily cleared up by desensitization.

In this area, as in most others, Exposure Therapy differs radically from the traditional approach. In classical psychological analysis, phobias are considered symbolic. The one phobia everyone has heard of is fear of snakes, which is typically interpreted as a fear of penises. According to the classical view, some people have developed a fear of the penis that they don't want to acknowledge, so they transfer it symbolically to snakes.

My own belief is that phobias are sometimes symbols and sometimes not. But even when they are symbolic, I think they are the result of a different mechanism from the one championed by classical analysts. For example, if you have been attacked by an animal in a wooded area, it's possible that the sight or smell of a woods will trigger a phobic reaction. Does that mean that the fear of woods is a symbolic representation of the attack you suffered, or is it just a generalized cue that precipitates an avoidance response because the attack itself is too painful to confront?

When I meet up with a phobia I usually consider it in terms of generalization rather than symbolism. A great many phobias are caused by generalization: fear transferred from spiders to scorpions to snakes. The human brain has an enormous capacity for generalization—it is designed to generalize, must do this to function.

In the classical approach a phobia is treated by attempting to build up the patient's strengths. The patient is made aware of his or her early life, of the patterns and basic needs of that life. Eventually it is necessary to review a good deal of what happened during childhood because, so the theory goes, the more the past is incorporated into the adult view, the stronger the patient gets. The idea is for the patient to become so strong that he or she will no longer need the phobia. The patient will, in other words, no longer need to symbolize a fear. This approach can take years.

Using desensitization, on the other hand, you can extinguish a phobia in a matter of a few months, weeks, or even, in some not very severe cases, hours. Phobias respond very well to the process, so I usually approach phobia treatment with a high degree of confidence.

WHAT WILL IT TAKE TO TREAT MY PHOBIA?

The treatment for a phobia will depend on how important the issue is in your life and goals. Do you want to get to like the thing in question, or just be able to tolerate it?

Sometimes a phobia is a big problem, such as people who are phobic about the idea of going to sleep—they are insomniacs. Their level of fear is such that it itself is a problem. They are afraid of hyperarousal.

Hyperarousal is hard to treat, and this is an intense fear because it is generated every night.

But most phobics (who are afraid of snakes, spiders, or whatever) just want to get back to work, or to be able to go to the zoo with their grandkids. Likewise, some people only have to fly occasionally, such as once a year or less to go on vacation. So it is no big deal. If someone had a phobia about snakes, and lived in NYC, I would recommend just getting them to the point that it was no longer bothersome. I would just do whatever had to be done to get things to workable. I might go to a zoo or pet shop with them to work on the behavioral aspect a bit. I would go a lot farther if it were something that was really going to affect their life. This is an example where the goal is minimal, established collaboratively. Mastery of snakes would mean more aggressive treatment, getting to the point where they never affect your thinking.

In treatment for phobias, the last step is to see if the person can manage to make themselves anxious over it. If they can't, the treatment has been fully successful.

Let's look at some actual examples of phobia banishment now.

THE UNFRIENDLY SKIES

Jesse is an example of someone who tried both the traditional approach and Exposure Therapy. He had a phobia about flying. Many of us are uncomfortable in planes. But when Jesse, a successful executive in his late twenties, with a handsome head of hair and a big friendly smile, came to one of my colleagues, it had been five years since he had even been able to go near an airport, much less an airplane. This was a hardship, for not only was he called upon to make business trips during which he had to cover a lot of distance in a few days, he was also under pressure from his wife, who wanted to take trips to places that were conveniently accessible only through air travel. He had been ignoring both professional and domestic demands to fly and had completely eliminated planes from his life. This caused a big and very noticeable gap in his lifestyle. Other executives in his profession thought nothing of hopping on a coast-to-coast flight, and other husbands as affluent as Jesse didn't bat an eye at a weekend trip to the Virgin Islands. So Jesse sought help.

For the first two months my colleague took the traditional approach, but Jesse became restless and annoyed at the lack of progress, so my colleague decided to try desensitization.

They started slowly because Jesse's anxiety was very great. At first he just imagined getting ready to drive to the airport with his wife, driving there and parking, and getting out of the car and walking toward—but not into—the terminal. Then they repeated these images several times until Jesse was able to go through them without stress. This took up a one-hour session. Then Jesse imagined going into the terminal with his wife, looking around, and going to the ramp to board the plane, and finally actually stepping onto it. This, with the repetition of the first set of images, took another session.

In their next two sessions Jesse and my colleague reviewed the previous images and this time Jesse went so far as to imagine getting into his seat, fastening the safety belt, and taking off. This was repeated many, many times. All during this period, it is important to note, Jesse was also visualizing the images twice a day, every day, on his own as well.

Then he imagined a very bumpy ride during which he was tossed from side to side, and the flight attendants spilled drinks and dropped trays, while the view out of the little window in the plane was of black and turbulent clouds. He also imagined that his wife, while accompanying him to the airport, was laughing at him for being afraid, and that one of the other passengers, as he stepped on the plane, said, "Oh, my, but we *are* scared, aren't we?" Jesse was acutely embarrassed by his phobia, and that is why we included this image.

After three weeks of all this Jesse was ready to fly. My colleague, who occasionally practiced what he called "action therapy," accompanied him on the shuttle flight from Newark, NJ, to Washington D.C, and then back to Newark.

As it turned out it started to rain and the flight to D.C. was bumpy. Both men voiced their anxiety and exchanged doleful predictions of disaster. As soon as they landed, however, they booked themselves on the return flight, which proved to be smooth and pleasant—almost fun. The whole back-and-forth trip had taken five hours.

Jesse was ecstatic. The very next day he called a travel agent and booked a weekend flight to Jamaica. Since then he has made many coast-to-coast flights and says he is even beginning to enjoy flying.

EIGHT-LEGGED AND AWFUL

In another case, Clayton, a young man in his twenties, had a phobia about spiders that we were able to get rid of in one day.

Most people are not fond of insects (or in this case arachnids). I myself dislike spiders and react more strongly to them than to, say, ants or cockroaches. But Clayton had such a strong phobic reaction to them that he would not even go to the cellar or attic of his home for fear of seeing them, and if one turned up in his room, he wouldn't be sleeping there that night.

To begin I had him imagine that he was in his house and saw a spider on the floor, a small one in the distance. It was not very threatening. After this image was repeated several times, I had him imagine that he moved closer to the spider and saw that it was somewhat larger than he had first thought. This was repeated several times. Then I had him imagine moving even closer, and seeing that it was quite a large spider, with hair on its legs and back and a large head. It began to move quickly in circles, and started climbing the wall. We stopped at this point and repeated the images over and over again until Clayton felt relatively calm.

Then I had him imagine that the same large, hairy spider was in a glass case with a hole in the top. I had him put a pointer through the hole and watch the spider crawl up the pointer toward his hand. We repeated this several times. Then I had him imagine that the spider actually crawled to his hand and onto it. Then he imagined that he took the spider and put it back in the case, then removed it again with his bare hand. I had him imagine showing it to friends and talking to it, petting it, putting it in his pocket and walking around with it. All of these images were repeated many times during the session with me, and Clayton went over them several times that evening. The next day he pronounced himself cured of the phobia, which he had suffered with since he was a boy. The following weekend he was willing to help his mother clean out the cellar!

"KEEP ME ON THE GROUND!"

Another common phobia is acrophobia, fear of heights. Caroline, a woman now in her mid-thirties, suffered from this to the extent that she was not even able to sit near a second-floor window without breaking into a sweat and tremors. She had been raised in a suburb where multistory buildings were not all that common, so up until the point I saw her she had not been too inconvenienced. She had, however, been forced to forego a number of invitations from friends for trips to various cities because she knew it was unlikely that she would be able to avoid multistory buildings. Oddly enough, she was able to ride across bridges, provided that the driver stayed in the middle lane and she did not look out the side windows of the car. In every other respect, however, her movements were confined to ground level.

We began the images cautiously by having Caroline imagine that she was planning to go to New York to meet a friend who lived in a tall apartment building. Even this image aroused some anxiety, so we repeated it several times until Caroline felt comfortable with it. Then she imagined the drive to the city, parking the car, and meeting her friend. This phase was repeated several times.

Then Caroline imagined entering her friend's apartment building, which had many flights of stairs and a window at each landing. She climbed the first flight of stairs and looked out the window. This made her very anxious, so we repeated the image about fifteen times. When she had become more comfortable, she imagined climbing up the second flight, and looking out the window. The same process of repetition followed until she felt at ease. Then on to the third flight, and fourth and fifth, right up to the tenth floor. After each floor the image was repeated until she felt comfortable. It took several sessions to get to the top of the building.

When she got to the top, I had her imagine leaning far out the tenth-floor window and looking down, watching all of the people below and the traffic. She also imagined tying a rope around her waist and stepping out onto the window ledge in order to get a better view. She was, of course, doing all of these exercises at home between our sessions.

After about six weeks she was able to go to New York and have dinner in a restaurant perched on a skyscraper. She felt only a little bit of initial anxiety, which soon gave way to exhilaration as she realized she had extinguished her phobia.

FEAR OF FORKED TONGUES

A fear of heights is not an entirely unreasonable fear. Many phobias relate to realistic fears. Fear of snakes, for example, is promoted in our culture by the media and word of mouth. Few of us see many real snakes, but what we read about them or see in movies and TV is not usually very good public relations for them. Rattlesnakes, cobras, and pythons probably lead the list in familiarity, and none of these is very endearing or appealing.

One of my clients, Susan, came to me with a snake phobia. She was a lively woman with a pleasant, open personality.

Susan had been in analysis for more than a year and had become fed up with the probes into her childhood. Her analyst was taking the classical approach that her fear must have been initiated by some infantile sexual trauma, but absolutely nothing in her past, as far as she was concerned, could justify this approach. She was becoming more anxious and fearful, not only because she was frustrated at the lack of progress, but also because she felt she was spending a great deal of money for no results. She had heard about me from one of my clients and decided that my method was worth a try.

During her first visit she was able to talk about her phobia with a certain amount of black humor. But what she described was a painful and very oppressive condition. She could not go into the laundry room in her house, for she was convinced that there were snakes among the piles of clothes and the coiled wires of the equipment. She often couldn't open drawers for fear of what she might find; occasionally she wasn't even able to open mail for the same reason. She was never able to go to the park because she imagined the woods filled with snakes. Once, while cleaning the master bedroom, she closed the closet door, and a belt hanging on it brushed her arm. She went into hysterics and had to be sedated.

A fairly recent event in Susan's life had aggravated her phobia. She worked in a large warehouse, the only woman among a number of men. The fact that she had been promoted over some of the men had caused a certain amount of resentment. One day, when the paychecks were being passed out, one of the men told her that her check was in a box in the office. She opened the box and reached in, and found the check covered by a coiled blacksnake. She was so upset she had to be hospitalized. Furthermore, she was unable to return to that job because even the idea of going back into the building where the event had taken place induced extreme anxiety. She had an intense fear of snakes before, which her coworkers had been aware of, but it was nothing like the phobia that developed after this cruel incident.

Just before we began our sessions she decided that she would no longer allow the phobia to rule her and she and her husband arranged to visit a snake farm during their upcoming vacation in New Orleans. But she saw a snake on the road as they were driving along, and this precipitated another attack of hysteria. They had to turn back. When she finally got home she was both anxious and depressed.

We started desensitization by having her imagine that she was going to visit the reptile house in the Bronx Zoo. Susan imagined making preparations to leave her house, going to the car, and driving to the zoo. This sequence of images aroused a great deal of anxiety, so we repeated it about fifteen times during the first session. Then we incorporated the preparations and trip into another series of images that led up to the entrance of the snake house. We repeated this sequence many times before going on. Then she imagined stepping into the foyer of the snake area and advancing to the threshold of the main room, where she just looked at the lighted glass cases but did not see any snakes. This was repeated. Then she walked to the case and saw a small harmless garter snake amid the twigs and leaves at the bottom of the case. This was repeated many, many times before Susan felt comfortable enough to go on to other cases with larger, more threatening snakes in them.

Not only was Susan repeating all of these exercises on her own, she also taped our sessions and then played them back at least once a day. This was extremely helpful because she was so anxious that she needed help to confront the images, and the tapes served as support.

Finally, after several months, Susan did make the trip to the zoo and did stand in front of the glass cages containing the snakes. Before this her anxieties had all but disappeared—she was no longer barring herself from the laundry room, or imagining serpents lurking in every drawer. Even so, it took a great deal of resolve on her part to actually make the trip to the snake house. Once there she was astonished that she was able to walk calmly around the large room, moving from case to case, as she said, "just as if I were normal." She added, "I'm so grateful I was able to go there—but it's not something I want to do every day." And that's normal too.

BIG DOG DISTRESS

Another of my clients, Kayla, had a phobia about big dogs. Dogs don't usually get the bad press that snakes do in our culture—quite the contrary. They are usually depicted as cute and lovable, man's best friend, and so on. Yet occasional horror stories do get circulated, such as incidents in which a large dog has mauled an infant, and many of us have

227

been menaced by a large dog while on a walk or whatever. So there is a cultural basis for an attitude of wariness toward the larger breeds. Furthermore, Kayla had been bitten by a large dog when she was working as a mail carrier as a young woman, and this very likely was the basis for her phobia. Her fear was not as constricting as many, but it still limited her movements.

She would not, for example, walk down a street if she thought there was a large dog on it, nor would she get out of her car if she saw a big dog loose somewhere, no matter how gentle it seemed or how unconcerned other people around it appeared to be. On her own she had bought a small dog, thinking that this might help her overcome her fear of the larger ones. But even with her own dog on a leash she remained frightened of larger ones and would still refuse to visit friends who owned them. Her phobia was a relatively minor inconvenience, but one that was certainly worth getting rid of. She finally came to me.

During our first session Kayla imagined walking down the street, seeing a medium-sized dog off its leash, and stopping and petting it. This aroused only slight anxiety, so we did no more than three or four repetitions. Then we kept imagining larger and larger dogs, until Kayla finally hit upon an image that made her very anxious indeed: a large German Shepherd.

So she imagined seeing this big black dog behind a strong fence, where it was sitting, looking friendly. After several repetitions she imagined the dog being friskier and more aggressive, but not necessarily hostile, and still confined behind the fence. This caused more anxiety, and we spent practically a whole session repeating those particular images.

Then she imagined that the dog climbed through a hole in the fence and chased her, and even nipped her leg. In the next series of images the dog got out through the hole, but Kayla chased it, whacking it with a large stick, sending it howling down the street.

After about a month, the phobia had cleared up, and Kayla bought a Rottweiler.

I believe that there are three common causes of phobias. One, a specific instance or incident has caused a fear. This was probably the case with Susan's snake phobia and almost certainly with Kayla's dog phobia.

Two, a phobia may be induced by cultural influences. This probably had something to with Susan's phobia, and also with Clayton's.

The third cause is a generalized fear in which the phobia is actually triggered by something other than what appears at first glance to be the cause.

HIDDEN CAUSES OF PHOBIAS

James was an example of this type of phobia. He initially came to me because he was afraid of germs that might give him some dangerous disease. As a result his life was dominated by a series of rituals. He washed his hands at least twenty times a day, and he was constantly cleaning any area where he happened to find himself, whether he was at home or in his office. He would compulsively brush away imaginary dirt from tabletops in restaurants, and polish the silverware relentlessly before using it. But even with these precautions, he would eat with profound misgivings, certain that he was being attacked by unseen microorganisms.

As we began desensitization we focused on this fear. James imagined sitting on his bed after he had awakened and saying to himself that he was not going to bathe or shave or make the bed that day. Then he imagined that he would not wash his hands or clean any part of the house. These images did arouse anxiety, but it was apparent to me that his anxiety was caused not so much by a fear of germs, as by a loss of control over his daily life.

His incessant washing of his hands was just one means of controlling his life, as was his constant scouring of his environment. As we became more aware of this, the images we had him viewing changed, until he was imagining people asking him to do things that he couldn't do, and then imagining that people laughed at him for his inability to perform the acts. In short, he imagined many situations in which he had lost control of his life, and where he was actually at the mercy of others.

The germ phobia, one small part of a larger problem, was cleared up in about three weeks. It proved to be the means to lead James to a confrontation with the anxiety about his need to exercise control.

One opinion voiced by more traditional practitioners is that if you get rid of the symptoms without going into the causes, other symptoms will just pop up. This argument is usually advanced in support of long-term and deep analysis. In James' case, certainly, there was a deeper cause of his phobia about germs than was originally obvious. But that does not mean that getting rid of it was a waste of time. It actually lifted quite a burden off of him when he was no longer compelled to wash his hands twenty times a day, and persistently scrub away at his surroundings. He was made more comfortable by the extinction of the phobia and was then able to concentrate on the problem stemming from his need to control.

So I believe that anyone who is suffering from a phobia should confront it head on, using Exposure Therapy, and not worry too much about what caused it.

There are a few additional aids that are helpful in dealing with phobias. Both modeling (observing others deal with the feared object or situation) and behavior rehearsal are invaluable. If, for example, you are working on a phobia about dogs, watch how other people act around dogs, watch how they treat the animals, and model your behavior on them. Then rehearse confronting the object of your phobia in controlled circumstances, just as Susan made the trip to the reptile house to see those creatures that had so terrorized her.

It is always important to go slowly when desensitizing, and especially so when dealing with phobias. Confront your images in small portions, just as Caroline did when she was climbing a long series of stairs, pausing at each landing, and repeating the climb until she felt comfortable enough to ascend to the next level. When I am using the process with people, I usually wait until they show signs of boredom before moving on to the next image. So when you are working alone, keep repeating an image until you are completely at ease with it.

If someone has a dozen phobias, there are two ways in which these could be treated. If they are desensitized one by one, the process gets faster and easier as you do more of them (you can't just take the time it takes for one and multiply by twelve to determine how long working your way through all of them will take).

If they have twenty or fifty phobias, you could work on desensitizing the person to the perception of anxiety in general, to anxiety in general, working on eliminating elevated heartbeat, and all of the other physical signs of anxiety, not necessarily confronting the phobic object itself.

PANIC ATTACKS

Panic attacks are one of the more dramatic forms of anxiety disorder, causing sufferers great mental anguish within a short time frame, often just five or ten minutes. Panic attacks may involve trembling, numbness or tingling, chills or hot flashes, shortness of breath and/or chest pain, and a sense of choking or dizziness, all accompanied by an intense feeling of fear or of imminent doom. Worse, once a person has had one, they worry endlessly about the onset of another such attack. Once they have had this experience, they often become so fearful of the situation where it arose that they become phobic of various places.

Fortunately, panic attacks are not just treatable but curable. People who have had panic attacks often are convinced that the panic just comes out of the blue. In reality, with the aid of a therapist, they will usually discover themes they are anxious about causing the stress that triggers the attack.

The first attack they have is probably the result of genetic predisposition, coupled with a great deal of generalized stress in their life. But the subsequent attacks are pretty much related to their fear of having another attack, and that is what causes them to have one attack after another. So I work on reducing their general level of stress, because that is effective, and on conditioning them not to overreact to an attack, by recognizing where it is coming from. Desensitization is very helpful in eliminating the fears of various situations that they have come to associate with the attacks. All of this gives them a sense of control over their lives, and often banishes the attacks completely within several months.

Let me give an example from my practice.

Virginia was in her mid-twenties when she came to my office. She was a tall, thin young woman, impeccably dressed, with a heart-shaped face and a model's high cheekbones. When she walked in she was a picture of upper-middle-class success: personable and friendly, self-assured and graceful. I was not surprised to learn that she had a full and satisfying social life.

She was, however, suffering from periodic anxiety attacks, usually one every other week or so, during which she would experience overwhelming dread and fear, and intense, nightmarish apprehension. She had no way to deal with these attacks. She was overcome by them and rendered helpless. Generally they came when she was unoccupied; she usually didn't experience them while working.

As she was describing the attacks she was embarrassed, as though she were confessing something shameful (this is frequently the case with people who suffer from generalized anxiety). She told me about the fear, trembling, and sweating; described how her heart would pound and she would become flushed and short of breath. The attacks, so far as she knew, had absolutely no reason behind them. During the periods between them she would feel mildly anxious, a nagging malaise—again, for no discernible reason. This anxiety influenced her behavior in all areas. For example, she was unable to use planes, and meeting new people made her uncomfortable. She had been subjected to these attacks, both the mild and acute ones, since she was a young teenager. For several years prior to coming to me she had been using a wide variety of tranquilizers. She had been sent to me by a physician who believed that these medications were jeopardizing her health.

TREATMENT FOR PANIC ATTACKS

During her first two sessions I took Virginia's history, found out how many and what kind of drugs she was using, and established rapport with her. Then I explained the desensitization technique to her. This was Step One, Education.

After she had become accustomed to me and relatively relaxed in my office (a process that was comparable to Step Two, Preparation), I guided her to the third step, Imagination. First I had her imagine that she was home in bed and that she began to feel anxious; she imagined that her heart was beating faster, she was sweating, and experiencing mild tremors. I had her describe these feelings in great detail. She repeated these images several times in my office, and I asked her to repeat them at least three times a day for the next four days before she returned for the second session. Repetition, the fourth step, is terribly important in order to exhaust and wear out the emotion. Of the five steps, in fact, repetition is the most important. Remember, that just confronting an emotion once or twice is not enough to extinguish it.

Then I had her imagine that she had absolutely no control over the anxiety, that she was completely powerless. This was repeated over and over again, about fifteen times.

In the next session I had her imagine that she was not only anxious at home, but also at work, and that, moreover, the attack did not end quickly. This was a new ingredient. I asked Virginia what she did when the attacks did not go away, and she answered that if her anxiety became particularly acute she would go to the hospital, something she had done several times.

"All right," I said, "imagine that you do go to the hospital, and that the doctor comes in and examines you. What happens then? What will the doctor say?"

"He says there's nothing wrong, that I'm OK, and that I can leave the hospital."

"OK, now imagine what you do next," I said.

"I go home."

"What happens then?"

"Well, after hearing that there's no problem I don't feel anxious any more. I'm OK…until the next time."

"All right," I said, "now let's go through the whole cycle again, only this time we'll go more slowly."

I took her through this scene rapidly the first time so she would know exactly where she was going, and this would prevent the anxiety the images were creating from getting out of hand. That is why I did not allow her to go through the doctor's whole examination in detail, but rushed to the conclusion. Once we had completed the cycle and she was aware of the outcome, then we could go into more detail without building anxiety.

In the next session I had Virginia go through the cycle more slowly and in much greater detail. Not only did I have her go to the hospital, but I had her imagine the doctor's examination right down to the last particular. Then I had her imagine that the doctor told her that the anxiety would not go away, that it was going to be with her for a long, long time, so she was going to have to learn to live with it.

At one point I said, "Imagine that the doctor believes you have something more than anxiety. What would he tell you then?"

"Well," said Virginia, "he would probably tell me that I have an incurable disease."

"OK," I said, "let's explore that scene…." And she imagined the doctor finding various incurable diseases. This brought to the surface one of the underlying causes of her anxiety. Though Virginia had undergone a number of almost ritual visits to doctors over the years, she still had grave concerns about her health. Many people who suffer from anxiety, I have found, will not believe a positive diagnosis when they visit a doctor. They feel that the doctor is holding back, or is incompetent, so their anxiety is not really assuaged. Since one of the symptoms of anxiety is accelerated heartbeat and a feeling of constriction in the chest, many assume that they have some heart disease. Of course, this fear only worsens the anxiety.

Virginia continued to use Exposure Therapy on her own to counter the attacks, and after three months they had diminished in intensity and frequency. After about another three months they had all but disappeared, and she was using desensitization as a matter of course on any problems that came up. She was no longer worried about the attacks catching her in a vulnerable position because she felt she could deal with them should they occur—and this feeling of self-sufficiency is in itself a great deterrent to anxiety. She could take planes now, and she changed to a professional position in which she had to meet people constantly. She now did so with comfort. She had resolved her difficulties.

Virginia's treatment followed the five steps of desensitization, which are, once again, Education, Preparation, Imagination, Repetition, and Relaxation.

One of the most painful aspects of an anxiety attack is the impression that you have no control over the situation. You can use desensitization very effectively on this feeling.

Imagine that you are completely powerless, without any ability whatsoever to alter your circumstances. Repeat whatever images you come up with for this several times in whatever way seems most effective to you. Exercises like this to extinguish your feeling of anxiety about lack of control will almost always alleviate the general anxiety symptoms.

Here I am working to desensitize a person's fear of being in situations where they might feel trapped. Once they feel that they have reached the point where they can handle a variety of situations in which they are likely to feel trapped, and they are not so concerned about whether they might have a panic attack in any of them, then their fear of these situations goes away.

Another feeling that can be extinguished by desensitization is a sense of hopelessness. Anyone who has suffered an anxiety attack is familiar with the feeling that it is going to last forever, that life is always going to be that way, that there is no possibility of recovery. Conjure up images of yourself as a perennial victim of anxiety, with no relief on the horizon. Imagine that there are others who are in similar situations who also seem stuck. Then imagine looking into alternative approaches—such as imagining you can overcome the attacks. You will start to boost yourself up, start to chip away at your pessimism, and start emboldening yourself. Now you are desensitizing your fears, negative feelings, and sense of hopelessness and becoming more positive, letting more optimistic thoughts in.

For most kinds of anxiety a person would have therapy once a week for six to twelve weeks. Treatment of panic attacks usually takes longer, about six months.

First I explain that panic attacks are caused by two things. The first attack is caused by the fact that the person has been under stress for a long period of time, six months or longer. That chronic stress triggers the first attack. After that first one, they become anxious, paranoid about having another attack. This is a phobic anxiety.

So they have two types of anxiety, one due to generalized stress, and the other a phobic response to the possibility of having another attack.

The general stress I deal with by discussing their life and circumstances and trying to get the stress down. This includes looking to see if there is a mismatch between their tasks and traits, and getting these things aligned a little better, which is one way of reducing stress.

Then I treat the anxiety about having another attack like a phobia, just like any other phobia. I go through the whole process of desensitizing the prospect of having another attack.

As I do this, the person feels less and less threatened. They get better and better at handling and mitigating attacks. Eventually, they get to the point where they look forward to getting one so they can practice on it. Now it becomes harder and harder to have one. Trying to consciously produce an attack is very difficult for most people—the very act of doing this is a confrontational approach that tends to reduce the anxiety that causes them. If you approach an idea with relish the brain picks up on this and the mind becomes increasingly confident. As the person becomes more confident, their anxiety goes down.

POST-TRAUMATIC STRESS DISORDER (PTSD)

PTSD is another anxiety-based disorder. Soldiers develop PTSD following battlefield traumas; crime victims are often traumatized by the experience; and serious health and financial setbacks can similarly affect us. At one time or another all of us have been traumatized to varying degrees. People are traumatized by horrific events such as things that happen during wartime, an earthquake or tornado, rape, mugging, torture, near-death experiences, and loss of a loved one.

The mind of just about every one of us harbors some traumatic memories—small, medium, or large. They cause a variety of distressing symptoms including uncontrollable replays of the event, nightmares about it, intrusive thoughts and recollections, and the desire to avoid anything even remotely connected with it. Traumatic memories are a special challenge because these memories are formed and stored in a more enduring way than others—as noted earlier they are permanently etched on the brain, because of the presence of adrenaline at the memory site when they are formed. The treatment outlined here has been developed and tested on severe cases such as war veterans.

Extraordinarily intense experiences are not stored like typical memory traces, which are subject to decay and forgetting. These experiences are indelibly etched in our minds—most likely as an evolutionarily developed safeguard—and so they cannot be forgotten. Unlike ordinary memories, which require many repetitions to gain access to long-term storage, traumatic events—for reasons that are obvious for our survival—are permanently stored after even a single experience.

Moreover, for reasons that have not been fully determined, the mind replays these experiences spontaneously, either as flashbacks or intrusive recollections that cannot be silenced. These are the thoughts in our head that haunt us.

My own view is that the brain is replaying these images as a means of desensitizing them, as well as prodding the person to prepare a response should they encounter a similar trauma.

The longstanding view of PTSD is that it is incurable and very difficult to treat because the person experiences flashbacks or sudden recollections, which they are not able to control. Any treatment regimen must take this into account as well as all of the secondary characteristics of trauma, which include depression, anxiety, guilt, and avoidance.

The fear generated by PTSD can be so intense it overwhelms traditional desensitizing techniques. Overreactiveness goes off the charts: people act first and think later. Research has shown that after significant trauma the amygdala, a part of the brain that is about the size of a walnut, can double in size, because of the amount of hormone being secreted in response to stress. No one is sure whether this is because the original fear was so intense, or because of damage done elsewhere in the brain. Shock waves, such as from the explosion of an IED for example, might damage the brain, adding a medical problem to the psychological one. This can reshuffle or revise all of a person's default mechanisms. You can't ask such people to imagine being in a foxhole, or even being on a plane going back over to Afghanistan or wherever. But trauma can be treated and substantially reduced by the measures I will describe.

For example, I treated a young woman who had been assaulted and raped on the campus commons near her dorm late one evening. When she passed a young man near her dorm, he pulled a knife, propelled her to a dark corner of the field, and proceeded to rape her there. Afterward, she was afraid to be alone, worried constantly about being attacked, and experienced distressing recollections and flashbacks of the incident.

People who have been traumatized, such as this woman, typically proceed through several stages.

They may find that there are some useful results of the experience. The person may reorient their priorities and values in a positive way—such as by emphasizing the importance of close relatives and friends, or by recognizing the greater importance of time spent with relatives and friends versus striving for material acquisitions.

But the most typical response is intense fear and avoidance of the cues and circumstances associated with the incident—e.g., people who experience near-death by drowning will avoid the water. This woman decided she wouldn't ever cross the commons alone again, and that she would avoid staying out late, as well as people and situations that she perceived as questionable or dangerous.

In time, what appears to be a logical and reasonable assumption, namely, that it is best to avoid potentially threatening people and situations, turns into an inflexible policy that restricts the person's social life, limits their freedom, undermines their self-esteem, and takes over their life. This rape victim now spent much of her time at home, refusing to go out unless she had to. She refused to stay out late, which interfered with socializing with her friends and family. She insisted that her boyfriend accompany her everywhere, which gradually pulled them apart. And she lost her sense of confidence and self-esteem.

Another woman who had been raped decided to avoid clubs and nightlife, or ever putting herself in vulnerable situations, only interacting with men under very safe circumstances. At first, this might seem reasonable and prudent, but in time the effect on her life—isolation, lack of relationships, loss of social confidence, feeling imprisoned—restricted her life in ways that were more detrimental to her than the original trauma.

Likewise, the person who almost drowned may find it difficult and disadvantageous to avoid the water, especially if loved ones or work are involved.

TREATMENT OF TRAUMA

1. The nature of trauma is explained to enlist the person's cooperation and active involvement in treatment, including an explanation of how the mind is programmed to respond to a trauma. People troubled by PTSD need to understand that they will probably never forget the incident, so there is no point in trying to get it out of their mind. Their emotional response, however, *can* be modified.

2. Next it is important to learn as much as possible about and from the incident—why it happened, whether it could have been avoided, who was at fault, what they could or should have done, what they should do now (such as perhaps change their approach to certain things, or their values and priorities), etc. The purpose of all this is to be sure the person gets whatever good can be gotten out of the experience, even if it is just an important lesson learned.

3. The next step is encouraging, actually summoning up the traumatic memories in a carefully regulated way that desensitizes them, gradually strips them of their emotional power, and thus their ability to arouse and upset the person.

   This step has several components.

- The brain will automatically bring up the traumatic images in an attempt to desensitize them. If possible, the person should just let the images come and go. If this is too stressful, just allow this to happen as much as possible, recognizing that the images can't harm them and will gradually subside. Even a minimal amount of exposure at first will gradually facilitate the desensitizing experience.

- When they can let these images come and go without a problem, they may start to gradually push them a little, take them further. For example, they may ask themselves what would have happened if they had acted sooner, or "I wonder what that person was thinking when he decided to attack me? "

- The person needs to be aware that exclusively focusing on how unfair the attack was, or how much they hate the culprit, will prevent them from exposing themselves to the trauma. This avoidance response is easy to indulge in, but ultimately preserves the strength of the traumatic images, much like avoiding flying on a plane preserves your fear of flying.

4. The person's assumptions and defensive strategies following the trauma are examined to assure a healthy approach to life free of overly restrictive and poorly suited practices.

5. When someone has suffered a trauma, it is not enough to desensitize his fears. He must also plan and enact an aggressive approach to the traumatizing situation in the future: actions that will build confidence in that situation and instill a feeling of mastery over it.

In the case of the woman raped at college, we discussed ways in which she could develop a sense of control and mastery of her fears. She took karate lessons, started carrying pepper spray, and eventually became a police officer. One way or another, the person develops a defensive strategy to enable them to deal with the traumatic experience if it should reoccur.

> The key to getting rid of flashbacks and intrusive recollections does not lie in trying to forget them, since this does not seem to be possible. Rather, it is better to desensitize them so that they cannot command our attention. While the horrific thoughts remain, stripped of their priority they lie dormant and helpless.

Desensitization of trauma can be accomplished in several ways.

1. By scheduling regular, leisurely walks of a half-hour or longer, perhaps several times a week, or more, if you want faster results. Let your mind wander. Don't try to focus your thoughts or regulate your thinking. Put your mind on automatic pilot. Soon the mind will naturally focus on the dreaded thoughts. As the mind repeatedly focuses on these thoughts, in the absence of any consequences, the emotional intensity associated with them will gradually diminish until they lose their ability to assert themselves. The images and the fear aroused by PTSD are often too strong to play with. It is not possible to summon the fear up or instigate it, and

trying would only lead to serious failure. Let your brain bring the images up and learn to tolerate them. Eventually, the brain will gradually stop bringing them up.

2. Another method, which should only be used with the aid of a professional, is to deliberately summon up these thoughts while in a safe place and time, and allow your mind to focus on them for varying periods until they lose their arousing properties. It is possible, by regulating the duration and intensity of the self-exposure, to overcome flashbacks and intrusive recollections at a pace with which the individual is comfortable.

The above goals will best be accomplished by allowing the mind to heal itself—prohibiting the mind from replaying the events will only delay the process.

For more on the process of desensitization see Chapters Four and Six.

AIDS TO DESENSITIZATION

Among the techniques that can be used to reinforce the process of regulating recollections through visual imagery are behavioral rehearsal (acting out the trauma) and modeling. These should only be done with the aid of professionals.

Acting out a trauma is often recommended as a way of determining which aspect of it is most disturbing to the individual. For example, a person may want to act out an argument they had with another person, recalling what they said and everything that was said to them, to help identify this.

Another way to act out a trauma is to visualize the incident. This way, again, you can determine which aspect of the situation was responsible for traumatizing the person. This is not that different from a doctor asking a person to demonstrate what hurts when trying to determine what the person's problem may be. In this case, the trauma is in your brain, not necessarily what actually happened.

I asked the woman who was raped at college what aspect of this bothered her the most. When she first saw the man who eventually attacked her she felt uneasy about him. When she tried to ignore him he followed her, grabbed her arm, and took her to a quiet corner. He told her to take her clothes off, and started pulling at them. Once her pants were down he put her on the ground and raped her, and it was done quickly. He had a knife to her neck, and told her not to look at him. When he was done he ran off.

She was shaken, but she got up, walked to her dorm, and took a shower. Then she called the campus police, who told her this had been happening in the area. The man was never caught.

We went over this experience many times, trying to see where the anxiety was coming from. What you might expect was oddly not the key. The key event was that when he told her to take her pants off, she apologized for the fact that she was having her period. She was most embarrassed by this, angry about it.

The issue was the degree of control she had—or didn't have—and the degree about which she was ambivalent about what to do when it was happening. She wondered if she should have had a weapon, started screaming right away, or have headed to her dorm earlier. Again, the issue is not necessarily what happened, but what you were most concerned about.

TREATING THE DEPRESSIVE PART OF TRAUMA

It the case of trauma you want to desensitize not only the fears associated with the incident, but also the depressive feelings. It is very important to note that depressive feelings can be desensitized, since this is unique to my therapy. Traditionally therapists analyzed the origin of depressive feelings, hoping to gain insight into them. My approach emphasizes that the emotional pain associated with depressive feelings can be desensitized without gleaning insight into them. Once the emotional pain is desensitized, the person's interest in gaining insight into it is greatly diminished.

"I WISH I'D ACTED SOONER!"

When thinking back on the incident in which they were traumatized, people often feel guilty because they didn't act sooner. This is a common characteristic of trauma. We have a natural tendency to give other people the benefit of the doubt, but you can be so concerned about not offending others that you put yourself in a precarious position. This is what a trauma victim may come to realize after undergoing a very bad experience.

Bernhard Goetz, the "subway vigilante," reacted very quickly in 1984, in fact too quickly, when asked by four teenagers whether he would give them a dime. Instead of handing over the dime, Mr. Goetz got down in a firing position, pulled out his gun, and shot them all. He then ran away.

The case became a sensation in New York City. When asked why he did this, he said he had been traumatized numerous times and had come to the conclusion that he waited too long and had been too kind in dealing with the people who had approached him in a similar way in the past. He was not acting in his own best interests when he did this, but simply trying to be nice to them. As a result, he resolved that in the future he would react much more quickly and put himself first rather than wonder what the motives were of the person who approached him.

This is a very common characteristic of people following a trauma. This is not a good practice because it would be seen as too hasty and irresponsible were it to be used on a regular basis. Courts generally do not review a person's past history in order to determine whether or not they acted impulsively in a given situation. As a result, many people who have been traumatized are accused of jumping the gun. If you react too quickly, you may end up in jail.

This kind of reaction can be seen in less serious circumstances, such as the case of the guy who cheated on the girlfriend he was planning to marry, by going back to his ex-wife and sleeping with her. Later, he and his girlfriend were talking about the ex-wife, and the moment her name came up, the girlfriend started screaming.

Unbeknownst to the fiancé, the girlfriend had spoken to the ex-wife, who told her about her tryst with her ex. The fiancé also admitted that he had cheated with his ex. He then had a long discussion with his girlfriend in which he answered all of her questions candidly. He also agreed to the temporary separation of their relationship she requested. He let her take her time to gradually get back into their relationship.

> The brain uses "transcendence" to determine whether it can trust someone. Transcendence is when a person puts someone else's interests above his own, without letting the other person know that he is doing this, thus he doesn't get credit for it. This act of selflessness usually implies a strong love for the other person. The fiancé displayed transcendence by allowing his girlfriend to control this situation.

THE FINAL STEP IN MASTERY

After they have confronted their fears and memories through desensitization and the other techniques described above, and gained some control over them, many people will want to go on to confront the actual circumstances in which they were traumatized. They want to prove to themselves that they have overcome their anxieties and can handle any such situation. This can be a real aid to recovery, if done carefully.

The young woman raped on the college commons, for instance, gradually reversed all of her assumptions—she started to go out alone, stayed out late, stared down criminals at work, and determined that she would rather risk being assaulted again than live in fear.

Once a person confronts their fears and gains a sense of mastery over them, they feel liberated and the intrusive recollections and flash-backs cease to overwhelm them and gradually subside.

AN EXAMPLE OF SUCCESSFUL TREATMENT OF PTSD

As noted earlier, PSTD can be very difficult to treat, but here is an example of a case that was treated successfully.

A young man named Clifford was drafted and sent to Vietnam. Before he went, he had his own business. He was a kitchen and bathroom remodeler, and doing very well in this. He also had a good marriage.

When he came back he had PTSD. Before his war service, his wife thought that he seemed normal and upbeat, well-adjusted and good-natured. Now he was depressed, easily angered, and abusive. He was an ambivert before (halfway between an introvert and extrovert), but when he came back he was more of a loner. He was very agreeable before, and now very irritable. His concentration was poor, and he had no spark or enthusiasm. He originally was very open to change; now he sought the comfort of structure and repetition. He was anxious at times, and depressed at others. Before he went overseas, he showed little sign of either anxiety or depression.

His brain had been damaged physically as well as psychologi-cally by the traumas he was exposed to—the constant bombardment of artillery and other blasts. He had not only the trauma of near-death experiences, the stress and strain of being in a war zone, but also actual physical damage. When the brain is damaged like this it's not unique to one area, but kind of a global problem. The brain protects itself by not taking on new tasks or undertakings and limiting activities.

The brain no longer has the energy to be conscientious, so it tries to skirt responsibility now. Cliff was no longer conscientious—he tended to wing it now— and he couldn't handle any kind of stress, so he was unable to continue running his own business. He took a job as a handyman for an apartment complex.

Desensitization could be used to reduce the anxiety related to his memories and flashbacks. I recommended it, and it did prove helpful. We also used it to work on the feelings of insecurity, inadequacy, and inferiority he had now. These are things that can be dealt with by the process, and we used it to treat his anxieties in all of these areas.

I told him that he would probably qualify for disability, and he should tell the doctors that he had PTSD. He ended being given 125% of his Army pay, because they determined that he had been damaged by Agent Orange as well. This was a sizeable check each month. It made up the difference between his income previously and what he was able to earn now. So he could reduce his workload in accord with his reduced energy, which helped him a great deal.

You can't change brain damage of the type Cliff had suffered, so I said, "Let's look at the new you." Then we created a new lifestyle to fit his present capabilities.

Before Vietnam, he was concerned with making money, having his own business, raising a family, and being successful. Looking at his predispositions now versus what they were originally, I suggested that he readjust his lifestyle in accord with what he was now capable of. He moved to a rural area, where there was less stress, and he and I continued to work on his anxieties with desensitization. I also got him involved in group therapy with other vets.

It was clear that he returned from Vietnam a vastly different person. This is why PTSD is clinically thought of as not being curable. This treatment was remarkably successful, and he referred many other vets to me, whom I also treated successfully in a similar fashion.

> When you understand your traits and predispositions, you can carve out a lifestyle that fits who you are and what you can do now. This is like living within your means. Cliff's life is much happier and more manageable now because of trait and predisposition analysis.

CHAPTER NINE

OBSESSIVE-COMPULSIVE DISORDER

Obsessive-compulsive disorder, or OCD, is more common than you might imagine. Approximately one in every forty adults and one in two hundred children in America have OCD. You've probably encountered many people with OCD without ever realizing it.

OCD is characterized by recurrent obsessions or compulsions that provoke distress and often interfere significantly with everyday functioning. Obsessions are unwanted thoughts that you can't seem to get out of your head. The more you try not to think about them, the more they stay with you. These obsessional thoughts can cause a person to feel compelled to engage in a particular action or actions in an attempt to reduce his or her discomfort.

OCD is commonly referred to as the "doubting disease." Those who have it are plagued with unrelenting "what if" thoughts. "What if I left the stove turned on and burnt down my entire home? What if I hit someone while driving home and didn't stop to help? What if I lost control and harmed my child?" Many people with OCD recognize that their thoughts and fears may be irrational, but OCD can make these things feel very real. It can fill you with constant dread that something awful is about to happen. Imagine if your brain was worrying about everything that could possibly go wrong, ignoring the question of how likely it was to actually happen, and disregarding any rational objections that might challenge these thoughts. This is what OCD is like.

OCD sufferers develop a number of different rituals to keep their anxieties at bay, and they expend a great deal of time and effort, mental and physical energy on them. The obsessions and compulsions may be directly related. For example, someone fears dying from a disease, so he/she engages in excessive washing rituals designed to remove "contamination." Or, a person fears being responsible for harm coming to a loved one, so he/she repeatedly checks to make sure all appliances are off and all doors and windows are locked when they leave the house. OCD sufferers may go to extremes to try to assure that their loved ones will be safe, such as waking up hourly throughout the night to check appliances and locks as well as checking water levels in the toilet to try and make absolutely sure that the home will not flood.

Other times, the link between obsessions and compulsions may be less clear, such as when the compulsion is counting to a safe number, arranging items in a certain order, performing a certain action (e.g., making a movement or sound, or speaking a sentence), or repeating an action until it "feels right" to try to relieve anxiety.

Compulsions do not have to be overt behaviors. Many OCD sufferers will engage in mental compulsions such as trying to "figure something out" or excessively reassuring themselves. For instance, mentally reviewing their thoughts to gain certainty on whether or not they may have contracted a disease when they touched an item in the store, or reviewing their actions to try and assure themselves that they locked the door on the way out of the house. Regardless of how many times you review or evaluate scenarios in your mind, however, you will never be absolutely sure about most things. Certainty is an illusion, as most things in life cannot be proven and there will always be a level of doubt as to what has occurred or will occur. Even if there is a significant amount of evidence to support a conclusion, OCD sufferers will question it. For instance, most people would be relieved to find out that their blood test results revealed they do not have cancer; however, someone with OCD may think, "My bloodwork may have gotten mixed up in the lab" or "My cancer may have not been detected by that test." This doubt causes endless mental ruminations and/or compulsions. People with OCD do not *choose* to have obsessive thoughts and they do not enjoy their compulsions. They perform them to try to get relief from crippling anxiety.

Research has shown that people with and without OCD have similar thought content; however, individuals with OCD have a strong emotional response to their negative thoughts, which causes them problems. For instance, someone without OCD who suddenly thinks, "What if I drove my car over this bridge?" will view the thought as odd or ridiculous and quickly move on. They will not become emotionally upset or view the thought as meaningful. Their brain effectively identifies this thought as insignificant and disregards it. On the other hand, a person with OCD will view the thought as being threatening and important. He or she will have a spike in physical discomfort (e.g., pounding heart, sweating) and will believe the thought is sound and meaningful. Thus they will change their behavior to protect themselves from the thought and try to make sure that what they have imagined does not actually occur (e.g., avoid bridges, drive very slowly, want another person in the car at all times).

> The problem in OCD is not the triggering thought (possible danger, health hazard), but rather the person's response to it.

THE THREE FEARS OF THOSE WITH OCD

People with OCD typically have three categories of fears, which include:

1. Events that they believe will happen immediately (e.g., "I will get sick if I don't wash my hands right now").

2. Intolerance of uncertainty (e.g., "I can't go on unless I am sure my family will be safe").

3. The fear that their distress will never lessen or be alleviated (e.g., "I will be anxious forever if I don't wash my hands right now").

Uncertainty lies at the root of OCD. Those who suffer from OCD have an intolerance of uncertainty and they want proof that what they dread and fear will not occur. Unfortunately, as noted earlier, few things in life are certain and it is impossible to prove that something won't happen. That is akin to predicting the future. At best, we can argue that something is very unlikely to occur, but there will never be proof that it will never happen. As a result, the person with OCD gets stuck in a cycle of trying to prove the unprovable.

OCD GETS WORSE UNDER STRESS

OCD is affected more by stress than just about any other mental health issue. As soon as the person is stressed they get a lot worse, and they do a lot better when the stress ceases. When they've gotten a raise or promotion, or are on vacation, things are going well for them, they will not feel the need to do their rituals nearly as much. But on the other hand, at difficult times, when things are not going well for them, they are unemployed, get a couple of big unexpected bills, or there's been a death in the family, at those times OCD can become more severe, even get out of hand.

This is a problem because by getting worse in bad times, the OCD can affect their ability to deal with the bad situation. For example, if they are in the hospital, or otherwise worried about themselves or someone else, the OCD will make them more stressed than they would otherwise be. This can raise their blood pressure and do other things that will adversely affect their health.

So one very good reason to deal with OCD is to reduce the possibility that it will come at the wrong time and complicate a problem, lead to further mistakes or a continuation of a problem long after it would have been resolved.

RITUALS: THE HALLMARK OF OCD

When anxious, people often gravitate to magical thinking, often involving rituals meant to assure a certain result.

Rituals were very common in pre-scientific society, less common as scientific cause and effect became more widely known. But even top scientists today often have some kind of ritual they practice. They may joke about it, say something like, "This is not supported by the literature, but I always like to wear this special watch when I start an important experiment." They joke about it, but they do it.

Many athletes, including top ones, have their rituals as well. They may bounce the tennis ball a certain number of times before they start to play, avoid stepping on lines, or touch certain parts of their bodies. And they often have special balls, hats, bats, or racquets that they think may assure success.

Gamblers have many rituals, too, rituals that often make them feel very confident, in control, superior. They show up at the casino wearing outrageous things because they are "lucky" things, associated with past wins. Gamblers often have a strong feeling that they are special, and they bask in this, but in reality all of this just encourages them to gamble more and lose more.

The rituals of OCD, however, are a whole different matter. As noted earlier, they are often elaborate and time-consuming enough to interfere significantly with everyday functioning.

Many studies have been done on OCD, and one of the first, many years ago, dealt with animals in large cages given periodic, random mild electric shocks (not strong or painful, more like a little bit of a jolt) through a grid on the floorboard. If they were in this cage for some time, they almost all developed rituals, idiosyncratic behavior, to deal with this. They walked in circles, or in a zigzag way, or touched the wall, or tapped the floor grid. All of these things, like our human OCD rituals, were meant to have some effect on stopping the delivery of the shocks.

People who have a high level of generalized anxiety, whether because of phobias or other triggers, have a more pronounced tendency to use magical thinking. This is possibly the basis of OCD.

> One of the tricky or problematic things about OCD is that people form a relationship with their OCD, they get to like it. It takes up time, and gives them something to do, as well as a tool they otherwise wouldn't have. It may also give them false hope, but that is better than no hope.

The positive aspects of rituals

The rituals of OCD do some things that are positive. The basic formula of OCD is that if I do something, which we will call A, then B will not happen (I won't lose my job, get sick, someone else won't get sick, the world won't end). B is usually something the person has worried about for a long time. They feel out of control with it and powerless to do anything about it.

So coming up with something such as A, even though it doesn't really solve the problem posed by B, it takes away this passivity, gives them something to do. It replaces passivity with an active response. Our brain feels much more comfortable making an active rather than passive response. Passive behavior is hard for the brain to learn, and difficult to train anyone to do. Withholding or inhibiting a response takes a fair amount of maturity. It's easier to teach children to go on green than to stop on red.

The compulsive actions of OCD can also take away the feeling of being totally out of control, give the person a sense of confidence.

They also distract the person from his fears to an extent, so that he doesn't have to keep pounding his brain with the dreaded thought. They take his mind off his worries, so he is not focusing on them without a break, which is too stressful, and give him some comfort.

Most people don't want to be embarrassed by their rituals, so they usually do them when others are not around. For example if they have the habit of rubbing their forehead or counting to ten when they are anxious, they may not do this during a job interview, when it might cost them the job. But then when they are done with the interview they usually make up for it.

In a situation like this the person may think to herself, this is an emergency, so I can bypass my ritual or do it a hidden way so that I do not draw attention to my behaviors.

The drawbacks of rituals

I treated a woman who had to check everything carefully before she could move on, especially before discarding anything, to prevent identity theft. So for example she would take anything with her name, address or phone number off of mail or junk mail, and shred it or rip it into tiny pieces before disposing of it separately.

To a certain extent this was rational and reasonable. But she carried it to extremes and spent an enormous amount of time on it. She was very meticulous in a number of respects—her family was like this too, she said, and she may have learned it from them. And she had heard horror stories about identity theft. But even if there were no issue of identity security, she wanted to protect herself as much as possible when it came to discarding things, and from anything that might be used against her.

As a result, since all of this checking took time, she accumulated a lot of things, because she had a limited ability to deal with all of the incoming material in her home. She overdid it, but felt she had a rational reason.

This is not atypical. Many OCD sufferers defend their activities as rational, not a problem, though others watching them might think so. But at some level they are aware that rituals can take an enormous amount of time. And they have to be sure they are done correctly because they also create a great deal of stress and anxiety when they are not.

The big question about rituals is: is this truly an effective way to eliminate anxiety? Often such things do not reduce anxiety, but merely delay or postpone it, or distract the person from it. Confronting it and stopping the response, letting the urge to make it wash over you and then letting it tail out is the only way to end the problem for once and for all, and relieve the person of the burden of rituals.

In OCD the power is out of the individual's control—it's in the process, the behavior, and the rituals. At certain times people might feel that they would rather have the process than the power. But once you shift the power away from yourself, put it in the hand of the process, you weaken yourself, and you want to be as strong as possible.

If you can go through an anxiety-provoking situation without relying on any of these things—any rituals—you will feel more powerful as a result. If you transfer that to a process, you will often attribute any success you have to the process, thereby undermining your own sense of control and success. It's a close call and many might say there is not much difference between these things. But I don't recommend that people believe in a process more than they believe in themselves.

This does matter, because things are always changing, the environment and circumstances, and if circumstances change, if a person believes in himself, he or she can adapt better than a process or ritual, which is not designed to change.

For example if a person is playing tennis, and it happens to be a very windy day or raining, the ritual may not work or be hard to perform under those circumstances. If the nature of a ritual is unyielding and unchangeable, it is hard to adapt.

> A big issue with OCD is that what starts out as a small compulsion, such as counting to ten, will not stay small for long—it will grow dramatically. This is because doubt will always creep in and the compulsion will never be enough. OCD is never satisfied and always wants more. Counting to ten will only relieve your anxiety for a short time before your OCD will fight back and say something like, "If counting to ten makes you feel better, imagine how much better you would feel if you started doing everything in tens." You need to get rid of a compulsion completely to break the association between A and B. Response prevention is the heart of OCD treatment.

TREATMENT FOR OCD

One of the first steps is becoming acutely aware of the lies of OCD.

OCD loves to lie. It will pretend to be a helpful ally who wants to keep you safe. But in reality, it is only manipulating you into performing more and more rituals.

Lies OCD commonly tells include the following:

1. Lie: **You have to know for certain**. OCD-related fears can vary greatly, but one thing they all have in common, as noted earlier, is an intolerance of uncertainty. OCD will tell you that something

bad will happen unless you have a 100% guarantee that everything is safe. Whether you check the stove multiple times or try to wish away unwanted thoughts, the goal is to feel certain that the feared outcome won't happen.

Truth: Certainty is an illusion. Ritualizing does not make you safer and it will not give you the certainty you crave. Instead of responding to your fears by ritualizing and desperately trying to achieve certainty, respond with "Maybe..." or "It's unlikely" and work on embracing the uncertainty. "It is unlikely that the house will burn down. My fear of fire is really covering up a more pervasive fear: I can't ensure my loved ones' safety because there are many ways they might come to harm. For all of the effort I put into my rituals, my loved ones are still at risk. I know that increasing my rituals isn't going to make us any safer, so I need to learn to live with the uncertainty of fire. Rather than focus on my discomfort right now, I need to remember how much more I will miss in the future if I don't fight my OCD. Because the saddest thing of all is that for all of the time and pain I spend on my compulsions, I don't ever get the safety I crave."

2. Lie: **This anxiety will last forever**. OCD tells you that the anxiety or discomfort you are feeling will last forever and that you need to do a ritual to make it go away.

   Truth: This is not only a lie, it is impossible. All anxiety will come down eventually. It takes a significant amount of energy to be anxious and as a result your body cannot maintain such feelings forever.

When working with clients, I usually have them create a hierarchy of feared situations. Situations are rated in terms of the amount of discomfort they may cause. For this purpose you will want to have a list of varied situations ranging from things that cause low to high anxiety (see below). For assistance with rating situations, you can refer to the

Subjective Units of Distress Scale (SUDS), which can be found online, and is discussed in Chapter Four.

SAMPLE HIERARCHY FOR FEAR OF CONTAMINATION/CONTRACTING AN ILLNESS:

Walking around a public place with hands in pocket: 2
Touching packaged items in a grocery store: 3
Looking at pictures of a hospital or doctor's office: 4
Sitting in a movie theater and touching the chair: 5
Touching grocery store cart without wiping it down: 6
Touching store door handle with bare hands: 7
Touching side of public garbage can: 8
Touching floor of a public restroom: 9
Using public restroom and opening/closing all doors with bare hands: 10
Note: Hands cannot be washed after the exposure

Once the hierarchy is created, we gradually approach each situation. I usually aim for clients to feel a distress level of 3–4 when actively confronting situations. Over time, the situations at the top of the fear hierarchy (rated from 7–10) will lower in discomfort so that they too can then be approached. It generally takes about twenty minutes for the client's discomfort to go down after confronting a situation. During this time, their attention needs to be on the situation as opposed to avoiding it and they cannot engage in any outward or mental compulsions. Engaging in a compulsion during this time will invalidate the confrontation process. Rating their level of discomfort during the confrontation process can help them see that their discomfort is going down. The same exposure will be repeated until it no longer causes a spike of physical or mental discomfort. In essence, the person's brain gets bored with the exposure and no longer views it as threatening. Once they reach this point, they are ready to move onto the next item on their hierarchy.

3. Lie: **You shouldn't have "bad" thoughts**. OCD may tell you that "normal or good people don't have these thoughts" and that you are bad person for having negative or scary thoughts.

    Truth: Everyone has weird, intrusive thoughts now and then. In fact, research shows that there are no differences in the thought content of people with and without OCD. The difference is in how people respond to their thoughts. While the average person will shrug most of them off and go about their day, people with OCD tend to overreact to these thoughts. As a result, they engage in rituals to reduce their anxiety, which actually makes the thoughts come more frequently.

4. Lie: **Thoughts = actions**. OCD tells you that having a thought or urge to do something makes it more likely to happen.

    Truth: You can't control the world with your thoughts. Thoughts are just thoughts. For instance, if I think of winning the lottery all day every day, I am no more likely to win the lottery than if I don't think of winning at all. People with OCD often fear losing control and acting on their thoughts. There is no research to support this. Even in the midst of extreme anxiety you are in control of your behavior.

5. Lie: **You have to control your thoughts.**

    Truth: We can't stop good, bad, or upsetting thoughts from coming into our heads. But we can change how we react to these thoughts. The more you react to a thought and try to stop thinking about it, the more you will think about it. The less we react to a thought, the sooner it passes. Do not fear your thoughts—let the thought stay in your mind until you get bored with it. By purposefully thinking of the thought and not engaging in a compulsion you will show your brain that you do not fear it and that it has no power over you.

6. Lie: **Possibility = Probability.** OCD will tell you that bad things are very likely to happen.

   Truth: Just because something is possible, doesn't mean that it is likely to happen. The feared outcome is usually highly unlikely.

7. Lie: **Your thoughts make you dangerous.**

   Truth: We can't choose what thoughts we have, but we can choose how we react to them. Your thoughts can't make things happen or stop them from happening.

8. Lie: **You have to do things "just right" in order to feel okay.** Example: If you touch the wall with your right hand, you must also touch it with your left.

   Truth: "Just right" is something OCD makes up. Giving into a compulsion only makes the obsession grow, which means you'll have to do the ritual even more frequently. Sitting with the feeling of discomfort as opposed to pushing it away with a compulsion will make the discomfort go away once and for all. You need to show your brain that the discomfort will go down eventually and that you do not need to do a compulsion in order rid yourself of the anxiety. Again, it is important to start with situations that cause low levels of anxiety and to gradually build up your tolerance of discomfort so that the process is tolerable.

9. Lie: **If something bad does happen, you won't be able to cope.**

   Truth: People underestimate their ability to cope with feared outcomes. We are far more capable of coping than we usually believe.

I work with clients on strategies for coping with bad outcomes so that they become less fearful of them. Visualizing coping with a bad outcome is more useful than evaluating whether or not the outcome will occur. It also builds up your confidence in handling negative situations. When you have less fear of the dreaded situation you will also have less anxiety about it.

10. Lie: **You'll never get better.**

> *Truth:* Recovery is possible and help for OCD is available. If you or a loved one are suffering from OCD, reach out to a professional with expertise in OCD and Exposure Response Prevention treatment.

TREATMENT OVERVIEW

Unfortunately, many people do not pursue OCD treatment because they're self-conscious, ashamed, or believe it cannot be treated. OCD is treatable and the first line of treatment is Exposure and Response Prevention, which in short entails gradually and systematically confronting your fears while at the same time preventing the compulsive behaviors you are accustomed to engaging in. You need to understand that we cannot prove that the feared event will not happen, but your compulsions are not keeping you safe and you will be able to cope with the feared event if it were to occur.

1. Label thoughts as being your OCD. This is an important first step, as it helps you to go against the thoughts that are currently controlling you. It also helps to take the power out of these thoughts. Remember, thoughts are not actions and the types of intrusive thoughts you have does not say anything about you (we will get into this more in a moment). Having a coping statement can also be helpful (e.g., "I'm stronger than my OCD, I won't let my OCD control me").

2. Gradually begin to do the opposite of what your OCD is telling you to do (i.e., confront feared scenarios).

3. Resist the compulsion your OCD is telling you to do.

It is critically important that compulsions be prevented when doing confrontational work on OCD. It is better to confront situations that are lower on your discomfort hierarchy and not do a compulsion than it is to confront a situation high on your hierarchy and do a compulsion. Compulsions reinforce the OCD and fuel your anxiety. Although many people believe that their thoughts/fears are the source of their discomfort, it is actually their response to the thoughts (compulsions) that is the root of the problem. Compulsions interfere with your brain's ability to desensitize you to the obsession. Suppressing or avoiding thoughts only makes them return more often and with greater intensity. You have to find ways of dealing with the thoughts and they will go away for good.

THE IMPORTANCE OF ACTIVE EXPOSURE

Rational arguments usually do little or nothing to reduce OCD behavior. In fact, emphasizing the absurdity of their behavior only serves to humiliate and alienate OCD sufferers. Obsessive-compulsive drives range from mild to severe, and mild to moderate cases can be effectively treated by professionals and with self-help such as I am describing here. Severe cases respond best to a combination of behaviorally oriented psychotherapy and medication.

Unlike some other types of anxiety, when treating OCD it is important to engage in active exposures. Examples of some common exposures include:

- Writing by hand (not typing) or saying out loud the feared thoughts, acts, statements, or sentences.

    o   Examples: "Maybe I left the door unlocked," "Maybe I will get a harmful disease," "Maybe I will lose control while driving." You will need to write out the sentence a number of times (such as 15–25) in order to reach the point that you are bored with it. The goal of the exposure is to confront the situation until your anxiety lowers without the use of a compulsion (for example, checking the door or providing yourself with reassurance that the door is shut).

- o Note: If you struggle with the urge to engage in mental compulsions (e.g., mentally retracing your steps or trying to convince yourself that you locked the door), you will want to talk out loud to break the thoughts in your mind. Talking out loud interrupts your thought process and will serve to prevent the compulsion in that moment. You can say a coping statement ("I'm stronger that my OCD)," sing your favorite song, or engage in a conversation with a friend.

- Deliberately going places where you will encounter the obsession;

- o Example: Going to a hospital or crowded place if you fear contracting a disease; driving on unknown roads or in increasingly crowded places if you fear hitting someone.

- Taking part in feared activities;

- o Example: Eating food without washing your hands first; driving at night or with music on; leaving appliances plugged in when you leave the house.

Remember, you want to confront situations that cause a 3–4 level of discomfort on the SUDS scale. You should not move on to harder situations until the items low on your list no longer cause discomfort. If your anxiety is at a level 3 when you first do an exposure, you should continue with it until your discomfort is at least cut in half (is 1.5 or 1). If you are initially struggling to engage in an exposure, consider bringing a support person with you to help facilitate your progress. In addition, exposures can always be made "easier" to help you confront them. For example, if leaving the house after plugging in an appliance is too hard initially, you can start by leaving the appliance plugged in while you are home, or sitting in your yard while the appliance is plugged in.

It is helpful to chart your level of anxiety during the exposure process. There many scales that can be used to chart your anxiety, such as the Subjective Units of Distress Scale (SUDS) mentioned earlier. Measuring your level of anxiety is important, as you want to confront situations that will cause a small or moderate level of discomfort. For instance, if you are measuring your anxiety on a 1–10 scale where 10 is extreme discomfort, you would want to confront situations that will bring your anxiety to roughly a 3. The goal is to be successful in the situation and to not engage in any type of compulsion. If you confront situations that are too difficult, you are likely to engage in a compulsion or the process will be so uncomfortable that you may not want to do further exposures. Measuring your anxiety during the exposure process (such as about every twenty minutes) can help you identify when your anxiety is going down.

My clients are taught that the discomfort they experience will go down on its own, and a compulsion is not needed to reduce it. Anxiety ordinarily begins to go down in about twenty minutes, although some clients will experience discomfort for longer periods. Your body cannot maintain a high level of anxiety forever as it uses up a lot of energy to be anxious. Therefore, at some point your body will register that you are safe and that the discomfort was a false alarm. It is critically important that a compulsion not be done during this time so that the association between obsessions and compulsions can be broken.

For moderate to severe cases of OCD medication may be useful to reduce the level of discomfort an individual experiences as well as reduce the frequency of intrusive thoughts. It is important to note that confronting feared situations and breaking the link between obsessions and compulsions is at the core of OCD treatment. Medication alone will rarely eliminate OCD symptoms.

CHAPTER TEN

DEALING WITH DEPRESSION— THE DARK SHADOW

Depression is a dark shadow over our lives that most of us have grappled with for short or longer periods somewhere along the line.

Depression is not a sudden affliction—it's something that happens gradually. It seeps into our psyche and can progress so gradually it's hard to be aware of, even when you've reached the point of clinical depression. This slowness of development makes it difficult to detect. Many people are surprised when they go to see a therapist and find out that they are depressed.

While it takes hold gradually, depression also waxes and wanes. It builds up, crests, and then may go into remission. You may have periods where you bounce back and feel better. There are periods of remission punctuated by periods of more intense negative feelings.

CAUSES OF DEPRESSION

There are many different causes of depression, but it is usually triggered by a loss or setback. Virtually any physical injury will engender depression commensurate with its severity and impact on the person's life.

People who suffer neurological injuries are especially prone to depression. Injuries to some parts of the nervous system are likely to cause depression, and virtually any head injury renders a person more susceptible to it. Once the body is injured, the brain wants you to withdraw— this is why animals often hide when they are ill.

Some depressions are also induced by hormonal changes, such as in menstruation, pregnancy, and change of life.

Diseases like Parkinson's disease and Alzheimer's can cause depression as well. You can have a double depression, from the disease itself and its impact on your life.

In many cases, as much as fifty percent of the time, when a depression is severe enough to be classified as clinical or major depression (Major Depressive Disorder, or MDD), it can occur spontaneously or for no apparent reason. In these cases, there is probably an underlying genetic tendency, and this is supported by considerable research that has shown a statistical link among family members of those who suffer from depression.

Basically, depression is caused by a slowdown of mental functioning. Mental images and information are processed by chemical reactions that occur between the neurological cells in the brain. Between these cells are a number of neurological fluids that regulate the speed and direction of this material. When a person is aroused or excited, the fluid levels rise to promote faster processing, and in turn, they drop when a person feels depressed. These fluid levels are extremely important in determining a person's mood. When a person is depressed, he typically feels unmotivated, tired, and usually but not always, sad. Depression is also usually accompanied by irritability, low tolerance for frustration, and pessimism.

Typically, the person's thinking slows down, as reflected in difficulty with concentration, a reduced level of mental energy, lethargy, and what clinicians refer to as psychomotor retardation, a slowing down of both thought and physical movements.

How did this system of speeding up and slowing down of mental processes come about? Every organism needs a means of assessing its environment to effectively navigate it and adjust its behavior as necessary. A fish swimming in the ocean has to react to danger, and at other times change direction to pursue more promising places for obtaining food. But fish, as well as all of the other lower animals, do not have the intellectual resources to understand and analyze their surroundings in the same way that humans do. These animals needed a simpler system for regulating their behavior, one that would speed them up and slow them down in response to triggers in their environment. In essence, the rise and fall of the neurological fluids in the brain seems to act like the accelerator in a car. When the level of gratification, as experienced by the brain, increases, the fluid levels rise, whereas when the animal feels a drop in gratification, then the levels fall off. In this manner, the brain regulates the animal's behavior by reacting to changes in the environment.

In higher-level animals such as humans, the brain is equipped with not just perceptual organs or senses but a sophisticated intellectual system as well that enable it to analyze its environment and anticipate changes, and govern its behavior accordingly. In essence, depression is a slowdown in mental activity, which slows a person down, discourages productivity, and promotes passivity and withdrawal.

One of the most obvious symptoms of depression is a drop in mental energy. When you talk to someone who is depressed one of the first things you will notice is that they do not show the enthusiasm, passion, and excitement of a normal person. They show little interest even in activities, hobbies, and pastimes they previously enjoyed.

Negativity is an important characteristic of depression because it allows the person to avoid doing things that they'd rather not do. Another symptom along this line is pessimism. By assuming that things will not work out in the end, the person then has a convenient excuse for not wanting to participate in some endeavor or activity. Pessimism is extremely useful in cutting off an undesirable activity at the very start. Skepticism, too, leads one to doubt whether it's desirable or likely to be fruitful to participate in an activity. Cynicism does the same.

Depressed people often withdraw socially, and this reduces conflict and contentiousness that can drain energy. They are often irritable, which causes people to avoid or withdraw from them. They do not have the emotional or physical strength to pursue a given thing or to interact with others, so they use irritability as a way of shooing people away. They have difficulty concentrating, and they laugh less and complain more.

People often confuse the two—irritability and anger. There is a significant difference between them. Anger is an emotion that is triggered by a perception of unfairness. If an individual feels he's been treated unfairly, this will normally produce an angry response from that person. Irritability, on the other hand, is precipitated by the perception that the brain is under strain—it has too much stress and too high a workload to function effectively. Unless something is done to reduce that workload, the brain might suffer a stroke or seizure. Irritability is actually attempting to prevent the person from experiencing such dire events.

Irritability responds favorably to a reduction in stress, so a person who is irritable will do much better if the pressure on him is reduced by leaving him alone, or somehow otherwise eliminating some of the things that are bothering him.

Reducing an organ's workload when it is injured is one of the brain's basic strategies for facilitating healing. For example, let's assume a person injures their knee. By making the knee inflamed and also painful the person is encouraged to avoid using that part of the body. The same principle applies to the brain itself. The symptoms of depression all work to alleviate the brain's workload.

As noted earlier, depression has a way of developing slowly in an individual so that the person is not very aware of it. It's not like other mental afflictions, which tend to come on more dramatically at first. It is often very difficult to spot the symptoms of depression even in oneself.

Living with a depressed person can and probably will make one depressed. Depression is very hard on relationships and is often a cause of divorce.

Symptoms of depression

Pessimism, negativity, social withdrawal, irritability, loss of pleasure in the things the person enjoyed previously, low self-esteem, and lack of confidence. Notice that these all in some way involve saying "no."

WHAT IS THE DIFFERENCE BETWEEN DEPRESSION, AND WHAT IS CALLED A DEPRESSIVE PERSONALITY?

True depression is probably a medical disease, like MS, heart disease, and gastrointestinal problems. It is a well-defined phenomenon with chemical as well as physiological roots, a cluster of behaviors, feelings, attitudes, and philosophies.

A person with a depressive personality has the behavioral symptoms of depression—except no drop in mental energy—without the underlying disease. Just as having coronary symptoms without the disease itself would be a pseudo cardiac condition, this is pseudo depression. For more about depressive personalities, see Grudges in Chapter Twelve.

Psychological depressions are depressions often (about fifty percent of the time) brought on by loss, and the depth of the depression depends on the size of the loss. It is related, too, to the ease or difficulty of replacing the lost thing.

BIPOLAR DEPRESSION

As many as half of the people who experience severe depressive episodes suffer from a chemical imbalance that is physiologically, and possibly genetically, based.

Bipolar depression, previously called manic depression, is a specific mental disorder, involving distinctive mood changes. The person is usually elated for two or three months and then depressed for six to nine. Some bipolar sufferers are always depressed, or eventually come to that after an earlier time of having elated periods as well. The sequence of the mood swings is somewhat variable. True mania is characterized by seven full days of uninterrupted mania, which then tails off into remission for a while, followed by depression or possibly another manic period. There is also a milder form of mania called hypomania, in which the person feels good and energetic without feeling out of control. Hypomania usually lasts for about four days, followed by a period of remission, and then a depressive episode or even another period of hypomania.

Bipolar depression can be severe—deeper than regular depression. It comes on suddenly and is very intense. The person may not be able to see beyond it. It may not respond to ordinary anti-depression measures like exercise, being with friends, or eating ice cream.

Medication helps to some degree, as does religion, and electro-convulsive therapy (a primitive technique usually used as a last resort). In the fifties doctors found that delivering an electrical current to the brain in some cases would sort of "reboot" the brain and result in significant improvements in depression. But this treatment often wiped out short-term and sometimes long-term memory, and had other side effects such as making the person very tired. Which is why it was used as a last resort. But sometimes it did work. The fact that it caused loss of memory caused it to go out of favor. Also, many doctors were reluctant to administer a treatment that seemed possibly harmful—delivering electrical current to a brain without knowing how or why it worked. It was a little like kicking the TV—sometimes it works, but you don't know why.

The more recently developed neuro-magnetic therapy is meant to be a milder version of the same principle. An electromagnetic coil is placed against a person's forehead, and a mild magnetic pulse is delivered to the nerve cells in the region of the brain involved in mood control and depression. Some studies show that used as a last resort, neuro-magnetic therapy sometimes seems to be helpful. More research is needed to see if this is true.

As for medications, lithium is fairly effective, but the line between toxic and safe levels of this medication is thin, and people with bipolar disorder are not good at compliance.

Antidepressants can also help with bipolar depression. They are not totally effective, but they can improve things.

TRAITS MAKE A DIFFERENCE HERE, TOO

Bipolar depression is a pathological condition, but it is also influenced by other factors such as a person's basic traits. If a person with bipolar disorder is of good character, for instance, he will be able to function much better in life. He will take his medicine, and be reliable and conscientious about his appointments and employment. When he sees that he is heading for a manic episode, or people alert him to that, he will tell his boss, "Listen, I'm entering a manic phase and need to take a break from work for a while. I'll be back in a month or so."

I had one client like this, a man of phenomenal character who was very trustworthy and honest. If he and his wife saw a manic phase or deep depression coming on, he would tell all of the appropriate people, including friends and relatives, who would know then to back off and also know what his needs were. He was particularly careful to do this with his boss. He was a systems analyst with a high-level job in his company. They needed him and respected him, so they were willing to work with him.

This was all possible because he was so reliable and conscientious. He also had an array of other people he was close to who were aware of his problem and were willing to be helpful as well.

What, on the other hand, if a person's character is poor, and they have a bit of con person in them? This is like putting the bipolar condition on steroids. The wavelike motions of bipolar mood from low to high intensified by other traits like this can make a person very hard to deal with. They will not be reliable or conscientious—they may lie a lot, and try to take advantage of others.

I saw another man with this problem. When he had depressive episodes he didn't tell his boss, just took off. When he had manic episodes he became very flighty, came in late, and criticized everyone and had arguments with them. He blamed others in his office for everything. When the boss called him on all of this, he didn't cooperate with him.

His life was a disaster. He finally came to see me because he couldn't even seem to handle simple day-to-day things like paying the rent and making sure his driver's license was renewed. And his habit of blaming everyone else for things was a big problem.

In therapy I was able to give some stability to his life. I gave him honest feedback on what he was doing and where he was going. This can work very well with a bipolar person because it calms them down and gives them a place to go for advice and suggestions, an objective view. When they trust someone through a therapeutic alliance this can be very helpful to them.

THE ADVANTAGES OF DEPRESSION

The mental and physical slowdown engendered by depression seems to confer several socio/biological advantages. Grief, for example, is actually a positive natural process that occurs in response to the loss of a cherished person, place, or thing. Depression is not just a feeling—as noted earlier it involves physiological changes such as slowing down of our thinking processes, a decrease in our mental energy, and even our physical stamina. We become withdrawn, passive, negative.

By slowing us down and making us more contemplative, depression causes us to relentlessly examine the nature and causes of our losses and setbacks. This enables us to learn whatever lessons can be learned from them, and take action, if possible, to prevent such things in the future. As a result, we learn from our mistakes and avoid repeating them.

It also motivates the person to pursue alternatives to the path he is on. If someone has been rejected by a lover, continuing to pursue that person in the absence of gratification would be counterproductive. Depression serves as a braking action. It strips a person of their incentives for pursuing worthless causes, and thus encourages them to move on. The same is true for those trapped in an unsatisfying job. Eventually, the lack of gratification not only causes them to look elsewhere, but in those situations in which a person feels trapped, as might occur if someone had a high-paying but unpleasant job, it enables them to overcome their fears by fostering a "whatever," or indifferent attitude.

This maximizes the likelihood that the person will find a way to compensate for their loss (e.g., the person who finds a new lover after a breakup), minimize its impact (the person who acknowledges that he cannot compete successfully in one sport and so moves to one he is more suited to); or even discover a means of undoing or reversing the loss (the person who discovers a cure for an illness or starts a new business venture).

TRAITS AND PREDISPOSITIONS THAT CAN CONTRIBUTE TO DEPRESSION

One thing a person can do to investigate this is check the photos of past scenes in their mind to determine whether or not they've had a tendency to be depressed.

Are many of the past scenes or videos you can see clearly in your memory involved with depressive situations—grief, losses, or lack of gratification?

One woman's father was always complaining about something, always had an issue, always saw himself as a victim. When he was down or depressed, asking him to do anything was a waste of time. Nothing would get done. Better to wait for his mood to change. His mood was more a factor in her happiness than her own.

Often people like this woman, without realizing it, may get used to someone like this and marry or become close friends with someone similar—what they are used to. If you find yourself in a situation like this, surrounded with depressives, you may well end up with a life filled with depression. You need to look at what kind of changes you could make in your life circumstances and attitude to change some of the things going on, and introduce more positive things and people to your life.

You can examine the strengths and weaknesses of your personality, too, to see if something here is contributing to depression. If you have a tendency to low energy, you may not have enough energy to provide gratification in various areas for yourself. When energy drops, gratification does too. If you don't do much or go many places, there will not be a great deal coming in by way of gratification. If you are not a self-starter, can't seem to get much done, this too will keep your rate of gratification low.

Also, if you are not very conscientious or open to change, this will further impede your chances of generating victories or a positive outlook.

If this is the case, see if you can modify these things a bit, and start associating with others who are more optimistic and have a higher level of energy, who are more inclined to want to do things. Depression can be contagious, and an upbeat attitude is too. Look at the people you are surrounding yourself with.

One woman reported to me that she grew up in a family that was always very positive, always looking at the bright side, looking for what they could do to change things for the better, and so on. This helped her enormously, she said. When she was going through difficult times or down because of losses, she would think back to how her parents had dealt with such things. She'd learned a lot of useful coping strategies from them.

Another thing you can do here is look at the times earlier in your life when you were happy—in a good situation, optimistic, resilient, when your rate of gratification was high. Look for periods when you did well, such as in school. Then see if you can find or create similar situations now. This can set the stage for a more upbeat outlook.

Something else to look at is how predisposed to anger you are. When someone gets angry at you, do you get very defensive, back down, capitulate, or does it generate desire to get back at the person? You don't want to be overly reactive or defensive in this way. But if you are too reactive to depression, too inclined to be thrown by losses, overwhelmed by them, you may want to use anger to justify putting a little more spunk in your responses, which could help reduce your depression.

If you grew up in a situation where there was constant anger, accusations, and battling, this is something else you may want to be aware of. Depressives are good at being angry. Anger itself is essentially a reaction to a perception of unfairness. If anger is not related to a desire to right wrongs, it may be being used to manipulate people.

Independent people get angry often, because they don't usually see the other person's point of view. They get very defensive, are very sensitive to being cheated or treated unfairly. Anger and depression go hand in hand.

ASSESSING DEPRESSION

Many people find themselves puzzled or upset when a loved one seems to have chronic depression. The person in question has his or her better moments, when they are more up, but generally they are just angry and depressed all the time.

Depression is contagious, and if you are in this situation, over time you may end up depressed as well, because you can lose a good part of your life in the process of trying to help the other person.

The general rule of thumb when it comes to helping someone is to "Throw them a lifeline—don't jump in the water with them."

If you watch a lifeguard going to save someone, what they usually do is bring a buoy with them. When they reach the person in danger of drowning, they toss the buoy so that the person can grab it, and it will hold them up in the water. Then the two can swim back to shore, even if the lifeguard needs the help of the buoy to pull the person back in.

The lifeguard is not likely to go out and try to help the person by himself, especially not in the ocean. If he does that, both may end up drowned.

This principle applies also to living with a person who is chronically depressed. If you think you can save them by jumping in the water with them, working with them and trying to help them get to their feet, this is probably not the best idea. You are better off looking for professional help, so you can find out whether the depression is the result of a loss or other circumstance the person has experienced, or is more chronic, even physiologically based. Often it is hard to determine if a depression is psychological or physiological. It can even be a mixture of both. Physiological depression can cause losses in a person's life that then cause psychological depression as well.

So if you find yourself wondering what is causing a person's depression, why it is hanging on so long, why they are having such trouble rousing themselves, you may want to call in a pro to determine what the situation actually is. You don't want to simply assume that it will resolve itself. You don't want to put yourself in a situation where you make assumptions that are not warranted. It's easy enough to go to a mental health professional so that the problem can be assessed.

Depression can also cause ripple effects and loss of control (see Chapter Eleven), so you don't want severe depression, especially, to go untreated for too long.

What we are dealing with in this book is losses of various types that we try to isolate and use desensitization techniques on, so that the person can move on—recognizing that this is sometimes not so easy. If a depression is physiological you will not be able to reverse it by desensitization—you will just frustrate yourself and waste time. If you are up against a physiological depression, desensitization will not work.

If you see that a loss is not responding to desensitization, that you or your loved one are not able to lessen the feelings of loss in a reasonable amount of time, it is not responding like a grief reaction, you should get a second opinion to make sure you know what you are dealing with.

If it turns out that the depression is physiologically based, the therapist or psychiatrist will talk to the person about medication, or some other form of professional intervention.

TREATMENT OF DEPRESSION

Mastering depression may seem more difficult than anxiety, but that isn't necessarily so. The basic process of exposure therapy can work well to relieve depression, as seen in its effectiveness in overcoming major losses such as in a divorce or the death of a loved one. The brain does seem to heal itself in a process called grief in which the brain brings down a depressing thought by repeatedly examining the cause of it until it no longer has any emotional life left to it.

But depression can be very resistant to treatment when it is not pure grief but a feeling of loss mixed with other emotions, such as anger. The combination can be difficult to treat.

The best treatment for most depressions

Sometimes it's hard to tell if a depression is psychological or physiological. Some types of depression respond better to one course of treatment than another; things may work for one type of depression and not another. Nevertheless, generally speaking, a combination of psychotherapy and medication is the best treatment for most depressive reactions.

THE COGNITIVE/BEHAVIORAL APPROACH

There are countless self-help books on depression. Most of them maintain that people become depressed because of faulty thinking and misconceptions that they have about themselves. According to the concept of "positive thinking," people become depressed not primarily because of what happened to them, but because of what they tell themselves about themselves afterward. For example, if a person was laid off from his job, that would not necessarily cause him to become depressed, unless he told himself that he was let go because he was an incompetent loser who probably deserved it.

These self-recriminations undermine the person's self-confidence and self-esteem, causing them to suffer from depression. This theory posits that people who are depressed hold numerous unrealistic assumptions, such as that they have full control over even events that are beyond their control, so they are nevertheless to blame.

Therapists who espouse positive thinking carefully examine the assumptions depressed people make, and then encourage them to change these assumptions to more realistic and logical views, which then establishes the basis for recovery. A few common misconceptions include the tendency to over-generalize (e.g., "If I did poorly on my test today, I will always do poorly; I will never be successful at anything"); to make faulty inferences from events in their lives ("She rejected me because I'm worthless and unattractive"; "He won't commit because he's never really cared for me"); and unrealistic expectations ("There's no use in applying for that position because even if I get it, they'll only let me go after a little while"; "Unless the woman I care for loves me I can't go on").

The depressed person is encouraged to analyze her view of herself and make the necessary modifications. For example, in the case of the faulty assumptions mentioned earlier, a person would be counseled to reassess her poor performance on a test by concluding that while she did poorly, she could do better if she tried harder, or even if she couldn't improve her performance, then she could still be a worthwhile person and shouldn't be disappointed in herself simply because she wasn't good at a particular thing. People are encouraged not to infer that they are bad or beyond redemption simply because someone doesn't love them or because things are not going their way.

The cognitive/behavioral approach has been popular because it gives people the impression that they can control their feelings simply by making a few relatively easy modifications to their thinking. The approach encourages an optimistic outlook and a sense of self-mastery. It has also made its mark in sports—many coaches believe that if you think you are not good enough to win then you will probably lose; winners win because they want to win more than the losers do.

LIMITATIONS OF POSITIVE THINKING

Animals get depressed, or at least they certainly seem to, and they probably don't make faulty assumptions. Take away the running wheel in its cage and a hamster gets depressed.

Positive thinking is also inconsistent with our day-to-day experience—it's not realistic to always think about things in a positive way. Things are in fact not constantly positive; there are plenty of negative things in all of our lives. Furthermore, the brain soon realizes that you are adopting this mindset consciously, and it loses its clout.

One of the things that positive thinking posits is that a person's change in thinking to the negative is what causes the depression. It's hard to imagine how someone's thinking could change so dramatically in a short time. It's usually the other way around. The depression causes the change in thinking.

People who favor cognitive-behavioral treatment claim that every emotion is triggered by a thought. So if you change the thought, you will change or stop that emotion. If you are afraid of planes, it is a thought that triggers this. You can't have a fear without a thought.

> But there are those who disagree with this. They say that if you are depressed it's not because you think you are a loser, or whatever, you are simply depressed. And it is this emotion that produces the negative thoughts.

A growing body of sports research has discredited the view that a winning attitude is the basis of good performance. In fact, the research shows that just the opposite seems to be the case—good results engender a good outlook and a positive attitude.

The socio/biological view of behavior has been gaining in popularity in recent years. It is not obvious what the socio/biological advantage would be for people to adopt counterproductive assumptions in response to setbacks. What is the evolutionary advantage of concluding that one is a loser, or doomed to loneliness in the wake of a lover's rejection?

Furthermore, positive thinking actually acts to discourage the suffering person from focusing on the thoughts and images associated with their loss. While this strategy may provide momentary relief (the way a favorite dessert might distract someone from the news of an IRS audit), the grief reaction is actually prolonged, since the curative process of exposure is interrupted, or aborted altogether.

Positive thinking may also limit learning from a loss so as to prevent future losses. In a *Newsweek* essay in August 1987, Julie Rose noted that after a miscarriage, many of her friends offered advice to help her get through the pain. "You can have another baby," one said. "The baby was too premature," noted another. Although this advice was intended to minimize the pain of the loss, Julie believed it did more harm than good. All of the advice seemed to imply was that she was overreacting, placing too much importance on the loss. She resented having the validity of her emotional reactions called into question.

What proved most effective for her was talking at length and in depth, again and again, about all aspects of her miscarriage. She reviewed the event from every perspective until the pain gradually subsided.

Positive thinking is useful in a situation like this only insofar as it encourages a hopeful outlook, and the replacement of morbid preoccupations with new, optimistic thoughts and activities.

In recent years positive thinking has been going out of favor. It is a simple solution to a complex problem, and most people are recognizing that. The method I will describe later in this chapter, by prolonging the focus on depressive thoughts, can facilitate the transition from one phase of life to the next, one circumstance or relationship to another. Failure to gain sufficient exposure leaves one mired in the past, weighed down by unprocessed negative experiences.

DEPRESSION—MY VIEW

Psychological depression is a naturally occurring process that evolved in response to the loss of a desirable person, place, or thing. A technically more accurate description is that depression results from a drop in the rate of gratification that we are accustomed to experiencing. Thus, we experience depressed feelings whenever we suffer a loss (the loss of a loved one, or of money, pride, opportunity, security, peace of mind, etc.) We are all accustomed to a certain level of gratification from our lives, which varies from person to person. Whenever we experience a loss, such as from a romantic rejection, the rate of gratification in our life dips, causing us to become depressed.

This type of depression seems to precipitate the following sequence of events:

1. Shortly after suffering a loss, the person experiences a physiologically based arousal response, which as noted earlier motivates them to either attempt to undo the loss, compensate for it, minimize it, or reduce its impact.

2. If the loss cannot be resolved, then the person continues to dwell on it, subjecting it to an intensive analysis that may uncover an adaptive means of dealing with it. In the event that truly nothing can be done, then they at least discover whatever lessons can be learned from the incident or incidents that brought about the loss.

3. As a last resort, the relentless rumination about the loss eventually dulls the emotional impact and desensitizes the person to the loss. It is interesting to note that while the process of repeatedly rehashing the loss weakens its emotional impact, it also acts to enhance our recollection or memory of the lost person or thing. This is especially important to survivors who want to resolve their suffering, but also hold on to the memory of the loved ones they have lost.

I encourage people to accept their ruminative thoughts of their lost loved ones, or whatever other loss may have triggered their depressive reaction. But I suggest that they structure their ruminative periods to maximize their effectiveness. At first, the emphasis should be on attempting to either find a replacement or consolation for the loss or otherwise mitigate its impact. Thereafter, the person should try to learn from the experience to minimize the likelihood of a recurrence.

And then, they should modify the way they think about the loss to maximize the effectiveness of the desensitization process. For example, a person could speed up the desensitization by increasing the intensity and duration of the ruminative periods or conversely, slow it down by spacing them more widely.

I have found that once people have an understanding of the nature and purpose of depression, they gain a sense of control and acceptance of the process that fosters recovery in a thoughtful and meaningful way.

THE DIFFERENCE BETWEEN DESENSITIZATION AND THE GRIEVING PROCESS

Grief often comes in spurts, and rolls in and out in waves, which can sometimes be very intense. The waves may be followed by two or three days during which the person feels somewhat better. These highs and lows can trigger poor judgment and bad responses, even suicidal reactions. This is because whatever mood you are in, your brain assumes it will be there forever—it draws a straight line way out into the future. So the person stricken with a deep depression from grief may think it's hopeless, and want to find some way out of it.

In any case, grief tends to be very hard on the individual, because the feelings come and go in such strong doses. They can be so intense that people seek to distract themselves from it, which causes the grief to go on and on.

> Grief is almost chaotic, as opposed to desensitization, which is scientifically structured and regulated. Desensitization is designed to be slow, gradual, and persistent. Thus it does not create the receptivity problems of grief, and is far more effective. It is carefully focused—a direct, steady stream, not too quick, not too slow, not too aggressive, not too passive.

Many of the problems of grief, desensitization takes care of, counteracts. Therapists can keep track of what's going on, measure your progress, and tell where you are having problems. They can separate out the anger or anxiety that tend to complicate matters, all of the complex interactions between the mind and brain that tend to make grief disorganized and ineffective. The anger calls attention to itself, but does nothing to help allay the grief.

A WORD OF CAUTION ABOUT
SELF-HELP FOR DEPRESSION

Exposure Therapy can be a big help with depression. My general rec-ommendation is to use self-help desensitization when depression is mild. Severe and even moderate depression are very hard to deal with on your own. Most people don't have the energy to do it. This type of desensitization does require some energy, as well as consistency and organizational skills.

A mild degree of depression shouldn't be uncomfortable or dan-gerous to desensitize on your own.

DEPRESSION VERSUS ANXIETY

It is rare to find one emotion in isolation. One of the purest examples of depression is grief over the loss of someone you love. This would cer-tainly seem to be clear-cut and uncomplicated. Yet mingled with this depression there is usually anxiety—worry about the future: How am I going to cope without this person; what is the future for me; how do others see me and my grief?

A saying that is frequently heard in clinics and classrooms is that depression is different from anxiety in that we become depressed about what has already happened, and anxious about what we think is going to happen. For example, a student on the way to an exam is anxious. If he fails the exam he is depressed.

This little adage is true as far as it goes and is useful as a guideline. But emotions, like people, are much too complex to be polished off so succinctly. In real life, the line between depression and anxiety is a very fine one and often difficult to find.

The symptoms of depression are, in many ways, the opposite of those of anxiety. When a lethargic and pessimistic person comes to me saying, "I'm not happy with my job. I don't like the life I'm leading, and I don't like my spouse," then it seems that the person is indeed depressed.

But then I'll learn more and find that the person is not happy with his job because there is a chance of being fired, and his lifestyle may be threatened in some other way, and his spouse may be at the point of running off with someone else—and what seemed like obvious depression begins to look more like anxiety.

Now this person will still be depressed, because the various situations do seem to involve losses, real or imagined, but there is also anxiety about failure and inadequacy.

Depression tends to make you passive and withdrawn, and if it were to exist without anxiety, it would leave you unmotivated. What makes you want to get rid of the pain is not depression but anxiety and worry.

Anxiety is nearly always recognized and acknowledged. It is so abrasive to the system that the body cannot tolerate it for long without taking steps to get rid of it. However, the body can accommodate itself to depression for years, and the symptoms of depression are frequently so subtle that they are not recognized by the person suffering them. This allows depressions to become ingrained and complex.

TREATING PSYCHOLOGICAL DEPRESSION

Here I will be talking about depressions precipitated by psychological conditions, in which a depression is related to a situation that involves some loss or change: loss of a loved one or a job, a change in status, or even a defeat in a tennis tournament—all can bring about depressive reactions ranging from passing to severe.

Carl, for example, was someone who had to seek help for his depression. When he came to me he was fifty-one years old. He was tall and very muscular, having worked as a logger for much of his life. Once, during one of our sessions, he picked up the couch in my office to prove his strength.

He was not hoisting couches the first day he came to the office, however; in fact, he couldn't stop crying. On the face of things he had a lot to cry about: he was deeply in debt, had marital difficulties, and had just been laid off—and these were only his most immediate problems.

He had been to a psychiatrist already, who had given him medication for his depression but not talked to him for any length of time. He was eager to tell someone about his childhood, which had indeed been rotten. His mother, who had been abandoned by his father, was a weak and ineffectual woman. She linked up with a series of loser men, who all took turns mistreating or ignoring Carl. The mother finally felt that she couldn't handle Carl, who was fighting all the time, so she placed him in a home for difficult children.

His life there had been a nightmare: he had been beaten, constantly medicated so he would be quiet, and had received no education. In fact, he would have lived his life out in state institutions if it had not been for a bizarre set of circumstances that managed to free him. While on a home visit he attacked one of his "stepfathers" so vigorously that he ended up in jail for two years. Carl was delighted. As he told me, "I was so happy, because that meant there was an end in sight. Before that I thought I'd have to spend my whole life behind bars."

After he was released he never again had any problems with the law, and he stayed out of institutions. He married, started working as a logger, and raised a family.

But over the next decades he suffered bouts of depression that kept growing more severe and requiring occasional hospitalization.

After talking to him for a little while, I realized that desensitization would be the most efficient method to use to relieve his symptoms. At the same time, I knew that because of the severity of his depression, he would be unable to sustain the strain of visualizing images for any length of time.

What I had Carl do was imagine situations and events that made him sad and depressed, and put himself into the images as best he could. He would do so, but he couldn't stand the trauma of the images for more than a few minutes at a time without crying or becoming almost paralyzed with depression. So we would change the subject and talk about something else for a while, and then go back to the same image and maybe take it a little further.

Moving at this rate, it took almost eight months to clear up his depression, a much longer time than desensitization usually takes, although a case like this would probably have been in traditional therapy much longer. But eventually his depression did clear up and Carl is functioning very well today. He uses the process on his own now when he faces emotional difficulties that threaten him.

Carl's depression was so severe that a clinician was helpful. Generally, if you are beset by mild depression, you can handle it on your own with desensitization. The steps for doing this are outlined later in this chapter, and in Chapters Four and Eleven.

A more typical instance of depression was the case of a very good-looking and well-groomed young man named Simon who came to me because "Things just aren't going well." Indeed they were not.

About year before seeing me he had been an affable, easygoing, yet ambitious man and quite successful in his work. He worked at a television station, and had been gradually treading his way up the ladder. He was finally told that his long-awaited chance at being a news anchor for the station had come. His manager and coworkers congratulated him, and Simon announced this to all of his friends and family. Then it just didn't happen. A flashy young woman from Atlanta ended up in the slot into which he was supposed to move.

He was shattered, humiliated, and angry. He began to brood on the injustice of the situation and developed rancor toward the executives involved. He also became more and more morose and lethargic, and was occasionally even incapable of action. He was, in short, depressed.

Unlike Carl, Simon had one specific cause for his depression, so it was easy enough to focus his treatment. I had him imagine how he felt when he knew he was going to get the coveted spot, then imagine being called into the office and being told that it was not going through. I had him imagine who was there, who had watched, how he and they had reacted, and whom he had told about his disappointment.

Then he stopped and repeated these images. After he had gone over the circumstances several times, I had him imagine going up to the head office and denouncing the executives, telling them they were insensitive hypocrites and double-dealers.

In a month his depression was pretty much cleared up. However, since he was still working at the station, and constantly seeing the people who from his point of view had shafted him, Simon's feelings of anger and depression were constantly being rekindled. It was a wound that refused to heal completely.

In order to counter this I had Simon use desensitization to extinguish his desire for the prestigious job that had been denied him, and even more, to achieve a kind of independence from his work. Many people derive their sense of well-being primarily from their occupation, and this can make a person's psychological well-being too dependent on the vagaries of the marketplace. So I had Simon work on concepts that would extinguish this reliance. I had him use desensitization to reduce his fears of looking for another job and for getting additional education and training. He used it to imagine job hunting, looking into other possibilities such as a part-time supplemental job so he wouldn't be so dependent on his main job. We also explored other possible areas in which he could find interesting employment and other sources of gratification to diversify his situation.

Because Simon's depression, with its attendant problems, was so clearly situational, he could very well have extinguished it on his own with desensitization. He did not necessarily need clinical help.

We all have a tendency to hold on to the status quo, unless it is unbearably painful, and nowhere is this more apparent than in someone who is suffering from depression. A depressed person may feel that the situation is hopeless and be determined that it remain so. In fact, one way of validating a depression is to have a therapist fail to root it out. So be aware of this: one of the earmarks of a depression is that frequently you don't really want it to go away. You are reluctant to go back into the arena and compete, and getting rid of a depression will mean that you have to return to situations that you originally found intolerable.

Another factor that frequently contributes to the staying power of depression is that it often brings secondary gains with it. One of my clients was a young man in his early twenties who withdrew from school and society and eventually just stayed home with his parents and watched television all day. His life became more and more constricted, until finally, when seen from the outside, it was grim indeed. But from his point of view it was not all that bad. He got up late, and did what he wanted all day. Nobody expected anything from him, and he had no commitments. These were, in fact, secondary gains that served to maintain and reinforce his depression.

When you have a difficult situation, it is only natural that you try to make the best of it. In its own topsy-turvy way a depression can give you a great deal. After a while you can adapt to it so well that it seems too much of a hassle to get well. These secondary gains are in part healthy adaptations that can bring some pleasure to you. There is no reason to feel guilty because you are able to create some little pockets of pleasure in a bad situation. On the contrary, recognize that there are some good things coming out of the depression. At the same time recognize that you will be much better off without it.

AIMING AT THE RIGHT TARGET

When using desensitization on a depression, or any emotion for that matter, be sure you focus your efforts in the proper direction. Following is the case of one of my clients who took it upon himself to extinguish all the wrong things, with bizarre consequences for him and his former girlfriend.

Dev was a young man who'd only been in this country for a few years. But having been raised in England, he spoke English very well. When he called and asked for an appointment, I told him I could see him the following week and asked if the matter would keep until then.

No, he said, it could not. His girlfriend had broken off their engagement and he just couldn't cope. He came by the next day.

He told me that his fiancée had just announced, out of the blue, that she didn't want to marry him. She returned his ring and added, for good measure, that she no longer wanted anything to do with him. When pressed, she said that there was no one else, but she had simply come to the conclusion that she didn't love him. Dev was devastated.

He began calling her two and three times a day, pleading with her, trying to change her mind. He would go over a whole litany of possible shortcomings on his part.

"Am I too aggressive?"

"No."

"Too passive?"

"No."

"Too dumb"

"No."

"Too ugly?"

"No."

In short, there seemed to be no particular reason for her breaking off their engagement. The woman had just decided that she didn't love him and that was that. Furthermore, after being barraged by phone calls for several weeks, she had grown to loathe the sound of his voice and would hang up the minute she recognized it. Dev was plunged into a painful depression.

In addition, he had become compulsive about making the phone calls—he could hardly bear to let an hour go by without making one more try. He would call, and if his ex-fiancée did not hang up immediately, he would beg her to come back, and frequently start crying. The woman would become furious and disgusted, scream at him to leave her alone, and slam the phone in his ear. This wouldn't deter him for long, however, because phoning her had become an obsession. Then he began stopping by her house, which only made her angrier.

Dev saw me about this problem at first and I worked on desensitizing both the positive and negative aspects of their relationship. He then decided to continue on with desensitization himself, just focusing on the negative, including his repeated attempts to see the woman since she left him. This only made him more brazen, since he managed to desensitize his fears of further annoying her and also of her calling the police on him. When this approach failed he returned to me and I again helped him desensitize *both* sides of their relationship.

In a situation like this I always desensitize both sides, not just one, although logically it does appear as if desensitizing one side alone might work. But it is confusing to do, and tends to backfire.

> In order to cure the depression from his loss, Dev had to extinguish his positive feelings for his lover. No matter how paradoxical it seems, dwelling on the fine qualities he had lost in a mate is what finally extinguished his grief.

BECOMING AWARE OF HIDDEN DEPRESSIONS

Another point I can't emphasize too much is that when you are depressed you may not be aware of the fact. Many therapists say that the most difficult condition to diagnose in themselves is depression. I can speak about this from my own experience.

When I was still in graduate school I was told that depressions were not at all unusual among people who had just received their degrees. I found this hard to believe. I'd been going to school just about all my life, and I couldn't imagine feeling anything but release and euphoria upon finally getting out. Then suddenly I graduated, my wife and I moved to a new town, and I had a new job.

On the surface everything was splendid. I was happily married, I had an excellent job, and I had the precious degree I had worked years to get. As they say, my whole life was before me. For months I kept reminding myself of my good fortune, and ignored the nagging feeling of despair that was lodged in the back of my brain.

It was true that my circumstances were auspicious—but things were much different after I graduated. As a student I was always hearing that I had done well and got constant feedback about myself. That stopped when I started teaching and seeing clients. Now I was telling others they were doing well, but nobody was patting me on the back. My wife and I had moved to a pretty town (though it was not nearly as nice as the campus we had left) and had found a pleasant enough apartment, but compared to the little house we had lived in at school it was cramped and dingy. We lost all of our friends in one move, and even our dog. We had, in fact, lost a whole lifestyle.

Yet I couldn't admit I was depressed because after all, I had what I had always wanted. Then a friend from the university came to visit us one weekend, and as we sat talking into the night, he kept repeating how lucky I was, and how I really had it made. I kept agreeing with him, but with an ever more oppressive feeling that things just weren't right. The day after he left I understood that I was depressed and had been depressed for several months.

I took inventory of my situation then and realized that I did have a lot to be grateful for, but at the same time I had lost a whole way of life I had found exceedingly congenial. To complicate matters, I could have returned to the campus and found work there, but the opportunities would have been far fewer and less enticing than those in my present location. So I decided that I did want to stay where I was, and having recognized that I had a depression I began to treat it with desensitization.

First, I imagined all the things about the university I liked—I saw myself on the beautiful campus, being praised, getting good grades, attending lectures, going to exams, meeting with friends, going to parties, going out in the evenings with my wife, and having friends over to our house. In short, I imagined all of the positive things that happened to me while I was a student. At least once a day, every day, I would take about ten minutes or so to go through a series of images of things I knew well and loved about the life I had left.

Then I went a step further by imagining that I was running committee meetings at the university, and was a popular lecturer on the campus. I was constantly surrounded by friends and admirers, and my wife and I were always being entertained by both students and faculty. I used more images to aggrandize the possibilities at the university.

When I began using desensitization on it my depression was about eight months old. After a month I felt the major effect of the technique, and the depression had pretty much been relieved. I continued using the process intermittently whenever I felt a twinge of pessimism or lethargy. And in another month the depression was completely wiped out.

Since it is easy to be blind to a depression even in yourself, you might want to be alert to these general characteristics: The depressed person slows down, thinks and moves apathetically. He feels sad, often loses his appetite, and has trouble sleeping. He may also lose some of his sex drive and begin to show a great deal of pessimism and cynicism.

If you are suffering any one of these characteristics, that is not necessarily a sign of depression. If you are suffering several of them, you might want to take a closer look at yourself.

THERAPY FOR THE DEPRESSED PERSON

Depression is hard to treat in a therapist's office because it is often not too productive a process.

To begin with, chronically depressed people often don't recognize their condition—it's become part of their personality or makeup. It intertwines itself into all of their values and thoughts, which gradually change. All of these changes are essentially trying to help the brain to do less work, as mentioned earlier. Depressive habits and ways of thinking become such a part of the depressed person's lifestyle that they don't see this as anything that even needs to be treated.

Often it seems as if not much is going to change this. Their friends adapt to their downer attitude, and are not necessarily too thrown by it. The person accepts it as well and eventually learns to live with it. And the people around him learn to deal with and around it.

When the depression finally lifts, and it usually does, is when they notice the difference. So now they may go for treatment the next time they get depressed.

How do you deal with a person who is depressed in therapy? A depressed person, as noted elsewhere, has little mental energy. Getting along with him or her is like getting along with a person who doesn't have much money. You don't want to put them in a situation where they have to spend a lot of money...or energy. You want to arrange things so that there is little need for that.

Since conversations with most other people usually take much more energy than talking to me does, a depressed person comes to see me because I am a low-pressure, low-stress sounding board for them. Nothing of what I do will cost them much in the way of energy. For example, I'm not going to ask questions, because questions take a lot of energy to answer and are a strain on the brain. Most of the time a depressed person is pretty negative and pessimistic. If you ask them what they want or how they feel, they are likely to give you an answer that even they don't like.

"Did you like the movie you went to?" Chances are they didn't like it, but they may not want to get into it, because they don't want to bum everyone out. They may just go along and say, "It was okay," and when you hear this you know that they just don't want to expend enough energy to really answer your question.

If you push them, it's like pushing a poor person to spend money. Eventually you will get a negative reaction from them, and that will just set things back, and it will take even more energy to rectify things.

When dealing with a depressed person, you can't ask too many questions because this creates work for the brain. You also can't suggest too many things—that they do this or that, such as join a club or take up a new activity. All of these things call for energy or effort on their part.

I make statements instead. Instead of asking, "What time is it?" so the person has to fumble around, I would probably just remark: "It seems late." Rather than "How are you?" I say, "You look good." Or, "I heard that you're moving to California. You know, If you guys are thinking of moving to California and doing it soon, I'd like be interested in hearing about that when you get a chance, when you feel up to it."

Again, I'm deliberately putting them in control so that they can decide how much energy they want to spend on a response. They don't have to keep up with my level of energy. This is the same thing I would do with a person I know has little money. I might say, "I'm getting kind of hungry. I'm not sure where we should go. Maybe eat home. But I'd like to eat before too long."

Then the person can say they want to go to that trendy new place at $500 a plate, or would rather stay home and eat hamburgers. He is in control, and can regulate his response.

If you talk to a depressed person like this, the person will feel more and more comfortable with you because they are constantly in charge. There is no social pressure to do things they don't want to do or can't afford to do. They also don't have to keep trying to keep up with your level of energy—they can decide what they want to do and when they want to do it.

Another thing to consider when talking with a depressed person is that they don't want to talk about happy things much. What they really want you to do is commiserate with them.

They might say, for example, that they went on vacation and it was just horrible. "The weather was terrible and the food awful and the service worse. I can't believe they allow people to run a resort that way."

They don't want to hear suggestions from you like, "Did you think of talking to the manager, or filing a complaint, or maybe suing them?" That would be too much work and energy for them.

What they want to hear from you is something like, "Yeah, I can understand that. Sometimes these vacations go south and it's a shame because we wait all year for them, and then some jerk at the hotel ruins the whole experience."

When they tell you a story in which bad things happen, what they want to hear is something like, "I can agree with that—I had an accident, too, and the insurance company was an incredible problem. They did everything they could to get out of it, and the lawyers were even worse. They didn't return calls or even seem to understand the case. Your life is hanging in the balance and the person who is supposed to be your voice, your advocate, is not very helpful. I know this happens and it's hard to deal with it."

Accidents, illnesses, problems with lawyers—these are experiences they routinely have and that make them unhappy. They don't want you to take the opposite view and make constructive suggestions. "That doesn't sound so bad. You can do this or do that." They don't want you telling them they need to change their attitude or their point of view.

They want you to agree with them, indicate that they are right about a lot of this, and that their perspective is not always wrong. They don't like anyone to oppose them directly: "No, that's a ridiculous point of view and you should never say that!"

Therapists who favor positive thinking often attack every one of a depressed person's views as being too pessimistic, too skeptical, too cynical. This is like talking to someone who is forever taking the devil's advocate position. A depressed person will never be comfortable talking to someone like this.

When you talk to someone, they like to hear a certain degree of consensus. If they don't get it, they won't talk to you for long. This is even more the case with the depressed.

> When you're depressed you do a lot of thinking. And most of what you come up with it seems logical and sensible. You lost your job, so you have no money, problems with the landlord and other creditors, and your wife and kids.
>
> Are you thinking negatively, or are these things true? They seem true, and may well be.
>
> But everyone else seems to tell you that what you are thinking is *not* true. They all say things like "The situation is not that bad, look on the bright side. All you have to do is_____."
>
> Everyone is telling them to think positive, keep trying, and they just have one failure after another. They feel like a fighter who gets roughed up badly in the ring, and his manager is telling him to go out there and punch his opponent in the stomach. But when he goes back in he keeps getting hit on the head. They get discouraged, feel like idiots. They get to the point that they don't want to talk to their friends any more.

Keeping all of this in mind while trying to make progress is difficult. Since you can't make suggestions or ask questions, you may eventually end up with long silences, which are hard on a depressive. If there are too many of these, they may drop out of therapy. So I try to keep the sessions somewhat lively, within all of these limitations and restrictions.

TREATING THE DEPRESSION/ANGER MIX

The brain deals very efficiently with grief: if you lose a friend, job, or whatever, in three, six, or nine months you have usually largely recovered. The brain's grief response, dwelling on the loss until it eventually loses its ability to upset you, works well for pure loss. The brain grinds it down and desensitizes it away.

> It would seem that grief is no different from most other depressions, but the brain doesn't do as well with other depressions. Why does the grief response work for some depressions and not others?
>
> Other grief responses are usually impeded, usually by anger. Anger is a hidden agenda here. Sometimes a person has other motivations that make him want to hold on to his depression as well, such as a desire for sympathy.
>
> You need to clear out the things that keep the brain from doing its job.

One of the most significant contributions I have made to the treatment of depression is the discovery that one of the reasons depression is so resistant to treatment is because most therapists end up not treating the depression itself but rather the anger that is often associated with it.

As noted earlier, anger is very resistant to desensitization. If you listen to a song over and over again, your emotional response to that song will lessen, and eventually cease. Most situations, if you repeatedly expose yourself to them, your emotional response to them eventually will become extinguished. Anger is one of the few emotions (the other is affection) that does not desensitize easily with repeated exposure.

Depression is often accompanied by anger because depression is usually caused by a loss of a person or thing. The primary cause of anger is the perception that one has experienced a loss unfairly. Often, but certainly not always, that loss is at the hands of another individual. For example, if someone promises to pay you back for a loss that you incurred as a result of their negligence, but then doesn't, that would make you angry.

Then people focus on the anger, which doesn't desensitize, while ignoring the depression, which would desensitize if it were processed.

When grief and anger coexist, the tendency is to focus on the circumstances related to the anger. For example, when one of my clients was cheated out of a good deal of money, he was preoccupied with seeking justice and thereby spent very little time grieving his loss of money. He even mentioned that he was not very concerned about his financial loss itself. He was mostly interested in getting back at those he felt had stolen from him.

In another case I was acquainted with, two people were in a car crash while driving to work on a day when every road was ice-covered. They were badly injured, and lost their jobs as well because of the accident. Afterward, they were mostly concerned with getting back at the employer who fired them.

During grief that is uncomplicated by anger, the continued exposure to the loss through rumination over time will desensitize the depressed feelings. But when grief is accompanied by anger—as toward a person who was drunk when they caused the loss of a loved one's life—the anger generated by the unfairness of the incident grabs our attention and we focus on that, more so than on the loss per se.

By dwelling on their anger, the person ignores the depressive material. The anger distracts them from the depressive material, serving as an avoidance response. Avoidance responses interfere with a person's exposure to whatever it is that they fear. People who are afraid of planes or spiders typically avoid them. In the process their avoidance perpetuates their fears.

In a case like this you need to work on separating the depression from the anger. If you can change the person's focus so that they concentrate on the depressive material instead, they will do a great deal to reduce their depression. By focusing on the anger, since it is so resistant to desensitization, they will not accomplish very much at all.

Q. Why do some women who have lost their spouse want to go to the prison where their spouse's killer now resides and forgive him? Why is this recommended by many therapists to get rid of their anger?

A. People who are depressed and also angry at the person who is responsible for their loss—such as a drunk driver—ultimately come to realize that being angry at the culprit does more harm to them than it does to the person they are angry at. Therapists, religious leaders, and those who treat people who are depressed have recognized this phenomenon for many years. Forgiveness helps the forgiver as much or more than the one he or she forgives. The reason is that forgiveness resolves the anger, or at least changes the person's perspective from focusing on the culprit to focusing on themselves.

If someone close to you is showing a mix of anger and depression, this is what I suggest: If the person gets angry at you, gets into an argument, say that you understand their point, but not why they need to get so angry. Focus on the word angry or something similar. The next time they blow up over some minor matter that could have been discussed civilly, again, focus on the anger. Say something like, "I can see that, I can make that change, but why do you have to get so angry?"

A depressive wants to get things done in a sense without having to pay for them. They get upset, want you to do this and that, and then they will no longer be upset. This is your reward. You don't want to reward them for not being angry. Don't go along with this or it will become an endless game.

Say, "I will do what you want, if it seems fair and reasonable, but the price of that is that you have to give up your anger and treat me more civilly."

After you tell them things like this several times, they will become somewhat sensitized to the issue and try not to get angry. You may say, "Are you going to start getting angry again?" And they will reply, "I'm not angry, I'm just mentioning that I want you to...."

This works rather well. Eventually they become so attuned to your ability to call them on their anger they won't even start to get nasty with you.

The problem is that at this point many people start to feel guilty for using this technique and stop bringing up the anger. They may even tell the person they are stopping, that they are giving this up. And the depressive person then goes right back to the same old pattern they used in the past. They get angry and expect you to do what they want.

If it is necessary to call someone on their anger like this, you have to keep it up, insist that they suppress their anger and act civilly.

CHAPTER ELEVEN

RECOVERING FROM LOSSES

Each year, millions of Americans lose a member of their immediate family, hundreds of thousands of men and women are widowed, and about half a million children die before the age of twenty-five. Not only death, but divorce, separation, and geographic relocation are often painful, disabling experiences.

Suffering a loss is what usually triggers a psychologically based depression. The loss can be of an individual, say a close relative, a relationship, an animal, even an object such as a favorite watch. The severity of the depression is directly related to the magnitude of the loss.

Loss is as much a part of our emotional repertoire as love. In the loss of a loved one, a relationship, a job, or some treasured object, we are wrenched from the people, places, and things we value. Yet we are so poorly prepared for this that we are unable to heal effectively: the natural healing process is slow, agonizing, and often incomplete.

People are usually well aware of the major losses in their lives. The man who lost his arm, the woman who lost her spouse, the executive who lost his job— they are all aware of the sudden changes in their emotional state and the causes thereof. But a loss can also be something such as the loss of pride, a reputation, or of the ability to look forward to a future pleasurable event, such as a wedding.

When the losses are not as obvious, such as in the case of those who leave an area they have long inhabited, or the letdown someone may feel after overcoming an extraordinary challenge, the change in mood and prospects is more subtle, and the losses in these circumstances are hidden, hence the difficulty in recognizing that there has even been a negative occurrence.

With more serious losses, we may remain in desperate pain, inconsolable and unreachable, wanting to move beyond the painful mourning that follows the loss, yet inexplicably stuck in a pattern in which everything reminds us of it.

In many cases, the reaction to loss may be more than withdrawal or emotional pain. A broken heart may be more than metaphoric: "Psychologically broken hearts often cause medically broken hearts," noted Dr. John Lynch of the Johns Hopkins University Hospital. Suicide prevention centers across the country report that close to eighty percent of their cases involve suicidal despair over the loss of a loved one. In some cultures, elderly persons don't survive the loss of a spouse for more than a month or two.

Some people, such as chronic depressives, are much more loss-averse than others. Women in general are more affected by losses, especially of relationships or people. Because women have a high attachment quotient, such losses hit them harder. You see this especially with the loss of a child—almost invariably the man is affected less. If his wife has a miscarriage, a man might say she can just get pregnant again. A woman would never think in those terms. Men, on the other hand, are more affected by job-related things. If a man walks in the door, I assume he has come to see him about anxiety or threats. If it is a woman, losses.

For many who suffer a grave loss, there seems to be no relief from the pain, and often they don't know where to turn. Well-meaning friends may discourage the grieving from discussing their feelings, in the mistaken belief that it is better to avoid or deny what is so clearly painful. Many people, confused and alarmed by the power of their pain, are ashamed to admit their "weakness," thus unwilling to seek professional treatment. The elderly are particularly vulnerable to this, and often are the least equipped psychologically to cope with their sorrow.

Some clinicians prescribe medication for people whose suffering seems particularly acute. With the reduction in anguish afforded by antidepressant medication, however, comes a disincentive to talk or even think about the loss. As a result, the crucial process of exposure is compromised. In addition, the "lessons of loss" are not learned, thereby increasing the risk of recurrences, such as for those who have been unsuccessful in sustaining intimate relationships or jobs. Rejected lovers, particularly, have much to learn from understanding what transpired.

The loss response is a normal and inevitable reaction to real events in our lives. Those who feel this response are not sick or crazy, but normal people who are experiencing the pain of loss. As Dr. Ann Kaiser Sterns observed in the national bestseller *Living Through a Personal Crisis Following a Loss*:

> "You will probably think of yourself and your loss more than you think of anything else. This is not illness, nor is it an indication of weakness or selfishness. It is simply human adjustment in the face of a loss. The greater your loss, the more likely and the longer you are to be preoccupied with your own feelings."

Although the loss response is normal, often our behaviors when we are suffering from the loss response are "dysfunctional." We may alienate our friends or other loved ones, perform poorly in our jobs, ignore opportunities for advancement, and generally experience a greatly diminished quality of life.

Loss response is associated with feelings of sadness, pessimism, negativity, hopelessness, despair, indecision, helplessness, powerlessness, anger towards others as well as oneself, low self-esteem, and even suicidal thoughts.

It can also include physiological symptoms such as chronic fatigue, poor appetite, sleeplessness, reduced sex drive, inability to concentrate, sporadic and seemingly spontaneous crying, and a decreased tolerance for frustration.

When we experience loss, our minds react out of anxiety, pain, and fear to try and find ways to cope with the situation. The common psychological responses to loss include:

- Reversal: in which we try to reverse the loss, such as by resolving a dispute with a loved one who is threatening to leave, or a frantic search for a lost object.

- Compensation: When the loss cannot be undone, we will often try to compensate for it, as with couples who immediately attempt to have another child following a miscarriage, or a person who files a lawsuit after a debilitating accident.

- Grief suppression: Keeping a stiff upper lip and not allowing the pain to show through.

- Grief minimization: Attempting to ease the pain by making light of the adversity.

People suffering from loss response are plagued by thoughts of the loved one. One woman who lost her husband told me, "It just comes over me like waves. I can't stop thinking about him. Losing him was horrible, but this incessant thinking about him is driving me crazy. If only I could get my mind off him."

This woman tried to get her mind off her late husband by distracting herself, another mental strategy for dealing with painful loss. She would call a friend, turn on the television and stare at sit-coms she ordinarily never watched, or overdo housework like scrubbing the kitchen floor, washing windows, and rinsing and re-rinsing glasses. This woman's response was psychologically normal, and indicated that her mind was in gear trying to resolve the loss.

I've seen many clients with such problems. Namely, an often irreversible tragedy that the mind can't accept or resolve. For example, a woman who had lost her son in the crash of a small plane challenged me to find a reason or explanation for why it happened. And why years later she still had made no progress in her search for closure. Another man wondered why his golden child committed suicide. The young man had everything to live for—he was intelligent, had a good job, sharp social skills, and a very supportive and attractive girlfriend. Why would someone who had all of this want to end it all?

After the tragedy, these people found that they couldn't stop thinking about it, and this was very painful. Why did they have to suffer through the endless recollections of what happened to them?

In order to answer this, one has to understand how the brain processes these experiences.

DOES TIME HEAL ALL WOUNDS?

We all know the adage: Time heals all wounds. But waiting is often excruciating and interminable. Isn't there any way of speeding up the grieving process? Can we control our own healing process in some way that will allow us to get over losses more quickly?

Exposure Therapy is a liberating psychological technique that allows people to successfully overcome the losses that punctuate their lives—rapidly and completely. It will work on everything from everyday setbacks to such pivotal events as the loss of a loved one. It can help you understand, confront, and overcome the pain of loss through the application of some fundamental psychological principles and self-administered therapeutic techniques.

Exposure Therapy—desensitization—is a uniquely powerful intervention for overcoming loss, based on widely accepted research findings in the behavioral and social sciences, and my own more than forty years of clinical experience. The result is an easy-to-follow and accessible step-by-step technique for people in pain.

Often, the psychological community pays little attention to the psychological response to loss because emotional pain, anguish, and despair are considered normal reactions, not a pathological condition requiring treatment. Many psychologists and psychiatrists claim that there is no reason to treat grieving people, since they will get better in time anyway. Many counsel the acceptance of this distress, suggesting that life goes on and that normal grieving, the "common cold of mental afflictions," should be treated just like the common cold: with plenty of rest and patience.

As a result, millions of people who experience the pain of loss are relegated to just "waiting it out." What they most often hear are the platitudes: "Time heals all wounds," "Keep your chin up," and "Let Nature take its course." But time, in and of itself, heals no wounds. People who have suffered a grave loss frequently report no easing of their suffering months, even years or decades later. Unbeknownst to them, their grieving has not proceeded normally—that is, they have not been able to extinguish their pain by the gradual, repeated exposure to distressing thoughts and images that is at the heart of the curative process.

Research in recent years into the nature of grief reveals that time alone does not heal. The resolution of grief, the gradual reduction in emotional pain associated with loss, is in fact the result of the mind's repeatedly summoning up and focusing on the thoughts and images associated with the loss. By dwelling on the lost loved one, opportunity, or object, the mind gradually extinguishes emotional pain, the same way that obsessing about anything eventually dulls its impact. There are only a handful of clearly established, definitive laws in psychology, and prominent among these is the Law of Extinction. Applied to loss, this law states that the emotional reaction to a loss is gradually and permanently eliminated (extinguished) by repeatedly focusing on the thoughts and images associated with it.

It is precisely this exposure to emotionally laden material that is the active ingredient in time's potential to heal. The passage of time itself, filled as it often is with all manner of activities, will do little in the way of grief reduction without this exposure.

Exposure Therapy is designed specifically to treat the grief reaction. It is designed to help us cope with the immediate pain of loss through a carefully monitored technique of controlled exposure that will drastically reduce the time it takes to heal.

THE THEORY BEHIND EXPOSURE THERAPY

Following a loss, the mind is beset with images and thoughts about the departed loved one, the money irretrievably dissipated, the leg that has been paralyzed.

There are compelling reasons for the mind's reaction:

1. Thinking about a loss enhances the likelihood of finding the best means of adaptation. Alternative strategies, such as refusing to think about it, can hardly be expected to generate means of undoing the loss, compensating for it, or finding substitute satisfactions.

2. From an evolutionary standpoint, attachments to others as well as objects are crucial to the survival of the species. People cannot survive alone. There is a powerful need to thoroughly explore every conceivable means of reestablishing attachments, or barring this, of making do without them.

3. By repeatedly thinking about a loss, we learn from experience, knowledge crucial to our survival as it serves to prevent recurrences and fosters ways of maintaining and strengthening remaining attachments.

4. Thinking about a loss actually increases retention of the lost person or object. Repetition enhances memory, which is a way of holding on to a person or object in a positive way.

5. Thinking about a loss gradually extinguishes the pain associated with it, which is especially important when there proves to be no adequate way to replace what has been lost.

The mind reacts inexorably to a loss by besieging the affected individual with recollections of the face of the loved one who is gone, his favorite chair, the time you and she were out rowing, her voice when happily surprised. But—and this is critical—the pattern of thinking about a loss involves waxing and waning, in which avoidance tendencies driven by the need for short-term relief interrupt focusing. As a result, the mind achieves only minimal, episodic, partial exposure to the thoughts or images necessary to overcome grief. Yet there is no reason this process of exposure to the loss cannot be harnessed, controlled so that healing can take place expeditiously, with the least amount of emotional or psychological damage accompanying it. This is what Exposure Therapy accomplishes by seizing the active ingredient in time that does heal—exposure—and subjecting it to scientific application.

Exposure Therapy allows you to control the healing process by systematically focusing on thoughts of the loss for specific periods of time. This gives you control over your own process of grief, and therefore a feeling of control over your life, even while you are feeling bereft from loss.

Exposure Therapy targets the loss—teaching skills that enable the person to better handle the pain that life will invariably bring. It is easily mastered by the use of several simple techniques, and does not require professional assistance.

TYPES OF EXPOSURE

I was involved in the psychological treatment of a woman who had recently been mugged. The police had asked her to accompany them back to the scene to search for clues, so she was forced to confront the circumstances associated with this trauma. Yet she experienced little if any exposure; mere proximity does not necessarily help a person to work through their trauma. On the contrary, in the absence of careful guidance and monitoring, the police action might easily have provoked an avoidance reaction. My patient dutifully accompanied the police, but she refused to process what was happening emotionally. Instead, she maintained a steady state of distraction the whole time she was there. Gaining exposure to the material pertinent to a loss requires a gradual, progressive approach so that avoidance tendencies are not inadvertently triggered.

Although actual exposure to a lost person or object is more intense than exposure achieved in imagery, the latter has the advantage of being more flexible, especially in situations where actual exposure is not possible. Gradual exposure is not as fast-acting as intense exposure in extinguishing an emotional response, but if the exposure is too intense, it will impair receptivity and provoke avoidance tendencies. Other factors, such as the frequency and duration of exposure, also have a bearing on receptivity as well as the effectiveness of Exposure Therapy.

AN IDEAL SELF-HELP METHOD

The essential aspect of exposure is that the person experience the thoughts or images emotionally and that the process not be followed by a traumatic event. Talking to a friend or therapist is usually sufficient to engender some exposure, but there are times when we are reluctant to express our emotions to others. Fortunately, exposure does not require a listener, although listeners tend to facilitate the process. Exposure Therapy is ideal as a self-help technique in this regard.

THE ROLE OF IMAGERY

As noted earlier, the same neural pathways in the brain used to experience and communicate information during actual exposure to events are used during imagery. Whether we speak to a friend or travel through the Rockies in actuality or imagery, the same processing mechanisms are used. Imagery allows one to manipulate and arrange events precisely as needed to derive optimal exposure, which is why it is so helpful in dealing with losses, which often cannot be confronted directly.

Consistent with the generally accepted findings, I have found in my own research and experience that people usually require about three or four years to get over the loss of a spouse late in life, about one year for the loss of a parent or sibling, and three months for a treasured object. In extreme circumstances such as the loss of a child or very close spouse, it may take longer than this before the person is back to their previous level of functioning.

These are, of course, only averages and they do not speak precisely to the matter of what it takes to get over someone. It is also the case, however, that only a tiny fraction of time during these recovery periods is spent focusing on the loss—less than one percent, I have found.

A major reason it often takes so long to get over the grief of losing a spouse late in life is because this loss involves so many other losses—the loss of friends, help at home and elsewhere, shared activities, income, and so on.

The loss of a child also carries over to other areas of a person's life. They lose not just the pleasure of the child's company and support in later years, but the legacy they represented, vicarious pride in their accomplishments, the sharing of their victories and difficulties, the children's friends, the parents of those friends, even loss of confidence in their parenting.

My clinical experience, again affirmed by the clinical literature, suggests that merely by encouraging the person to focus on the loss for discrete intervals of five or ten minutes twice a day, healing time can be significantly reduced. People can readily be taught to concentrate a year's worth of exposure into four to six weeks. The overall time spent thinking about the loss is roughly the same, but the person's grief is resolved in a fraction of the time, thereby minimizing the deleterious effects of lost opportunities and other complications that commonly occur when grief persists.

Unlike psychotherapy, which can be a long and drawn out process, Exposure Therapy can deliver emotional relief in a fraction of the time and at virtually no cost.

I have also found that patients who have learned through exposure to overcome their emotional pain are freer to take risks, such as by getting involved in new relationships. When grief resolution occurs in a shorter time, the individual will be more fully functional a year later than another who has needed all that time simply to begin to get back on his feet.

PREPARING FOR EXPOSURE THERAPY

Preparing for effective sessions of desensitization to treat losses usually involves the following when I conduct them myself:

1. First comes a discussion of the circumstances and nature of the loss in great detail, looking at and reviewing the loss from every perspective, including what led up to the loss, the effects the loss has had, the nature of the attachment to the lost person or object, the things the person did and didn't do to prevent the loss from occurring, etc.

2. Now we need to determine significant themes: What does the person's mind spontaneously think about, which thoughts recur, which cause the most difficulty, which are most frightening, embarrassing, distressing, and so on.

3. Then I explain the nature of grief to the person, whereby his or her mind is drawn to particular thoughts and images related to the loss in an attempt to resolve them, and in the process,

extinguish the emotional pain that accompanies them. The crucial point to highlight is that most losses can never be fully resolved or compensated for and that intellectually based strategies for adapting often come to an impasse. For example, a spouse may find that she has done all she can to restructure her life after her husband's death, and yet she is still besieged by thoughts of missing him.

What follows now is systematic exposure to the troubling thoughts related to the loss with consequent extinguishing of the pain.

THE FIVE STEPS OF DESENSITIZATION

As described earlier, a five-step self-help procedure will help the individual to maximize exposure.

Step 1: Education: A review of the research on the effectiveness of Exposure Therapy, from my own descriptions in this book or the articles listed in Appendix II.

Step 2: Relaxation involves creating a proper setting to achieve concentration. This may involve no more than finding a comfortable chair where you can sit without distractions for at least ten minutes.

Step 3: Imagination involves summoning up images of the lost loved one, situation, or object. This includes attempting to recall as many details about specific events as possible, as well as the qualities of the lost person or object that you miss most. Do this for regular periods of five to ten minutes twice a day.

When you focus on the images, make this a slow, gradual, process. Just allow the thoughts to sit by your side, be next to you for a while. Don't push them on yourself or try to block them out, either— just let them sit beside you so that they stay in your mind long enough for the brain to desensitize them in a gradual, safe way. Give the brain the time to think about the material without focusing on it too intensely. Let your mind regulate the grief, thinking about it in a relaxed, easy manner, just letting it wash over you gently.

Step 4: Repetition is learning to hold your focus on the images and summon them repeatedly until they begin to lose their emotional power. As you repeat the guided imagery of Step 3, holding on to the painful images for longer periods of time, their intensity begins to diminish.

Step 5: Relaxation is the point at which you will return to a relaxed state by thinking about some unrelated, pleasant scene and immersing yourself in it.

In this way, with regular exposures of twenty minutes a day, someone can experience as much therapeutic exposure in a week as would ordinarily be achieved in months of spontaneous recovery.

The longer and more often one thinks about specific highly troubling aspects of a loss, the greater the relief. The same is true for images that are progressively more vivid and intense, the development of which can be taught (and measured) with a high degree of precision. Exposure is expanded within the limits of the person's capacity, until highly charged themes lose their power.

By way of illustration

The woman who lost her spouse was instructed that each time she thought about him, she must resist the urge to divert her attention, as she had been doing in an effort to reduce the hurt. Instead, I encouraged her to allow her thoughts and images to proceed unchecked, to immerse herself in them for a little while: "Let yourself think about what you would have been doing today if he were alive. Discuss your concerns with him as if he were there. Imagine what you would have done with him if…" These enjoinders reflect the thrust of this process, leading into a prolongation of the exposure for up to five to ten minutes at a time. (Longer if this can be accomplished without undue upset.)

Then I told her to expand her thoughts about her husband anytime she found herself thinking about him at all. The overall duration of exposure, time spent in concentrated thought about the loss, will have been dramatically increased in this fashion, so that the person will have spent as much time thinking about the lost person or object in say a week, as would normally be done in months.

BENEFITS OF TREATMENT

The benefits of this strategy are enormous and quickly realized. They include the following:

1. Instead of being subjected to the spontaneous occurrence of thoughts about the loss, now the person initiates them, giving them a powerful sense of control.

2. The speed of extinction (reduction of the emotional reaction to the loss over time) is dramatically increased.

3. The person will have a new understanding as to why his or her mind has been summoning up thoughts about the loss, and in turn, will feel less at odds with the process. He will comprehend the essence of "grief work," and will get to it, efficiently and effectively, with greater appreciation and respect for the process and less bewilderment and resentment.

4. By taking control of the mind's need to focus on the loss, the person can structure periods of contemplation into discrete time slots at his convenience, and at a self-regulated frequency and intensity suited to his needs.

SOME OF THE GRIEVING PEOPLE IN MY PRACTICE AIDED BY EXPOSURE THERAPY

- A middle-aged woman who was childless and had been told by her physician that she was now unable to conceive. Prior to Exposure Therapy, she would have become sullen and withdrawn, and begin to cry each time she passed a woman with a baby in a stroller on the street.

- A fifty-five-year-old man who retired early from his own cleaning and maintenance company. After several months of puttering around the house, he felt unaccountably depressed. After years of giving orders on the job, he felt at a loss. Exposure Therapy enabled him to become free to appreciate the stage of life he had arrived at by working through the loss of what had come before.

- A young mother whose infant was stillborn. Obsessed with thoughts and images of the child, she felt isolated and withdrawn. Her son was angry because "She couldn't get over it," and her husband was frustrated because he wanted to have another child. Her friends tried to distract her with hobbies, to help her "get her mind off it."

- A middle-aged man whose teenage daughter committed suicide. He was haunted by images of driving up to their suburban home and seeing all of the police cars and neighbors, and then seeing his daughter lying lifeless on her bed.

- A woman who lost her wedding ring a few weeks before her fiftieth wedding anniversary. She became so obsessed with finding the ring that she was unable to sleep or eat. She turned the house upside down looking, and compulsively retraced her steps during the days preceding the discovery of the loss, over and over.

- A young man who was laid off from his prestigious and well-paying position in a real estate management company after a major downturn of the real estate market. Accustomed to the wealth and power of his position, he was overwhelmed by a sense of inadequacy and found it difficult to motivate himself to look for a new job.

- A teenager adopted at birth who began to feel a painful yearning to meet her biological mother, who was living in another state and experiencing similar yearnings, which she kept secret from her new family. On her daughter's birthday, this mother was given to sitting alone in a darkened room, smoking cigarettes, eating junk food, and crying.

These cases illustrate the wide range of people who suffer from losses. Two further cases more fully illustrate the therapeutic procedure used with all of these people.

A LOST LOVE

George displayed all of the classic symptoms of loss response. He felt tired all the time, but had trouble sleeping. He had no appetite. His friends complained that he never wanted to do anything with them anymore. He couldn't even muster up the interest to watch television.

A strong-featured and mannerly middle-aged man, George had been a state senator for many years. His ready smile and quick quips reflected the skills that got him where he was. But inside there was only emptiness. He was spinning in a downward spiral of distress and self-hatred, avoiding his friends. By our third therapy session, he revealed himself to be at the edge of desperation.

Almost a year had passed since his wife confessed that a long-simmering affair with a colleague at work had become a full-blown romance, and she asked him to leave the home they shared with their children. George moved in with a friend, but continued to hope that things would eventually work out. He did everything he could think of to win his wife back, lavishing gifts on her and offering trips to places she'd always wanted to go. Then he began to call her frequently, "Just to see how she was doing." He persuaded his wife to see a marriage counselor with him, but when they did, after a number of sessions they seemed to get nowhere.

George consulted a psychiatrist, but balked at taking the antidepressant medication prescribed, just as he was averse to spending the time it appeared it would take to delve into the roots of his personality. All he wanted to do was get his wife back. "Sophie is all I ever lived for," he said. "Not even the children matter like her. There is no life after Sophie."

I began our fourth therapy session by telling George that it was time to look his problem "squarely in the face," and to begin thinking about Sophie in a more productive way. "Are you kidding?" he asked, startled. "All I ever do is think about Sophie, about her and her lover."

At the outset, I explained that most people are haunted day and night by thoughts of a serious loss. "You are assaulted and bombarded by thoughts and images of Sophie, but you have never invited any of this. These thoughts and images are not under your control. They occur spontaneously throughout the day. When they arise, you focus on them momentarily, feel the pain, and then divert your thoughts to something less distressing. As a result, you don't entertain the images long enough for them to work themselves through and burn themselves out." I reassured him that by the use of the desensitization technique we could produce a rapid and substantial elevation of his spirits. This therapy could not bring Sophie back, but he had everything to gain from feeling better.

Work with George proceeded as follows. I asked him to describe an image or thought involving Sophie that frequently came up spontaneously. Apparently, she liked to rendezvous with her lover at a seaside hideaway the man owned in East Hampton. While George had never been there, he'd often imagined what it was like—a table set for two on a big deck overlooking the ocean, waves lapping gently in the distance, and the two of them cuddled together later on a plush couch inside the little bungalow.

I asked George to close his eyes and summon this image, and then to hold it as long as he could and look at it from every imaginable angle. By the end of the session, he reported being able to project himself into that beach house on command. I suggested that if a troubling thought or image of his wife should occur to him during the week, he should stop what he was doing and stay with the distressing image for five to ten minutes without distraction, in order to extinguish the thought. The more this occurred, the less bothersome that particular thought would be, and his overall sense of loss would be commensurately diminished.

In contrast to spontaneous exposure, controlled exposure, wherein the individual sets him or herself quite deliberately to focusing on disturbing scenes, is vastly more efficacious in discharging negative feelings.

When George returned for his next session, his mood seemed slightly more upbeat. He had followed my instructions and was now able to imagine Long Island love nest scenes with equanimity. We spent the next twenty minutes creating a more disturbing portrait: Sophie and her lover sitting in the family room of his house, holding hands and watching television with George's children. The scene was approached gradually and intensified until he was able to visualize it without being overly upset, and I asked him to continue this at home during the week.

After four sessions, George was tremendously improved. He was able to conjure, without distress, a wide range of scenes involving his wife and her lover. He reported that the frequency and intensity of the bombardment of spontaneous thoughts of her had dropped dramatically. His general functioning showed strong signs of recovery: renewed job satisfaction, a significant increase in energy, and even interest in other women.

There may have been nothing George could do to win Sophie back, but there was a great deal he could do to change his reaction to the loss of her. Exposure Therapy enabled him to concentrate his attention and confine his ruminations to discrete time slots, so he could remain relatively free of these thoughts the rest of the day, while substantially reducing the duration of his grief. He might have fleeting images of his wife, or other manifestations of the loss response, but they no longer had the power over him that they once did.

CASE STUDY #2

Marilyn came to see me on her son's recommendation. She had lost her husband in a boating accident in Michigan more than a year ago. Although gaunt and drawn, Marilyn was an attractive and well-dressed woman in her late forties, who was clearly in distress.

"I hate to admit it, but I feel destroyed," she said. "If my son hadn't insisted that I get dressed up and kept begging me to trust him, I would never have come to see one more…shrink. Sorry," she said. "That just slipped out."

Since her husband's death, Marilyn had been unable to get out of bed, care about her appearance, or resume any of her formerly active social life. She sat in her bathrobe in a darkened room, stoic yet pained. She had little appetite and virtually no interest in the world around her.

Marilyn's loss was serious, but she, too, responded well to Exposure Therapy. As with George, we proceeded to concentrate and focus on the thoughts and images associated with her pain.

After about eight sessions, I received a telephone call from her son. "I stopped in to see Mother today and found her nicely dressed and ready to go out to the Garden Club. It's the first time since Dad died that she wanted to see her old friends. She's even been working in her flowerbeds. And she was so pleased to see me. For the first time in months I could see a brightness in her eyes."

And indeed there was. After a few more sessions, I told Marilyn that she had enough understanding now of the techniques of Exposure Therapy that she could now help herself. She left my office smiling, sure of her ability to control and further extinguish the pain of her enormous loss, without relinquishing her fond memories of her husband.

Exposure Therapy is not a gimmick to speed up forgetting. A grieving person does not want to forget a loved one, but rather do the opposite, hold onto the memory but relinquish the pain. Exposure Therapy allows us to retain our feelings of attachment—repetitious thinking of the lost person or object enhances retention—while letting go of the pain and anguish that the loss entails.

DON'T LET LOSS LINGER

One of the most common aftereffects of loss is finding yourself alone and lonely, where you seem to have no one in your life, and no means of socialization. You find yourself walking around as if you are the only one left on the planet. Trying to reach out can be difficult, and you can be seen as desperate.

All of this can affect your judgment and more.

This loneliness can be caused not just by the actual loss of a loved one we shared our life with, but by the fact that when we are depressed, we become negative and irritable, so that people tend to shy away from us. We also withdraw from society by our own choice.

So when you have a loss, you want to be sure that you don't let your anguish over it go on too long. Jump on it and see if you can resolve it as quickly as you can. This doesn't mean you have to put everything else aside to go straight into experimenting with ways to overcome your loss, but you can work on desensitizing your of loss of spouse, job, or whatever. You can get yourself back to the point of balance, so you don't end up isolated and lonely. The drive for companionship is strong, and if you find yourself all alone you may not be able to tolerate it indefinitely. Then your judgment goes out the window.

So losses are serious and have to be dealt with promptly—they shouldn't be allowed to fester indefinitely.

THE RIPPLE EFFECT OF LOSS

During normal grief people repeatedly think about and eulogize the lost person. Gradually the loss diminishes as this rumination, repeatedly thinking about the loss, has a desensitizing effect on their grief, leads to resolution. And eventually they feel better, return to normal.

But some forms of grief are so severe that even the desensitizing effect of repetitive thinking about them can take years to accomplish extinguishment, and even then it is not fully resolved. It may be significantly improved, but not eliminated. People often report that they never fully get over a serious loss.

One reason grief continues on after the normal period is that one loss can lead to another, and then another, a ripple effect that ripples on and on and sometimes can't be stopped.

For example, the person who was lost might have owned a family business, and he is not replaceable. Other family members start leaving the business, new hires are not as good as the original, and the business goes down. This can cascade to a situation where lives can be changed permanently.

Another possibility is that one loss may lead to a situation where everyone feels victimized. In one such case a widow died after an extended illness, and she had eight children and quite an estate. The children started fighting among themselves over the inheritance, and this became so intense that they ended up all at odds with one another, not even talking to each other. Some felt that because they had helped care for the mother, they were entitled to a bigger share. Others felt that all shares should be equal. All had their own point of view, and no one was able to rally all to a just solution. Eventually, any sense of family just disappeared.

In another case a young woman lost her life in a train derailment, and things really got out of hand. Her parents had planned to go into business with her, and now they had to stay at their jobs, which they didn't want to do. The woman's two siblings ended up feeling so disenfranchised by the whole thing that they moved out of the area, and the couple had marital troubles, and ended up divorced.

A lot depends on how the people left behind handle a loss when it occurs.

If they come together, support each other, and help heal each other, it builds morale, camaraderie, and closer bonds, and thus loss has a constructive effect.

The opposite can also happen, and then grief is a more destructive process.

WHEN GRIEF IS MIXED WITH OTHER THINGS

If a loss is straightforward it can be desensitized by repeatedly thinking about it, as described earlier. Desensitizing is very effective with grief under normal circumstances. When it is not, it's usually because there is some contaminant such as a ripple effect or some form of anger involved.

One reason people often have difficulty allowing the grief process to extinguish their grief is that they unknowingly distract themselves from focusing on their grief by instead focusing on the anger that often accompanies a loss. It is not uncommon for those who experience a loss to blame it on someone else. The sense of injustice that follows causes the person to become angry. As a result, he spends more time focusing on his anger and desire to get justice than focusing on his loss. For example, a couple who lost a son to his opioid addiction may spend most of the time they are in grief focusing on the people who were responsible for enabling their son's addiction.

Early on in the history of the accepted treatment of grief, clinicians would typically encourage clients to vent their anger at the people or circumstances that they felt were responsible for their loss. The assumption was that this would enable them to move beyond their anger and thereby focus on and relieve their grief. Unfortunately, this usually didn't work and the client usually only experienced momentary respite from their distress. Clients would often leave the session feeling relieved, but the feeling of relief wouldn't last. This is because as noted earlier, anger, unlike anxiety and grief, is very resistant to desensitization. Anger is best resolved by helping the client to find constructive ways of getting justice. This is attested to in the ubiquitous presence of courthouses throughout societies down through the ages. Apparently, perhaps because of the ever-present scarcity of goods and services, nature came to regard justice as a basic need, much like hunger and security. As such, like all the other needs (drives) people have, one can't simply extinguish them by desensitizing them.

My approach is to encourage people to separate the loss from the contaminants such as anger or ripple effects, which should be dealt with separately, and allow desensitization to heal the loss.

I saw a woman who lost her son in a hunting accident, and she had a lot of anger about it: anger at her husband, at the people who were with her son and didn't do the right thing, and at people who acted inappropriately to her afterward. The woman especially missed her son because he was the one who had been bringing all of the new things into her life—he was "the spark of her life." But she always gravitated to anger in our sessions, so she didn't make much progress on the grief. The trouble with anger is that you vent, feel better, then the next day are back to where you started.

When people come to me complaining about some previous therapist, where they don't think they made any progress, it always turns out that their issue was anger-based.

LOSS CAN CHANGE ATTITUDES

Another example of how loss can cause a ripple effect is that it can change one's outlook. It then has a downstream effect because of that.

Once I treated a young woman who had lost her mother as a young teen. During the later stages of her mother's illness she had a relationship with a guy who wanted all of her attention focused on him. He was so concerned with his own needs that he interfered with her relationship with her dying mother, and her ability to be there for her.

After her mother died she realized that she would have been much better off if, rather than placating her boyfriend and his endless needs for attention and support, she had spent more time with her mother in her final year of life.

The loss of her mother triggered a ripple effect. The stress of all of this caused health problems for the young woman. No sooner had her mother died when she came down with insomnia and stomach ailments.

She also changed her view of men, seeing them now as very needy and always wanting what they wanted. Her boyfriend's endless desire for sex, attention, and approval all interfered with what she now felt she should have been doing.

She was more self-focused now, and angry. She felt victimized, and her attitude toward men changed dramatically. She had trouble meeting guys now because they would pick up on this. She was quick-tempered when they made demands, rather than accommodating.

So you see loss can become complex over time.

Going over her loss, resolving and desensitizing her grief and depression in therapy, helped. We were able to separate the secondary issues from the primary one, and were then able to focus on her other issues, such as her stomach problem. This too was improved, although she would need to take medicine for a while to fully resolve it.

She also revisited her attitude toward men, and reestablished a more positive attitude toward them, especially since she wanted to have a relationship with a man, and to develop a family with one someday.

This all happened because we were able to focus on her grief, and pluck it out of the equation. We allowed the grief to take place, and treated the secondary issues as separate ones, rather than all combined with the grief.

In Chapter Twelve you will find a very interesting case that shows that a loss can be multifaceted, creating depression and anxiety that has far-reaching effects, including drastic change in attitude.

LOSS CAN CLOUD YOUR JUDGMENT

Another example of the complicating effect of loss is a woman who found that after her husband of many years left her, she was unable to put her life back together. She found herself compromised financially and otherwise. This, according to her, led to not being so careful about the person she decided to date and then eventually marry.

She was so preoccupied with her needs and problems and limitations, that when she met someone who seemed to be kind, helpful, and considerate, it was a tremendous relief. She quickly fell in love and then married him without fully understanding the nature of the person she was getting involved with.

She soon discovered he was seriously limited emotionally—to the point of being almost totally self-absorbed. She was unaware of this originally because during their whirlwind courtship they were both buoyed up by the interesting things they were doing and good times they were having, and both infused with the hormonal stimulants of the mating ritual. So he was much more emotional then than he normally was, and she was too emotional herself to see and assess things clearly.

Over time she became more and more stressed by his inability to reciprocate her affection and show compassion and empathy. He never really understood her points of view, and tended to minimize her concerns. She found herself drifting into a situation where she felt more and more alone, and more and more stressed.

This is another example of the ripple effect.

At this point she was not in a position to do much about it. She was in her early sixties, and felt too discouraged to look for someone new. Or to go back to work and become autonomous again, as she was previously for many years.

The ripple effect of loss in this case was the contamination of perspective, the ability to see clearly what you are doing and the kinds of choices you are making.

> Clinicians recommend that you allow at least a year to let grief be resolved before seeking a new relationship. Looking to introduce a new person into your life as soon as possible is not the solution to loss.

The desensitizing effect of time, coupled with the mental processing I have described, is a more realistic way to get over a loss, overcome the grief, than a new relationship that is supposed to immediately solve all of the problems that the grief is creating.

AN EVEN MORE SERIOUS LOSS: LOSS OF CONTROL

Often an initial loss, or the fear of it, puts you in the position where the loss you are going to experience is loss of control over your own life, and this can be devastating.

This loss is often not so obvious at first because most people tend to focus on what they want rather than what they are losing in the process of trying to get it.

A typical example is: You meet someone you become very fond of, who seems just perfect for you. But at some point the relationship stalls. The person is not willing to go on. Now you have to decide what to do—back out, give up all the time and energy you have invested in it, or cut your losses and leave.

Many feel they can't leave, that backing out now would be a disaster—they would never find someone else nearly as good.

One woman I treated had met someone who seemed ideal. Both were Olympic-level skiers, so they were able to travel to many interesting places together to practice their sport. They also did many other things together, and had similar outlooks and points of view. But after the relationship reached a certain point the man decided he wasn't ready for marriage.

She was left wondering what to do. She had what seemed like the perfect man for her—everything seemed ideal. She wanted to go forward, and she had expected the relationship to go forward. But it was stalled. Should she abandon this seeming dead end, or hope for the best? Not an easy situation.

In her case the relationship gradually deteriorated because her mood got worse and worse over time. She felt more and more resentful and couldn't get it out of her mind. The loss triggered anger and the anger became the driving force, to the extent that she was forced to leave the relationship for her own health. She was bitter about it afterward—all of the wasted time, the lost years of her life.

In such situations it is easy to deceive yourself that the person will come around. This is not always the case. In one case I was involved in, the man of the couple did eventually come around, after dragging his feet for years. But the problem the woman did not foresee is that when they did finally get married, the problem of loss of control cropped up again when she wanted to have children. He dragged his feet about this forever as well. She spent years and years trying to get him to agree to it, and never did succeed.

Sometimes a loss like this puts you out of control. You get so preoccupied with getting over the initial situation (failure to get married or whatever, feeling that if you could only get "X" resolved the rest would take care of itself), that you don't realize that the reason things are out of control is probably factors related to the nature of the relationship itself.

Just resolving the loss, by coaxing the other person into what you want, or hanging in there, will not solve everything. The same problem you had in regard to the relationship will pop up again in other situations such as getting a house, a different job, having children, and so on.

> Many people put themselves in situations where they are out of control. Such as never knowing how someone important to you feels about you, or being in love with someone who is not sure they want to get married. Waiting for a situation like this to resolve itself can go on for years and be very depressing. Putting yourself in a situation where you are out of control, where things are out of your hands entirely, is a dangerous thing to do. It puts you in limbo, and is very likely to cause you to become depressed.

Here is another example of how loss can lead you to be out of control, which can go on for a long time, delay your progress, and serve as a big speed bump in your life.

This is when the other person is not fully committed to something, may actually be looking to get out of it, but is not likely to come out and say so. In this situation people can find countless reasons for which they don't want to go ahead with a relationship, get married, resolve an uncertainty, etc. They are constantly pointing to this and that as the reason.

All the while the other person is trying to resolve all of these problems so that the situation can go forward.

Often when you see this, one excuse after another, excuses that are always different but often seem sound and logical, you have to question whether the person simply doesn't have the assertiveness to tell you directly what they really want.

I had a case like this—a man and woman, both personal trainers, who met and were very attracted to one another. They had a great time together, went on vacations together, and all seemed fine.

But she said she couldn't leave her husband because they had young twin sons, and she didn't want them to be fatherless. It eventually became clear that she had no real regard for her husband, was just using him as an excuse for her own lack of desire to go forward. The husband had issues with drug use and other things and eventually developed more and more serious problems. He eventually lost his job and moved out of the area.

She was left alone with her sons, and the person in love with her figured that now they could finally get married. Only to find her saying that she was now reluctant because she was afraid of what negative effect that might have on her children, she wanted to wait a few years, and so on.

Ultimately what he found out was that she really didn't have strong enough feelings for him to marry him. She had a lot of doubts and wasn't as committed to the relationship as he was. He had overlooked one thing after another, without stopping to realize that she really didn't love him enough to actually tie the knot. The excuses she gave, first her husband and then needing time because of her children, were just that—excuses. This became glaringly clear when she met someone else and got married in short order. Someone who was more ideal for her, more of what she was looking for.

What the original lover missed in his need to see things the way he wanted them, his need to have her, was that her inability to assert herself, to hurt anyone, kept her from letting him know what was really happening, and this perpetuated a problem that went on and on.

Another young woman I treated was in love with a guy who was very charismatic, lovable, friendly, and likeable, but had a great fear of being trapped, and he thought of marriage as a trap. He didn't want to discuss this with her because he was embarrassed by it. So he kept giving different reasons for why he was hesitating, to delay the reckoning, when he would have to make a decision. She took this very personally and wondered if it was her appearance, her intellect, her job, and so on. He wanted to hang on to her, but didn't want to be committed.

In all of these cases involving loss of control, essentially what happens is that the person gambles that if they hang in there long enough they can win, get what they want—the other person will do what they are looking for them to do.

When you allow yourself to lose control of a situation, it can have a pernicious effect on many areas of your life. You should desensitize yourself out of the relationship if you are losing control, so that you can move on. This can get you to the point where you can live with a loss and it no longer affects you so strongly that you can't make proper judgments. Grieving the loss of a person like this so that you can get your own life back is highly recommended, though often very difficult at the time to see in these terms.

TWO MORE CASES OF LOSS

Bryan was my second client one morning. I was just settling in to one of my typical long days in the office—ten hours or more. I'm never fazed by this since I've always found doing therapy enjoyable and invariably interesting. My client, who was there for his first session with me, began to describe the last ten years of his life, which had been spent in and out of courtrooms litigating the artful attempts of others to redirect his money to their own accounts. In short order he outlined his strikingly successful career as a novelist, which had been followed by his attempt to salvage whatever was left of the amazingly large amount he had earned over this time. Two ex-wives, a literary agent, the producer of a movie based on one of his books, and the lawyers of all of the above were the culprits.

Bryan was very bright and psychology-minded—he enjoyed analyzing himself and others, and somewhat defiantly challenged me to figure out how to resolve his problems. He couldn't stop thinking about the injustices he'd been subjected to and was still being victimized by. These thoughts had been running around in his head for quite a while now—he told me he had tried every conceivable way of looking at what happened to him in the last decade in an attempt to come to terms with it. Each new perspective came with the hope that it would settle his mind—and it did, but only for a week or so, sometimes a little longer, but never for more than about a month. Each time he would find himself poking holes in his latest analysis until this supposed killer insight lost its ability to pacify him. He wondered if I could do any better.

This is another example of loss leading to loss of control. True, this client lost a great deal of money because he was cheated out of it by agents and lawyers. But he became so involved in lawsuits about this—trying to get even, and get back at them—that he lost control of his life by putting it in the hands of lawyers and judges. He did recoup some money, but it was at the enormous expense of having lost a good part of his life during which he was constantly upset by the anger associated with the lawsuits.

In Chapter Twelve you can read about another case where an impending loss caused great problems for a young woman who lived to play soccer.

LOST TO ADDICTION

Two other cases come to mind in this business of loss of control. Two people whose spouses each had an addiction problem, one using drugs, the other alcohol.

In both cases the spouses were convinced that the person could resolve their addiction problem and that the marriage could be mended and life could go on in a positive way.

Both had tried to fight the influence and effects of these addictions. They eventually thought about all of the problems involved and realized that a person who had been taking a drug all along in effect had a relationship with that drug, and it was actually stronger and deeper than their relationship with them. There is an old country song that says, "If whiskey was a woman, I'd have a better chance." This is a woman involved with an alcoholic lamenting the odds. In other words, if her man was having an affair with another woman, she'd have a better chance of getting him back, than going up against alcohol.

People involved with any drug tend to minimize and deny its effect, its importance in their lives, their dependence on it. They usually want to keep their spouse because their lifestyle creates many problems and a spouse is handy to have around to help out with some of this, help solve these problems.

But eventually the spouse realizes that the person is just using them, and that their partner's real relationship is with the drug. Unless that is broken and they return their focus to the spouse, there is not much hope for the relationship.

Keeping a relationship going with a person who has an active addiction is extremely difficult. The question is, do you want to lose control of your life on the gamble that you can fit what amounts to a third party into your lives? An intense addiction is no different than if the person brought an affair into your lives, and was actually living with a third person. If a person continues to take the drug, it is his fundamental relationship, and more important than you.

Again, here you are putting yourself in a situation where you lose control of your life, gambling that you can get your partner to the point where he will heal himself and resolve his problems. And underestimating the severity of those problems.

> In a relationship with an addict, you will always be second in line.

JUGGLING LOSSES: WHEN WE VACILLATE

Our reaction to loss—even potential loss—can have effects beyond the grieving process.

What do we find ourselves doing when we are torn between two equally compelling courses of action? We vacillate. To explain why we do this, and what it accomplishes, let's consider the following story.

A woman comes to see me who's been having difficulties with her husband for many years now. She's thinking of leaving him for someone she met a while back.

She's been seeing this other man for some time now and feels she has gotten to know him very well. She thinks that he is probably better suited to her, overall, than her husband is. Maybe she should leave her husband and children and go off with him. At first the decision seems simple and obvious. "This is the perfect man for me," she thinks. "Why ruin my life by spending the rest of it with someone I am no longer interested in or attracted to? It seems to be a clear-cut decision—I should go."

The guy is willing to leave his wife as well. Both could just ditch their spouses and take a chance. They believe they have the right person now, so things should work out well.

But no sooner do they attempt to embark on this when their emotions step in.

The woman's mind, for instance, seems to be saying that from a logical standpoint, leaving her husband and going off with her lover is the way to go. But emotionally this is very difficult to do. She no sooner takes steps in that direction when she starts to question herself. She becomes very anxious and fearful of the problems involved. She realizes that she would have the children less, the whole thing would be a big problem for them, and they might not do as well in school. Maybe divorcing would simply be too selfish a thing to do. Perhaps it would be best to wait until the kids graduate. That would probably be another ten years. This is not a very satisfying temporary decision, but she makes it.

She mentions the difficulties she is having to her lover, insisting that it's not that she loves him any less, but they need to slow this down, go back to the drawing board. "I'm going back and forth," she says. "Everything points to leaving with you. But given the fact that it is going to impact the children negatively, I don't think I can do it." He understands this, because he faces the same problems, the same tradeoffs.

They decide to postpone the idea of leaving and revisit it in the future. Meanwhile, they continue their relationship, thinking they have come to a resolution. They are going to continue their affair and perhaps give up the idea of ever moving out. Their decision to stay now (the opposite of their original decision) seems satisfying.

But after a month or so, they really can't go through with it.

She has suffered interminably with her husband, and has nothing in common with him anymore—her life is vacuous. He has the same problems with his wife.

"Let's revisit this. Let's find a solution. Maybe there is a way to break this down in terms of all of the problems involved and come up with solutions to these problems so we can proceed."

This seems to be a good idea and they again feel that they have reached a resolution.

But it's just a matter of time before they go back, and find themselves feeling again that the idea of leaving their families is too selfish, too dangerous.

In the woman's case, her children have already gotten wind of the fact that things aren't going so well between her and her husband, and they are already starting to show some issues in school. She can't subject them to this. So back she goes. He's going through the same thing. Back and forth and back and forth.

After a while they start questioning their ability to even come to a decision. They joke to each other about being "out there"—having lost the normal ability to analyze problems and then figure out how to go about things from there. They have entered a realm they didn't even know existed, where logic is not necessarily the deciding factor, emotions come and go, and are sometimes very intense. Sometimes they even find themselves getting panic attacks over all of this.

They don't really know what is happening. What they do feel is that their minds are not handling the situation, not making things better.

They are both strong-willed people who are used to having strong opinions and telling themselves what to do. They've often criticized others who seemed unable to make a decision, thinking of them as just weak. Now they themselves are in a situation where they can't seem to make a decision easily, if at all. They find themselves questioning whether they are as strong as they thought they were.

Their self-esteem plummets.

The man, for example, can't believe that with the woman he loves so much within his grasp, he is vacillating as to what to do.

She is vacillating just as much, going back and forth and back and forth. She too always considered herself a very decisive person. But faced with this dilemma, she seems unable to come up with a solution, to have any way of even effectively analyzing it.

The two begin to show a little depression in their thinking. Their brains start to wonder what's going on. This dilemma is consuming so much time they aren't doing so well in other areas of their lives—at work, at home, with their children.

The reason for all of this back and forthing is that their brains are gradually desensitizing the fears of losing either option.

They have ended up on a seesaw, because they are saying to their brains in essence, I want to solve a problem that doesn't really have a solution. I want to determine which person I should live with. Each has advantages and disadvantages—it's like comparing apples and kumquats. There is no real logic to which is the better choice, no clear way of arriving at a solution.

Faced with this dilemma, the brain goes to a strategy it has developed over the course of many centuries: basically, it is a form of vacillation. The brain finally decides: "Let me take this over—they're not getting anywhere and it's causing an enormous amount of grief. Let me step in and see if I can help out."

So far the reasoning part of their minds has been the major factor in this vacillation, going back and forth, considering all these different factors.

What the brain is saying to itself now is that obviously these two options are about equally good. It would not be vacillating if there were a vast difference between the choices. But in this case the difference is scarcely discernable, so this is essentially a 50/50 situation.

Over the course of evolution this kind of dilemma has popped up countless times and ways.

Should I believe in God or not?

Should I become a basketball player or a scientist?

Should I move or stay where I am?

Etc., etc.

The brain has had a tremendous amount of experience with this kind of situation. A person caught between two different choices, not seeming to be able to decide which one is better.

A big part of the problem is that losses affect us more than gains. Consider a simple example. Let's say that you buy a lottery ticket and find that you have won a million dollars. In the afternoon of the very same day, however, you lose a million, because you lost the ticket. What happens? Do you feel that you are just back where you started, and just go on with your life? Or get frantic and depressed, since you lost the chance to solve many problems in your life? "How could I have done this? What's wrong with me?!" This kind of loss would really stress many people out. It could take a long time to recover from it.

Historically things like food and supplies, and for that matter close relatives and friends, were in short supply. The brain is very reluctant to accept a loss without a concentrated effort to reverse it. After centuries of scarcity, the idea is not to lose things, and if you do, the brain will prod you to try and recover them.

To go back to our seesawing couple, if the woman decides to go off with her boyfriend she is going to put herself in the position of losing her husband and all of the advantages that come with him. They have a longstanding, steady relationship, he's strong and successful, and they have a good life, and good friends. But staying with the husband would mean losing the love of her life, all of the possibilities of a fantastic relationship; the person she now sees she should have married, the person she would love to come home to and be with forever.

The pressure from a possible loss and the need to prevent it are far stronger than the need to acquire some gain. So the brain is immediately drawn to the fact that maybe we should prevent that loss.

If she prevents it, the boyfriend is now the thing to be lost, and the husband what will be gained. Faced with that, the loss of the boyfriend is more impactful than the gain of the husband. So it's going to swing back in the opposite direction.

Now it flips the situation, and we are now worried about losing the first option. This back and forthing has one very helpful and decisive effect. It gives the person a chance to imagine and visualize, experience, see what it would be like to actually live with one option, go forward with it.

Then they can go back after a while and do this in reverse, experience, live the other one out. Doing this gives the brain a chance to examine both options in depth.

Also, as you experience one option, you desensitize your fear of losing it. Going over it in the absence of any consequence sets the stage for extinction of the emotions associated with the loss of option one. When you flip it, you set the stage for extinguishing the loss of option two.

As you gradually go through this you get the feedback you need, experience each choice emotionally as well as intellectually. You also get the benefit of the desensitization that occurs from the process of going back and forth.

Over time the fear of losing either one reaches the point that it is not really that difficult or anxiety-provoking. At that point, you can probably make a decision.

The brain has come up with a solution. What it has done, in essence, is reduced your fears to the point that you can more readily go with what you logically think is the best thing to do. And not have to worry that the emotional reaction will spring up again and cause you to reverse yourself all the time.

TREATING LOSS IN THOSE WHO WON'T TALK ABOUT THEIR LOSSES

I had a client, Janette, who suffered many losses in a bad car accident. She had serious facial scarring and some brain damage, and now walked with a limp. Whenever she talked to me I had to keep changing the topic back to her. She kept changing it to me and other people. Finally I came right out and said that she wasn't focusing enough on herself—she needed to be considering herself more and making plans to improve her life. People were yessing her—they don't usually mind you changing the topic to them. They will go along with it, even enjoy it. People love to talk about themselves.

People with the agreeable trait like Janette don't like to burden other people, so they don't like to talk much about themselves. If a person is agreeable and depressed, he will often quickly switch the conversation to you. A therapist has to watch out for this. They often want to talk to a therapist about his own issues. You try to get them to talk about their losses and they say, "I know what you're saying, but Jimmy, a friend of mine, has it worse. He has this problem and that problem." It's hard to get their mind off of other people.

They have a very pronounced tendency to distract themselves and others, so that they don't focus on themselves. They circumvent, go around issues, rather than confront them directly. They need a lot of reinforcement in therapy to keep talking about themselves.

It took a while before Janette began to make the change. But as she became more assertive, her depressive tendency and personality were improved dramatically.

CHAPTER TWELVE

OTHER DEPRESSION-RELATED PROBLEMS

There is an odd cluster of complex emotions that crop up rather frequently in relationships, and routinely screw them up. Many of us do our best to avoid them because they are so irksome and difficult to navigate.

This chapter explains their makeup and underpinnings, as well as how to deal with them and their often lingering aftereffects.

DEPRESSION PLUS ANXIETY

Depression is often accompanied by anxiety, and in fact, the two can work into a kind of seesaw effect with each other. The hyperactivity of intense anxiety, for example, finally fatigues us to the point that we sink into depression as an escape mechanism. Eventually we become so disgusted with the nihilism and lack of accomplishment of that state that we vault back into anxiety again.

An interaction between depression and anxiety is fairly common and where this occurs what usually happens is that the anxiety serves to act as a lid on the depression and once the lid is removed, such as when a person is with people he is more comfortable with, then the depression reenters the picture.

For example, say a person who is both anxious and depressed is in a foul mood when he is stopped by a policeman whom he perceives as strict and unreasonable. He would probably control his frustrations and be polite to the officer. He may well express his frustrations, however, when he gets home. The reason: His anxiety would tend to control his depressive negative mood when he was with the officer, while his relatively low anxiety when he was at home would make him prone to vent his anger at his family. When a person like this is with an authority figure of any kind, or a friend, his anxiety is usually sufficient to inhibit the depression so that it doesn't come out. Oddly enough, the anxiety in this particular case tends to be a positive factor, inhibiting the person from revealing his depression at times that might cause him an immediate problem.

When someone is both depressed and anxious their behavior varies a lot, so they can be hard to read. Dealing with someone like this is difficult, because they oscillate between the two moods, and you never know which you are going to encounter. This causes people to back off. When in a depressed state, a person can say some nasty things, and then people will go out of their way to avoid him or her. When they're in an anxious state they usually don't do this. They're not as outspoken, because they don't want conflict and contentiousness.

Someone who is depressed has a tendency to accuse other people of being at fault for whatever difficulty has arisen. Initially, people assume that if they're nice to a person who is depressed, he will react more favorably, but they soon find out that this is often not the case. Acting pleasantly to the person, perhaps allowing him to assume that his accusations that the issue in question is really their fault are correct, inadvertently removes the anxiety that would tend to serve as an inhibitor of the depressive mood and opens them up to getting more accusations thrown at them.

This is a pattern we see often—when depressed people are with friends, teachers, colleagues at work, and so on, they function much better because they are a little anxious. Outsiders may give rave reviews of

343

their behavior. When at home with the family, and other close people there is no anxiety, thus no inhibitory effect, and the result is outbursts. This might be the origin of the expression "We only hurt the ones we love." Many people show this pattern, including alcoholics and drug abusers. They can be hell on wheels to live with.

Here is a real-life example of this kind of relationship between anxiety and depression in action.

Andrea, a high school about-to-be senior, had suffered seven injuries over the past three years playing soccer—ankle, knee, and tendon injuries, as well as two concussions.

She'd always been good-natured, friendly, and agreeable, but her parents had noticed a big change in her. Now she was irritable and easily frustrated. She denied this, but as we talked, it was obvious to me, too, that this was the case. She insisted this had nothing to do with soccer, although she was obviously very concerned that her soccer privileges would be taken away from her. At this time she was being told that her doctors would probably no longer allow her to play, which would be a major loss to her. She not only enjoyed soccer immensely, she was the team captain.

I thought that her brain was showing signs that it was unable to tolerate all of the frustrations and hassles inherent in exchanges with other people. I decided to see if there was some way I could help her with this problem.

One possibility was that when she felt herself becoming irritated she could walk away and wait until she calmed down. She did this and it did work, but it took time and patience. She also found herself walking away more and more.

Then I suggested going over the things she wanted to discuss with others in her mind first, including things that would be very contentious, such as her desire to continue with soccer, before discussing them with parents or doctors. Soccer was a very hot topic because she was very intent on playing again.

These techniques did help her considerably, but she had to prepare for them and think about them (such as how to present things),
which took a fair amount of time.

After a while we discovered that when she was on the anxious
side, such as dealing with an authority figure, she did considerably better. Whenever she was intimidated, uptight, or concerned, she was able
to control herself. Her fear of losing her friends or the respect of other
people was more than enough to stifle any outbursts. When her anxiety
was low, such as when speaking to family, very close friends, and others
who were not very threatening, she often lost her temper. Those she felt
she could get away with such behavior with, who wouldn't abandon or
reject her for a fit of temper, took the brunt of her irritability.

One way to deal with this was to desensitize the irritability itself,
and that's what we did, by going over things that were bothering her,
such as her parents' reaction to her refusal to stop playing soccer, and
her fears of not playing. This all had to do with a potential loss: of her
ability to play soccer.

Her impending loss of her favorite game was causing her to act
out. As we worked around it, as we reduced the strength of that loss,
including by considering the fears in her mind about not playing, and
how she might get along without soccer, the better she got along with
her family and others she was close to.

We also worked on preparing her better for conversations with
such people. We tried desensitizing the situation when she was speaking to people she knew very well, and the process was very effective. She
showed significant improvement in how she dealt with her parents and
siblings, and it gave her much greater control.

When you have a situation like this, you need to extinguish the
depressive feelings causing it so that you don't have to worry about
whether or not anxiety is present to inhibit the person or not.

OTHER INTERACTIONS BETWEEN DEPRESSION AND ANXIETY

If a person is depressed, a little anxiety may help in that it will tend to demonstrate to the person that their depressive mood is having negative consequences in many areas of their life. It may also mobilize the person to act in such a way as to minimize the negative effects of his depression on himself and others.

If a person is extremely anxious, he may find himself becoming depressed because the brain, recognizing that the anxiety is getting to intolerable levels, helps the person reduce his anxiety by modifying his thinking: such as by sidelining his fears that he won't achieve his goal, and his feeling that the goal is very important. Depression is often at the heart of the give-up response if a person's fears become intolerable.

Say you are pondering some difficult decision, such as switching jobs or going back to school. You are very anxious about it, but being forced into it, either by outside forces, or yourself.

For example, you have been offered a fancy book promotion tour by the publisher of the book you wrote. You would love to do such a glamorous thing, and it would benefit your book, but you don't want to have to leave your family and pets for an extended time to do it. This is known as an approach/approach situation.

So how do you deal with the problem? If the conflict is serious enough, say the publisher keeps raising the ante, offering more and more perks for the tour, you will eventually become depressed and find all kinds of reasons to not do it. All meant to reduce your anxiety.

> If our anxiety is too high or we are in a panic, our brain goes toward depression to knock the anxiety down some. It adds a little depression to make us lose interest in what we feel threatened by.

346

This can lead to another kind of psychological seesaw effect.

Say that you join the Air Force, and decide that you want to become a fighter pilot, because of the adventure and prestige that seems to offer, and the fact that your girlfriend is also in that program. You are ready to go ahead and do it, to sign the papers.

But then upon reflection you start getting anxious, and then more and more anxious: this is something high risk if not death-defying, and you are already on the bombardier squad. You've always had a problem with details, and a fighter plane cockpit is nothing but details. And maybe you don't need all of that glory, especially since your girlfriend has now decided to be a homemaker.

But as you get ready to back out, the reality of losses hits: a lost dream, loss of prestige, and your girlfriend has now changed her mind and is going to go on to become a pilot.

If you don't get back into that program, you are going to lose all of these things.

TREATMENT FOR DEPRESSION PLUS ANXIETY

When a person suffers from both depression and anxiety, in therapy we usually try to get at the anxiety first, even though it tends to hold the depression in check. This runs into the problem that when the anxiety is reduced, the depression is likely to spill out. Thus removing it can cause the person a problem, so we point this out to them early on.

Usually we work with the person to decide which to treat first. Mostly it is their anxiety.

Depression is hard to treat, another reason why we usually treat the anxiety first. There is greater likelihood of success, which may buoy the person on to help with the treatment of their depression.

GRUDGES

Grudges, a form of anger, are often seen in close relationships and are in essence a deep, lasting hostile stance that one adopts toward another person.

Grudges are usually at the heart of families that break up. My experience with grudges has been mostly with families that have developed schisms. For example, I treated two young men who had been rejected by their parents because of grudges. In another case, a woman had a grudge against her mother, whom she felt did not protect her from her stepfather's sexual abuse. I also saw a family where there was a break between sisters caused by a reason they would not tell me. Eventually one of the sisters was on her deathbed and still the alienated sister refused to even go to the hospital. I role-played with them to enable them to deal with this situation.

Often grudges are based on disputed facts and trust issues are common. Without trust it is difficult to get at the truth. Relatives who are former business partners are good candidates for grudges. There are no easy answers for problems like these, and if the parties go to court this may well aggravate the hostility between them.

Grudges are usually very resistant to intervention. But understanding the dynamics involved can be very helpful in easing the suffering grudges can cause.

Grudges are often held by depressives, who are especially well suited to holding on to anger. Some people use grudges to create a barrier between them and those they want to protect themselves from. A person who is angry with someone he feels treated him unfairly may form a grudge that prevents the unfairness from being rectified and thereby maintains the separation that was secretly sought. Grudges are often manipulative techniques for maintaining distance.

Depressives can hold grudges interminably. Most recognize that they get a lot of secondary gains from this. For example, it enables them to feel self-righteous and morally superior to their victims, whom they hold in contempt. This acts to allay any sense of inadequacy they might have felt stemming from their rivals' accomplishments. Holding grudges also enables them to feel that they are victims. As victims, they feel entitled to compensation from their rivals while they consider themselves free of any responsibilities. Moreover, depressives often become very adept at manipulating others with their anger.

Depressives find interpersonal relationships inherently stressful. They have become accustomed to emotional breakups—having conflicts with others and terminating relationships with them is a regular feature of their lives. Depressives find that getting angry is a convenient means of gaining an advantage over others. If they find an opportunity to hold a grudge—and they are always on the lookout—they can use this as a bargaining chip.

Depressives often see themselves as powerless due to their mental sluggishness, negative outlook, and passive nature. Thus grudges and anger offer a unique opportunity to gain power over others as well as their own lives. Moreover, grudges can be formed rather easily, and usually the effort is richly rewarded.

WHO STANDS TO GAIN?

One of my clients woke up one morning to realize that his sister had invited everyone to her big summer cookout except him and their parents.

Why? That was never fully answered. She didn't call or visit anymore. When asked about this, she said she was angry at them, and that she had her reasons (they didn't seem to be very substantial). Just the year before she had spoken very eloquently about how much she loved them all. This was an odd switch over a short time, and without much backing it up. Why would she do this? What was there to be gained from a grudge against her family?

I talked to the sister, and got nowhere.

The question became who else was involved in this, and how might they benefit? Whenever there is a grudge, usually someone has a motive for it.

It turned out that the sister's husband resented her family, and this was the real cause of the problem. So the sister found herself in an untenable position, in the middle between her husband and her family. She didn't have the strength or wherewithal to stand up to her husband, so she just passed her husband's hostility toward her family on. The sister needed to be candid and say to her family, "My husband has a problem with you, but I don't want to divorce him or have him leave me." She didn't, so the grudge was maintained and everyone felt awkward. The husband wouldn't admit he was generating the hard feelings—he just acted dumb and as if he were not any part of this. The parents and brother were frustrated, because there seemed to be no way of resolving this, which was a difficult situation all around. This is why grudges tend to stay in place.

I was involved in another case that seemed similar. A son seemed to have suddenly alienated himself from his family—now they were fighting bitterly, had nothing to do with one another.

"Why are you so angry at your parents?" I asked him. He came up with some reasons, such as that they never helped him out much, but that was long ago, in the past, and only now was he angry.

I asked the parents about this, and found that they loved him and wanted to get back together, didn't want this separation. They were very cooperative.

Again, who has a motive?

It seemed to be the daughter-in-law.

She had a good relationship with the son, but for several reasons she was feeling insecure. And he was always talking about going to see his parents, and the things he did with them.

Look for the motivated party—this is how a grudge is analyzed.

In another case, a woman came in with her husband and insisted that her husband's parents were impossible, she couldn't get along with them. Every time they came over all they did was criticize her, and so on. When I listened to her complaints about them, they didn't really hold up, and she couldn't even describe them well. She would start an explanation and then descend into, "Well, you know what it's like, what goes on. You can't do anything with those people," etc.

When there is a fight between a mother-in-law and daughter-in-law, it all depends on how the son handles it. If he takes a strong stand and gets involved, examines the situation and determines what should be done, the situation may be resolved. Expecting the daughter-in-law to resolve it in a situation such as this is unlikely, since her motivation is not to solve the breach but to perpetuate it.

TREATMENT FOR GRUDGES

Grudges are very, very hard to change. Therapists are forever trying to find new and better ways to deal with them.

In grudges, it is difficult to get at the underlying motivation because it is usually claimed that the other person did terrible things, it's all their fault, etc.

Since grudges are based in anger, they don't desensitize easily and can go on interminably. After a while people get used to living without the other person, because when there is a grudge they don't deal with them at all. The grudge stays in place over time, and ten years later it is hard to even think of changing things.

When dealing with grudges we try to find and work with the motivated party, the one who wants to end it and get the family back together. We at least start with this party, the one who wants to get it over with.

The grudge bearer may not be motivated at all. He or she doesn't want it to end. If you approach them about this, they will very often dismiss you and tell you outright that they are not interested. Undoing grudges generally involves determining the nature of the underlying resentment and the person's motive for seeking separation.

While anger can be undone by correcting the injustices involved, grudges require unearthing of the motivation for longstanding schisms. Often, the victim of a grudge is frustrated and confused, since most direct approaches at rectifying the injustice are rejected by the person holding the grudge.

A good example is the case of Melissa. Melissa was short, but trim and fit. She was attractive, energetic, and quick to see the humor in things. She was also optimistic and readily engaged others, so she was easy to like, and had many friends. She enjoyed her friends and the deep bonds she had developed with them.

She tried to avoid conflicts with others, mostly because she loathed the way it made her feel—anxious and very eager to resolve matters. She was not good at maintaining ill will and animosity towards others, even when it might be justified, and she would stretch herself to find the middle ground. While she could be assertive, this did not come naturally to her and she had to work at it. Overall she was well grounded psychologically and enjoyed a fair measure of self-esteem and confidence.

Melissa's brother was her polar opposite. He was eighty pounds overweight, out of shape, and described himself as a couch potato. His disposition was markedly depressed, whether because of circumstances, or more likely, because of temperamental and genetic factors. Like most people who suffer from a depressive personality, he showed a variety of secondary characteristics of depression, which had a profound impact on his life.

To digress for a moment, people who have a depressive personality show many of the secondary characteristics seen in people who suffer from depression, but not the primary ones. One speculation about this is that depressive personalities have had depressive episodes during which they adopted secondary behavior that became habitual. Also, there is often a low level of the primary characteristics in depressive personalities, which do not rise to the level of a clinical depression, yet trigger the secondary characteristics.

The primary characteristics of depression, as noted earlier, include a marked slowdown in mental energy, physical fatigue, which impairs a person's ability to concentrate and engage in mental activities, anhedonia (the inability to experience pleasure from activities or circumstances), and withdrawal. Many depressed people also report a feeling of sadness.

The secondary characteristics, which stem from the primary ones, reflect how depressed people interact with the people and circumstances in their lives. These characteristics include pessimism (seeing the glass as half empty, if not empty) and a pervasive sense of negativity, argumentativeness and interpersonal conflicts, low tolerance for frustration, and irritability. Such people are also overly sensitive, easily angered, and feel victimized.

Melissa, who was only a year older than her brother, found it difficult to get along with him. During their childhood they didn't share many activities beyond family trips to relatives and vacations. As they got older Melissa went to college, where she excelled, and she eventually became a PR person for a large cosmetics company. Her brother went to work right after high school and married several years later. Melissa married shortly after graduating college, and before long had two sons. Melissa was close to her mother when she was young, but they grew apart while she was in high school and college. They seemed to get along much better after Melissa had children, especially when they were preschool age. Thereafter, her mother and her children gradually grew apart, with neither showing much interest in the other by the time the children were in their early twenties. At this point her brother's children were still young and her mother had developed a strong bond with them.

When Melissa reached her early thirties she noticed that her relationship with her brother had become increasingly troubled. At first, she attributed this to the dissimilarities between them, and the close bond that seemed to exist now between her mother and him. But there was more to it. Melissa realized that she had a lot of difficulty dealing with her brother's negativity, pessimism, irritability, low tolerance for frustration, and all of the other characteristics common to people with depressive personalities. She knew that he had a hard time with her optimism, enthusiasm, and cheerfulness. Moreover, she found her relationship with her mother increasingly strained. While Melissa had always had a good relationship with her father, she now noticed that even he was distancing himself from her.

While Melissa was troubled by her growing estrangement from her brother and mother, she never suspected what was to come. One day, she learned that her son, who was a football star at his high school, would be playing with his team in a special demonstration game against a team of well-known pros—all proceeds to charity. Melissa's son managed to get tickets to the event for his brother and parents and chose to give the two remaining tickets to his friends. Melissa's brother and her mother were incensed and let their feelings be known. But Melissa accepted her son's decision and refused to intervene. Soon her family issued an ultimatum: either the grandmother and uncle were invited or else—which turned out to be several angry rebukes, followed by the silent treatment. Melissa was subsequently shunned by her brother and mother, who established an alliance against her.

Melissa initially didn't take the matter very seriously and assumed that her mother and brother would get over it. But to her amazement their position gradually hardened. Melissa tried all of the obvious approaches to this situation to no avail. When she phoned her mother, she was told that first she had to apologize to her brother. But her brother refused to accept any of her apologies—citing a litany of past offenses as well as the present one. Moreover her father, who often mediated disputes, now refused to even talk to her on the phone. Melissa tried using other relatives and friends as intermediaries, which also did not work.

It soon became apparent to Melissa that nothing short of major groveling on her part would undo the enmity her brother and mother felt for her. Melissa did not see this as an option, and she didn't think that it would even work. In fact, when subsequently she did barge in on her mother at home and try to ask for forgiveness she was told to leave, and that her mother never wanted to see her again.

Upon reflection, Melissa realized that these relatives had routinely played the anger and grudge game on her as well as others throughout their lives. Her mother had a longstanding split with several members of her family, including her own father, whom she had refused to see even on his deathbed.

Afterward, which was now going on two years, Melissa's head was cluttered with anger, sadness, anxiety, guilt, and remorse. When she was at work, she was usually too distracted to think about it, but at night, often before she went to sleep, she would think about it over and over again. She would examine countless scenarios of what she could or should have done, which resulted in no obvious gain, although it did keep her up many nights.

She tried minimizing it—assuming that it wasn't all that important, and should be overlooked. After all, her brother and mother were probably more of a hardship and burden than a blessing.

She tried compensating for the problem by trying to get closer to her husband and own children and enlisting their support to help offset her loss.

Unfortunately none of these things brought relief for more than a short time before she was again assailed by feelings of distress.

Finally she decided to seek professional help.

MELISSA'S TREATMENT PLAN

The first step involved determining which emotional responses she was having the most difficulty with.

In Melissa's case, there were several.

a. Anger, toward her brother, mother, and to a lesser extent, her father.

b. Depression—associated with the loss of her original family.

c. Anxiety—about the ramifications of the situation: how this would affect her children and husband, as well as her ability to work and relate to her friends?

(There were, in addition to this, a number of secondary emotions—guilt, resentment, and hostility.)

We applied desensitization to the problem. Melissa gradually and progressively imagined confronting her brother and mother, living without them, discussing her fears with her husband and children, talking to her supervisor at work about the toll the problem was taking on her, and discussing the matter with other relatives, especially those partial to her brother and mother. By summoning up these images and allowing them to provoke an emotional reaction, she was able to gradually eliminate her fears and anxieties. She imagined seeing them at family gatherings and feeling sorrowful, allowing the feelings of loss to pass over her until this no longer provoked a feeling of sadness.

To help resolve her anger, Melissa acknowledged that she had been treated unfairly. She no longer looked to appease her brother and parents since this was self-destructive. Once her fears and anxieties were quelled and she no longer felt oppressed, she was able to view the situation more clearly. This brought a number of realizations.

She realized now that her outlook, attitudes, and concerns were generally antithetical to those of the problem family members. Melissa had an upbeat, energetic personality. She liked to initiate activities, while her brother and mother were chronically short on mental and physical energy. In the past, they had often found themselves in the uncomfortable position of having to come up with excuses to decline her initiatives. Melissa asked a lot of questions, and she also liked to talk about her activities, her accomplishments, and her new ideas, all of which her brother and mother found stressful. Melissa's optimism and cheery outlook were also a problem, because they preferred consoling each other with discussions of their problems and hardships.

In essence, Melissa's brother and mother found her personality very stressful and whatever misgivings they had about rejecting her were compensated for by their sense of relief when she didn't come around anymore. Her brother and mother intuitively understood each other and were able to get along with each other well to form an alliance against her.

Love versus control

Melissa had always thought that her brother and mother loved her, which they did to an extent. But they also shared a need to control others. In part, this was due to the insecurities they had regarding relationships (because of the problems depressives have getting along with others). And in part, from their need to regulate the stresses they experienced from interpersonal relationships. Melissa's brother and mother juggled their love and need for control until their love dropped. The need to control others is a form of abuse and is incompatible with love. Melissa realized that her brother's and mother's pathological need for control was a major factor in their rejection of her.

Taking action

Part of Melissa's recovery involved examining her own anger toward her brother and mother. As noted earlier, she felt manipulated and mistreated by them. She realized that her parents were old and in poor health and wouldn't be around much longer. She was also aware that they had a relatively large estate that was largely directed to her brother. Indeed, she often questioned her brother's motives for holding so tight to his grudge, given the pettiness of his complaints. She wondered if his grudge was no more than a convenient pretext to establish an alliance with their parents and thereby gain complete control of their estate.

The path to recovery when one is treated unfairly is to take corrective action. Thus, Melissa decided that when her parents died she would ask the courts to determine whether her suspicions were justified that her brother was exercising "undue influence" on their parents. Realizing that she would have her day in court relieved her of the burden of determining whether she was in fact mistreated, and mitigated her sense of helplessness.

> The people holding grudges don't think much about them. The grudge has accomplished their purpose—not having to deal with the person or persons, so they don't process it much anymore. They won't even think about it, unless they are getting a lot of pressure from the other party to reestablish the relationship, in which case they may possibly reassess the situation, or even come to therapy.

THE URGE FOR REVENGE

Revenge is similar to regret in that both are a complex combination of emotions (depression, anger, and anxiety) and thoughts about something. When one seeks revenge, he feels angry with those who have harmed him; depressed because of the losses he has incurred; and anxious or fearful because of the resulting threats to his survival.

As with regret, the treatment of those suffering from persistent thoughts of revenge involves first determining the strength and significance of each of the major components.

Often the problem is that the person pictures himself as a victim and the other person or persons as a culprit. The result is a tendency to see things as pretty black and white.

When someone wants revenge, they are blinded to the other person's point of view. If they wanted to reduce their anger, they might try to understand the other person's position. If the other person apologized or offered a rationale for what they did, those things might help. But they deliberately close themselves off from this, don't want to hear about it. They are not interested in the other person's point of view; they just want to get back at that person.

They dehumanize their opponent, refer to them in very derogatory ways and often not by name, or even as a human. This makes resolving the issue by therapy difficult, because the mind is not involved—this is a very emotional or visceral kind of response.

If you talk to people looking for revenge, and mention that you are interested in the other person's point of view, they get very angry. "You ask him! I don't know why he did the stupid thing that he did!" It stirs them up.

People seeking revenge don't usually come to therapy. They have usually thought the matter through to the point where they have eliminated most of the other possibilities, such as discussing the matter with the other person. They are not only angry, they want to get even.

For humans only?

Most of us take revenge on people, not things.

If a tree fell on your car during a hurricane, or your house was swallowed up by boiling lava from an erupting volcano, you probably wouldn't get angry at the hurricane or the volcano, or want to take revenge on the tree.

But if someone hit your tree and caused it to fall, that would be a different story.

Revenge is usually an interpersonal matter—the brain doesn't see a great need to get revenge on nonhuman sources. Many people who seek revenge say that they want to teach the other person a lesson. The fact that you can't teach nature a lesson may be a factor in this.

There are no simple answers when it comes to counseling someone bent on revenge. Often, the urge is so overpowering that they dismiss those who advise against revenge, while enlisting the aid of those who support it.

The desire for revenge is particularly acute when the loss involves a loved one. Love is a powerful emotion with bonds that transcend a person's concern for his own safety. Thus, the person may not care about whatever consequences he might suffer in his attempt to either "rescue" his loved one or harm the person who stole him or her. In the early 1900s, the courts accepted the idea that a person could experience an "irresistible impulse" to harm or even murder someone who had committed a horrendous offense against them, such as raping their wife or killing their child.

Not that long ago, a father was acquitted of murder when he tracked down and killed the man who had raped and killed his daughter. While the courts no longer accept the concept of irresistible impulse, juries often consider it in their deliberations.

Love is the only emotion that engenders transcendence—the tendency for people to place the needs and safety of loved ones above their own. Grandmothers have been known to jump into canals to wrestle with alligators who are attacking a grandchild; soldiers often risk their lives for one another, and so on. When it is a component in the desire for revenge, love can have a very powerful incendiary effect. People seeking revenge are often driven to commit audacious acts to quell the ruminations that plague them. A Palestinian soldier reported that he couldn't sleep for months after discovering that his wife and children had been killed in an Israeli attack. Eventually, obsessed and tormented by the need for revenge, he blew himself up in a terrorist raid on an Israeli town.

From a socio/biological perspective the urge for revenge probably evolved from our ancestors, and was linked to survival. At this point in time, revenge is more often destructive and counterproductive, giving rise to sermons and books on the importance of forgiveness.

DEALING WITH THE DESIRE FOR REVENGE

Both revenge and grudges involve anger toward the person who committed the act that you are angry about and the process of holding on to the anger. Elsewhere in this book I mention that anger is very difficult to desensitize and suggest alternate ways of dealing with it. The brain is for the most part programmed to want to have revenge in the form of getting even with the person. Getting even is a quicker, easier, and surer way to resolve this than the alternative, blaming yourself or looking at your own possible role in the matter. Few of us are willing to do this, because it is hard, and not as satisfying.

See you in court

Revenge is commonly dealt with in the courts, because it doesn't play out well in therapy or other areas. So it ultimately ends up in court, where it is just a battle to see who will win. When I was working for the courts people came in all day looking to get even, for revenge.

The court system was probably developed to provide a means of resolving anger in a more civilized way. Otherwise, people would resort to taking it out on the other person on their own and this would lead to significant problems for society. The courts try to regulate the way anger is managed in our society. If a person is found guilty of harming another person, the victim gets even because the culprit is punished. If the matter is civil, the victim ideally gets even by being rewarded a financial settlement.

> **The urge to get revenge**
>
> Is primitive and unsophisticated, and may not always be justified, but it is the heart of our legal system, which is essentially civilized revenge.

Getting together to get revenge

Often revenge-oriented groups are formed because people can't go after the specific person who caused them harm, so they go after everyone in that category, hoping to snare everyone they can in that net, including perhaps the very person who harmed them in the process.

Revenge is probably at the heart of MADD. Members are usually women who lost a child or other loved one to drunk drivers. So they take a very strong stance against drunk drivers. They enact laws against them, do everything they can to get them off the roads, and won't allow permissive legal policies regarding them.

America's Most Wanted is another example—the man who started this lost his son to a pedophile. He went on a rampage to get back at not just pedophiles but eventually all criminals. The program netted a great many bad apples over the years. Once you were featured on that show, it was not easy to stay hidden. Again, someone driven by anger and the need to get even.

Megan's Law is another example. It originated in the case of a young girl kidnapped by a neighbor while playing in her yard. The parents took no special precautions because they didn't know that a sexual predator had moved next door to them. So a law was passed that all sex offenders now must register, and they are put on the internet, so that you will always know it if a predator has joined the neighborhood.

We see this with the Parkland students, too, who banded together into a national organization to go after the NRA. That organization's loose policies about guns, in their eyes, are at the heart of what happened in their school. The person who came into their school to wreak deadly harm, from their point of view, was assisted by the NRA.

Tragedies don't always make the best laws. People who experience a tragedy may be so blinded by anger that they are not in a good position to assess all aspects of the problem. They often take a very black and white view, filled with the urge for revenge.

NATIONAL TRAGEDIES AND THE URGE FOR REVENGE

Studies of the mass murderers of recent years show how they usually arrive at the point where they decide to mow down innocent people.

They go through several stages.

1. They start off very depressed.

2. Decide that life can't go on like this, they will never get relief, so they are looking to end it all.

3. Now they are clearly suicidal and rather than try fight it, they accept it.

4. Once they fully accept it, the question becomes, how will they do it? Why not do it in some dramatic way? In the past this might have meant jumping off a bridge. Now they want to take others with them. They're miserable and not too happy about the fact that there are other people out there who are enjoying life, thrilled with things. They may even blame them for their unhappiness. So they will seek revenge.

5. They pick out a group they are angry at, such as the other students at the school they attend.

6. With their suicidal thinking in the background, they are liberated from concerns about other people, and the fact they themselves might get caught.

7. Suicidal people who have nothing to lose find it easy to get guns, and satisfy their urge for revenge, at the expense of many other people.

Put oily rags and matches together, and you will have an explosion. This is the prototype of the person who becomes a mass killer.

TREATMENTS FOR THE URGE FOR REVENGE

People rarely come into therapy and say, "I want to get revenge on someone—can you help me out?"

The tendency is to want revenge quickly, so often there is no chance to think it through and understand exactly what they are doing. They could make a lot of mistakes in the process. They may act impulsively and make things worse, end up in more trouble. So you want to try to help them improve their judgment.

Generally, it's a lot like treating anger. You want to attempt to get the person to understand the other person's point of view, which tends to ameliorate the need for revenge. You want to give them time to think about the situation and try to understand it, so you ask a lot of questions to prompt this.

The more time they take to think about it, the greater the chance that the frontal lobe or thinking, intellectual part of their brain will analyze the situation, and they won't just be acting out of raw emotion.

Exposure Therapy won't remove anger, although it may give some relief. Anger and the desire for revenge are so hard to desensitize it is hardly worth the time it would take to do so. Better to take some action to resolve this, getting back at the person in some way. Historically, scarcity was a major issue in survival, and it was not easy to make up a loss—it could potentially be fatal to lose things. So the brain wants you to rectify a problem like this, not desensitize it. Go out and get the horse someone stole from you back!

If you had a longstanding grudge against a boss for sexual harassment, it would take forever to extinguish, be exhaustive, and not work all that well. Getting even would be better, such as by writing a strong letter to management or the appropriate authority about this. One can get even without breaking the law.

PROCRASTINATION

Procrastination was originally believed to be the result of a person being poorly organized—a procrastinator was someone who had difficulty anticipating and planning properly. Some psychologists also thought that procrastination might be caused by some sort of attention-deficit issue.

When studies were done, however, it seemed that procrastinators were not ill organized. They simply had a tendency to focus on themselves and their own personal needs. So the root cause is self-absorption, and the lack of consideration for others that follows.

For example, imagine that a procrastinator is getting ready to leave the house so that he can meet his friends in fifteen minutes. As he's walking out the door he notices that the final of an important sports match is about to be played on TV. At that point he will decide to watch the event, even if it means that he will be late, rather than go meet his friends on time. Someone who is other-person-oriented would be on time or early.

A procrastinator wants to do what he wants to do, when he wants to do it. Procrastinators tend to be strong-willed, and don't like to be told what to do, or bullied. Often they don't do things on time because there are other things they could do, things they would prefer to do, rather than get the car washed, clean the house, or get that paper written or form filled out on time.

Given a choice of things to do, a procrastinator is inclined to pick something that suits his needs rather than someone else's. If you don't get things done for other people on time, it is because they aren't that important to you. An other-person-oriented individual gets things done quickly and without inconveniencing others.

A few other reasons for procrastination:

- Another common reason for putting things off is to avoid anxiety-producing possibilities—something you don't want to do, are afraid of doing, or have mixed feelings about, such as putting your affairs in order or taking an intimidating medical test.

- Procrastinating something that has a deadline due date may be based on fear of standing out, or even excelling.

- If you have the conscientious gene, you will feel awkward and uncomfortable if you don't do things on time. If you don't, it's hard to get things done in a timely manner.

> **Not doing things on time:**
>
> If this happens once in a while, it is probably situational.
>
> If a person is late with certain things but not others, it may be anxiety-based.
>
> When it happens all the time, across the board, it's because the person is attending to his own needs and not those of others. The core element is self-absorption.

The underlying psychological dynamic

Procrastinators usually suffer from a combination of anxiety and depression. The mix of anxiety and depression varies from person to person, with either one or the other being the dominant force. Those who are more depressive by nature usually avoid working hard, tend to be sedentary, and enjoy consumption more than productivity. Their depressive tendencies account for their reluctance to expend the effort needed to get things done. Their mental energy is often insufficient to meet their needs and so they look to take advantage of others. They often train the people in their lives to look somewhere else when it comes to getting something done. Their procrastination is often aimed at forcing others to do their work for them.

The ones who are predominately depressive are hard to motivate. They often don't have a strong incentive to change. These people usually seek treatment when the people in their lives rebel and refuse to carry their load. They may also be motivated to change by their employer. Treating their depression may involve restructuring their lives so that they are less stressed and have enough energy to meet their needs. Some require antidepressants.

Those who are more subject to anxiety are similar to those with anxiety-based problems discussed in Chapters Six and Eight.

Treatment for procrastination

When treating procrastination, we explore the tendency to be self-focused versus other-person oriented. When working with procrastinators, we start along those lines, and try to examine why and how they came to feel the way they do. We also try to develop more of a sense of empathy and concern for others. If someone is inclined to see themselves as the focus of everything, it's hard to put others' needs before their own. This is a difficult change to make, so the problem often persists.

When the other person is in a position of authority over them, the problem generally disappears. When the person they are inconveniencing is below them, the problem is hard to eradicate.

When people lose regard for other people, it usually means that their empathy is down, so they are less concerned about others, about peer pressure, or what others think of them. This "could care less thinking" usually comes about because they have reached a dead end, are depressed and have nothing to look forward to. It can help in this situation to reduce the stresses in their lives, the number of people and things they are involved with, which reduces the workload on the brain.

TO RECAP THE STEPS FOR TREATING DEPRESSION

The treatment of depression typically proceeds along much the same lines as the treatment for anxiety. Psychologically based depressions are generally caused by a loss, and the greater the loss the deeper the depression.

A major obstacle to recovery that people face when they are traumatized, whether the experience left them suffering from anxiety or depression, is their tendency to employ behaviors that enable them to avoid having to deal with the unpleasant emotions that accompany their condition. For example, a person who was traumatized in a pool accident may decide to avoid pools or never go into deep water. While avoidance behaviors are a problem when treating people who suffer from anxiety, they much more commonly go unrecognized in people who suffer from depression.

The most common avoidance response used by people who suffer from depression is to focus on the anger they have toward the person or thing they feel is responsible for their situation. The loss of a parent can be expected to engender a moderate to severe depression. If there are no complicating circumstances, such as guilt for not assisting the person, then the depression, generally referred to as grief, usually lasts from three to nine months. However, if the loss was attributable to the irresponsible actions of another person, then the grief-stricken party may be more likely to focus his grief on the anger he has toward the person who was responsible for his loss. So although a simple depression will as for three to nine months, a complicated depression (especially one that is heavily influenced by anger) can go on for years. The reason for this is that while depression will gradually desensitize with age and the frequency of the person's rumination on the loss, anger, on the other hand, is very resistant to desensitization. Anger is triggered when someone perceives themselves as being treated unfairly. Anger is very long-lasting because nature seemingly determined that one's survival would be severely jeopardized by allowing someone to get away with letting someone else treat them unfairly. Society has learned that unless the inequity is rectified, the need to get even or get justice will persist. When depression is mixed with anger, the two emotions must be dealt with separately. Depression responds to time and allowing (and encouraging) the brain to self-correct, while anger responds to techniques that allow the person to get justice.

The treatment of depression is to facilitate the person's focus on their loss, while providing compassionate support and discouraging them from unjustifiably blaming themselves and adopting false assertions such as they are not a good person or they are a complete failure. The anger is treated by encouraging the person to seek fair and reasonable ways of obtaining justice.

STEP 1: Here is where the use of guided imagery can facilitate the desensitization of depression. Under normal circumstances, a person will naturally focus on their loss on and off throughout the day. But this focus tends to be random and brief, as the exposure can be unpleasant. In treatment with a supportive therapist, or in self-treatment, the focus can be prolonged and organized into compartmentalized segments that are far more effective and will effectively reduce the duration of the desensitization process. Controlled and organized grief can be much more effective in a fraction of the time. Two or three ten-minute sessions a day will be much more effective than the usual erratic process carried out for months. The level of improvement at this point is 75%, with the remainder assumed to occur naturally over time.

STEP 2: As the person continues their exposure to guided imagery, they narrow the images down to ones involving the parts of the grieving memories that still cause distress.

The creative use of techniques to reestablish fairness when warranted is also important to reduce the likelihood of enabling the anger, if present, from complicating the depression. If properly executed the depression (grief) should be minimized. The level of improvement at this stage is about 100%.

STAGE 3: MASTERY: Mastery is achieved when you get to the point where you can successfully maximize the power of the desensitization process, when still needed, at will. Decoupling the anger from the depression and seeking out resources to facilitate coming up with creative ways of getting even when warranted is also an amazing improvement on the normal process.

CHAPTER THIRTEEN

GUILT AND REGRET
THE BURDENS OF LOOKING BACKWARD

When Henry Fonda was on his deathbed, his final words to his daughter Jane were that he didn't regret anything he did, though he did regret a few things he didn't do.

When we reach the later chapters of our lives, guilt and regret are two of the big themes we find ourselves contending with. Things we did that we aren't proud of, and things we didn't do but wish we did. Both of these issues are hard to deal with. When they come up earlier in life, we tend to keep putting them off, so they pop up at the end as a result. We tuck them aside earlier because we are too caught up in our current situation and its problems, and now there is no longer much later to defer them to.

It's a good idea to try and resolve guilt and regrets before you reach this point, so you don't end up adrift in a sad sea of maybes and "if only's."

REGRET

Most of us have our share of regrets, either because of things we did or failed to do, or things that did or didn't happen to us. Regret is not an emotion in its own right. Rather, it is a combination of feelings having to do with choices we made in the past that we have now come to feel differently about. Regret has as much to do with what we *think* about something, as what actually happened.

People who suffer from regret typically feel depressed (because they have suffered a loss as a result of whatever happened); anxious (because of the implications the loss has for their well-being, now and in the future); and angry (because they often feel that the outcome was unfavorable to them and unfair).

Overcoming regrets is therefore a complex process of first reducing the experience to its essential emotional underpinnings, and then determining the best way to resolve each of them.

For example, suppose a woman regrets not having a child. The analysis and treatment might be as follows:

1. She may feel depressed because her decision not to have a child in retrospect may constitute a loss.

2. She may feel anxious because she fears her decision may leave her lonely or without assistance in her old age.

3. She may feel angry because she feels her predicament is unfair due to circumstances beyond her control.

Let's assume that the woman feels angry because the man she was engaged to kept putting off getting married and having children until it was too late. She probably feels she was treated unfairly by him. Venting her anger toward him may bring him down a notch and thereby make him as miserable as she is—a form of justice. But this is probably not the best way to overcome the sense of unfairness she feels. If she is right in her assessment that he in fact did treat her unfairly, then she could advance a good case for him to acknowledge it, and consider changes in their relationship that would somehow compensate for this. Otherwise, she may have to seek other remedies for the part of her regrets that make her angry, such as deciding to move on to another man who might make her happier, as well as designing a lifestyle that is as fulfilling as loving and raising her own child. Maybe she could adopt a child, work with children, or otherwise find a meaningful outlet for her need for a child.

> Everyone has regrets, although some deny it. There are women who didn't have children, who in later years wish they had. There are those who have had children, who wish they never did. There are people who have made bad investments, and others who have offended friends and family. But of all life's regrets, the two that stand out are the failure to select the right career and get the education needed for it, and the failure to pursue a relationship with someone we later feel would have been our true mate.

I spoke to one woman on the subject of regret and she looked at me in puzzlement. She said she couldn't imagine why people would regret anything. She said she just made decisions, the best ones she could make at the time. She recognized that at times things wouldn't work out, but her inclination was not to look back and regret what she did, but just chalk the results off to fate, and go on with her life.

For most of us, it's not that easy to just attribute our losses and setbacks to fate or bad timing. We tend to take such things out on ourselves to some extent, feeling that if we had perhaps consulted more people before we made that decision, or relied on ourselves more, or done more research, or been more diligent, we might have prevented the mishap. If we had stayed within the boundaries of our own rules and guidelines, if we had done what we should have done, or whatever, things would have gone differently. In the face of bad consequences, there is a tendency to examine and find fault with how we handled a situation, to attribute blame to someone, if not ourselves, and then follow up with some form of punishment in the form of a negative attitude, a drop in confidence, an alienation from ourselves, or the like. For many of us, this is not a process we feel we have much control over. It seems to unfold on its own, and once we are caught up in it, it is very difficult to get out of.

> Many men have told me that they are torn between the pressure to work hard to provide for the family and the pressure to spend time with the family—a very difficult balancing act. Women report the same problem with the need to care for their children, and at the same time often work to help support the family. So many people in our society find themselves in a situation where there are no good answers and they are forced to make a choice that will cause them regret no matter which way they go.

A personality characteristic that is very much associated with regret is depression. Depressed people tend to live in the past, which is of course where regrets originate. They are also more inclined to be aware of all of their losses and setbacks. Much of the depression I've seen in clinical practice is the result of losses and setbacks. So it is only natural for people to look at those losses, think about the things that could or should have been done to prevent them, and attribute their depression to either their own failings or perhaps those of the people they consulted. Depressives also have a tendency to examine their lives, and reflect on the various turning points and crises in it. The result is often interpretations that call their own actions into question.

A good example of this is a person named Amy, who had always done exceptionally well in school. She'd gone to one of the best colleges in the country, and when she graduated she had a straight-A average.

She'd always loved animals, and wanted to go on to become a veterinarian now. And sure enough, she was accepted into one of the best vet schools in the country.

During her first year there, she was an outstanding student. Her teachers all praised her. She decided to specialize in animal internal medicine, and was looking forward to it. Her mother was very proud of her (her father had died earlier), and all was going along according to plan. Toward the end of her first year, however, her mother became severely ill, and given the family's limited finances and the children still at home, she asked Amy to come home and help out. She'd have to take a job in the local area to do this.

Amy was devastated, but had always been a very responsible young woman, so she did go back home. At the end of her first year she dropped out of veterinary college and went back to her family in Binghamton. She took a job at a used car sales network, where she made a modest income, but it helped.

In the next year or so she was quickly promoted, which earned her considerably more, and enabled her to assume full responsibility for her family's income. Eventually, her mother passed away. But by this time, she had spent quite a few years working her way up in the car sales company. She didn't feel it was possible to go back to become a veterinarian at this point, so she stayed where she was, and over the next ten years, rose to the level of regional vice president.

During that time, she married a man who was also very bright and talented. He worked from home, running a company that guided trophy hunters and fishermen, and together they developed their life and had a child.

For the most part, they were so involved in proceeding with their life together that Amy had little opportunity to look back on the fact that she had never completed veterinary school. After about ten years of marriage, however, her husband had a bad accident on an ATV. He developed severe health problems afterward that required a lot of surgery, medication, and physical therapy, but even so he could no longer do the things he once did. As time passed he stayed home more and more, and his mood began to dip. He became more and more inclined to pessimism and negativity. He didn't have the energy to help take care of their child, and often complained about the demands that were put upon him. At that point he stopped working, but still felt that he couldn't keep up with all he had to do. As he slipped deeper and deeper into depression, he became more and more argumentative and sour.

Eventually, coming home became a living hell for Amy. She spent more and more time at her job to avoid her husband, and the more she did that, the worse he greeted her when she came home. She dreaded going home, and spent as little time as possible there. She began to become severely depressed herself, which only contributed to the arguments between her and her husband. After about ten years of constant strain and stress, and arguments over every imaginable thing—including lack of communication and lack of camaraderie—her husband had a stroke and died.

At this point the couple's son was in college, and didn't require much in the way of care. He was well on his way to his own career. Around this time Amy started looking back on her life, and thinking about the fact that she had never completed her veterinary training.

She felt that she had been dealt a bad hand that prevented her from pursuing her ambition to be a vet. She found herself having more and more intrusive thoughts about this. During the day while she was working on her computer at the car company, she would imagine herself as a vet with a full waiting room, and seeing dogs and cats and the occasional rabbit or ferret. When she took her own pets for their medical checkups, she would often find herself wondering what it would be like if she were the doctor, instead of the one bringing in the patient. She became obsessed with talking about her failed veterinary career, and how many problems she could have avoided if only she had gone through with it.

At this point, she was fifty-eight years old, and it was probably too late for her to go back to vet school. Did she want to pursue a volunteer position at the local humane society, or take courses in animal-related areas at the local college? She was so depressed that although she complained bitterly about her situation, she didn't feel in a position to do anything about it.

Shortly thereafter, she met a man whom she ultimately married. They are still married and have a wonderful relationship. He is ideally suited for her. He doesn't seem to be unduly put off by her obsession with vet school, and he puts up with all of her other quirks and peculiarities seemingly without missing a beat. He himself tends to be upbeat and positive, and he has rejuvenated her. And she has come to appreciate him and love him deeply.

In all of my time treating Amy, I couldn't help but notice that on the days when things were not going so well, such as when she was having trouble with her son, the obsessiveness kicked in, and she talked quite a bit about becoming a veterinarian. On the other hand, when things were going well, when the stock market was up, she'd gotten an interest check, her son had gotten an award, or she'd gotten another promotion or bonus, things were, in other words, looking up, she tended to talk much more positively. And when I asked her about her regrets on those occasions, she tended to take a more existential view of them, saying that things happen, she recognized this, and now she'd learned to live with it.

It might be only a week or so later before things turned around, and she was much less inclined to look at her situation philosophically. Now she resumed her brooding over her lost chance to be a veterinarian. The quality of her life at any given time seemed to be a predictor of how she would feel about the regrets in her life. As the quality of her life dipped, she was more inclined to become obsessed. And when the quality of her life was up, she denied that such things were much of a problem. This is not an uncommon phenomenon.

For older people, the treatment for regret is often focused on changing internal perceptions. It is much more difficult late in life to change one's circumstances, as Amy found out later in life when she regretted the fact that she had not finished veterinary college. It was too late for her to resume working toward that profession, so at this point she had to work on changing her view of things. She had to think more in terms of improving the quality of her life and recognizing that what she had done as a young woman was the right thing to do, which was very important to her. It was more important than self-actualizing and achieving everything that she could achieve. Her sense of duty and righteousness was more important than accomplishments or achievements.

WAS THAT EARLIER CHOICE REALLY WRONG?

Studies that have examined regret closely reveal that when a person makes a decision, and then many years later decides to look back at it, there is a tendency to think that the first decision was wrong, and to regret it.

But many years later we tend to have a biased view of things, and are not usually under all of the pressures we were back at the time when we made the original decision. And there may have been other things going on at the time, affecting us initially, but not now. We overlook these things now, twenty or whatever years later.

From today's perspective it may seem that that earlier decision was wrong.

But research has been more inclined to show that the original decision was better than the one, twenty years later, that you wish you had made.

A BETTER CHOICE THAN REGRET

People often come to therapists with a dilemma they face, such as whether they should go on to a particular professional school or not. This is often a question of what is going to happen if they make the wrong choice.

Psychologists often say that if you have a choice between regret and guilt, choose guilt. Guilt is usually not as complex, as will be explained later in this chapter.

If, for example, if you wonder if you should go to law school or not, and you are not sure, it may be better to go. By going you will find out whether in fact it is a good idea. You will experience it—the first year, the second year, and so on, and you might even graduate. Even if you don't like it or find out that you never will be good at it, you may waste a year or two on this, but you will know exactly why you didn't stick with it. You will know for sure that it wasn't the right choice. There will be a specific and clear-cut outcome.

If you don't go, you will always wonder if you should have gone, and not have much information as to how it would have worked out. If there was some limitation or problem, could you have coped with it, or might other options have come into play?

Guilt is often easier to deal with than regret, because you know the whole story. With regret you don't. Guilt is a straight line—you know what the outcome was, and it is the only issue, while with regret you can only wonder how things might have turned out, and you usually have to desensitize far more possibilities. With guilt, you only need to concentrate on what actually happened.

FACTORS THAT INCREASE REGRET... OR DECREASE IT

There are a number of things that have a bearing on a person's likelihood to feel regret, as well as on how severe that regret may be. The following are some of the better established of these.

Were there alternatives?

Were there alternatives to the regrettable act? People tend to feel more regret when alternatives to the regrettable act were possible. The more alternatives there are in a given situation, the more likely people are to experience regret if things do not go well. For example, one of my clients was a woman whose son had died during an operation to remove a rather large hernia he had. He'd been checked and tested by his doctors before the operation, and assured that everything would go okay. Yet for some unexplained reason, during the operation, his blood pressure became extremely high and he died as a result.

Her mother felt that not all of the necessary precautions had been taken. She thought the doctor could have been more conscientious in monitoring her son's blood pressure, not only during the operation, but before it. She had talked to other doctors who spoke of other techniques that could have been used when the crisis developed, which might have managed to save him. She spoke of how her son should have had regular checks of his blood pressure, which did tend to spike at times. If only he'd had the hernia removed while it was still small, so that the operation would have been shorter and simpler, and on and on. The more alternatives that could have prevented a tragedy, the more likely a person is to experience regret.

Another example involves a woman named Adele. A couple of years before she came to see me, her husband had developed skin cancer. He'd had a lot of sun exposure in his life, and especially since he had a light complexion, she tried to keep him mindful of the danger of this disease. She prodded him to self-treat any possible precancerous spots on his face, neck, and elsewhere yearly, with a preparation that reddened his skin for a while, but did help. He didn't like these treatments, and sometimes skipped them. She also tried to keep alert for any suspicious-looking spots anywhere on his body, when she had the chance.

One day when he was having a routine physical, his doctor noticed a darkened area on her husband's back. He suggested that it be checked out by a dermatologist, and when it was, it turned out to indeed be skin cancer. Her husband arranged to have the spot removed by a local dermatologist, and was relieved afterward to feel that he had dodged that bullet.

Eighteen months later, her husband was suddenly unable to continue reading the newspaper he'd been perusing. A trip to the emergency room and then a large hospital in the nearest city afterward found a doctor telling Adele two days later that her husband had stage 4 melanoma, which had spread to his brain, stomach, lungs, and liver. Six months later he was dead.

Adele was overwhelmed with grief at the fact that her husband had contracted such a horrible disease. She looked back at her actions and began to blame herself. If only she had made sure he *always* did the self-treatments. If only she'd watched him more closely, and seen the spot on his back. After the spot was discovered, she should have insisted that it be removed by a better-qualified and more expert dermatologist. If only they'd kept checking afterward to be sure that the doctor had "got it all," and that it wasn't being harbored elsewhere in his body. She went over and over all of the actions she should have taken—how easy it would have been to do these things. When alternatives are plausible and readily available, a person is very likely to experience regret.

On the other hand, when there are few alternatives, there is less regret. For example, a person I know was caught in an avalanche in unexpected circumstances. He had taken all of the necessary precautions, and it was just one of those flukes that occur. He wasn't killed, but he was severely injured. When I asked him if he regretted anything about that day, he said not really. Before he left to ski he had been cautious, checked everything out, and consulted with the ski patrol—done everything he thought he should do, and just assumed it was bad fate. So here is a case where low mutability resulted in little regret.

Did you have to do it?

Regrets are much more likely when it's easy to imagine not performing an act that turns out to be regrettable.

For example, in the case of a young woman who had a car accident and was very seriously injured as a result, it was very easy for her to imagine not having performed that act. She could have just been more assertive, and told her boyfriend that she was not going to come to see him in a down moment he was having one night, when she knew he probably didn't truly love her, was just using her. Her regrets were intensified by the fact that the act she regretted, driving in the middle of the night to his aid, was so easy to imagine not doing.

If, on the other hand, someone is called into action in a situation where they feel they have no choice, when perhaps a family member is stranded by the side of the road somewhere, they may feel they have to come pick them up. If they have a problem in the course of something like this, it usually isn't a regrettable act. While they had a bad experience as a result, they had to come to their family's aid.

Were you under pressure?

Regrets are less likely to occur when you feel that you were under pressure to do whatever you did that was regrettable.

For example, in the case mentioned later in this chapter involving Janet, she felt that she was under a lot of pressure to leave her childhood home. Thus she did not experience much regret over her decision. Even though she ended up divorcing the man that she married, she felt that she needed so badly to leave her mother that she didn't have much of a choice.

In another case involving a boy studying to become a dentist, he wanted very much to have a girlfriend, because all of his friends had one. The fact that he decided to put this off and concentrate on preparing himself for his career (and earning the money to help put himself through college) meant that he didn't have much of a social life during his college days. But the pressure he felt to move forward toward his eventually very lucrative career reduced the sense of regret that he experienced over this.

Doing hits harder now than failing to do

In the short term, regrettable actions tend to be more severe than regrettable omissions.

In the short term, people are much more likely to experience regret when they do something that results in a problem, than if they fail to do something that causes a problem. For example, I saw a woman named Patsy who asked her girlfriend whether she would mind if she went out with a guy her friend had recently broken up with. Her girlfriend said fine, they were no longer together, and there was no reason she couldn't go out with him. So Patsy decided to do that, and for a month or two, she and the fellow had a fairly good relationship. But during the course of that, her girlfriend saw less and less of her and rarely called her.

When she approached her girlfriend about this, the woman said that she was horrified that Patsy had decided to go out with her ex-boyfriend, and said she now felt that she couldn't trust Patsy with any of her boyfriends. Their relationship seemed severely strained, if not terminated. Patsy indicated that she deeply regretted having done this—she hadn't realized that her girlfriend would be so upset. She thought that she had covered all the bases, but later she realized that she had not been fully sensitive to her girlfriend's feelings.

> The reason that regrets in the short run tend to be more associated with actions than omissions is that when you do something that leads to bad consequences, it is often obvious shortly thereafter. But when you fail to do something, there is usually a time delay before you realize that you have made a mistake. The most serious regrets are usually associated with omissions, such as not having gone to college or chosen the right life mate.

Omissions will get you later

Regrets in the long term are more often associated with passivity or omissions.

It usually takes some time before it becomes apparent that some failure to act was a mistake. In the case discussed earlier, involving Amy who wanted to be a vet, it was many years before she realized that she probably should have gone back to college right after her family crisis was resolved.

In another case, a man named David had a love affair with a girl in his high school. They were both considered to be among the most beautiful people in the school. He was very successful on the basketball team as well as academically, and she was one of the prettiest girls in the school. They had a charmed romance and life together. They both went to Ivy League colleges, and until their senior year were planning on getting married. At this point, David began to wonder if they should date other people, just to make sure that they were right for each other. Before long they were on separate paths, never to meet again.

Dave now looked back at his decision to get more exposure to and experience with other women as a huge mistake. He felt that he never should have allowed himself to entertain that kind of thinking, and never should have suggested it to his girlfriend. But this feeling of regret didn't come about for many years.

In the meantime, he had married another woman and had two children. The first five years of their lives together were good. However then there was a downturn in the economy, and he lost his job. He had been an executive in an ad agency, and was now forced to take a job as a PR person. This was a big setback for him, because it was a much lower-level position than he'd had previously, and the work didn't really interest him. So he went to the office each day progressively more depressed, and came home every day after not being very successful. His wife began to get on him because of all of the bills and problems that were mounting up at home.

Before long, their relationship deteriorated, and in a few years, they decided to get divorced. Looking back, he felt that the biggest error in his life had been when he let his high school sweetheart go. He should have stayed with her. She was much more upbeat, was preparing for a better career, and together they could have handled these kinds of vicissitudes much better than his subsequent wife, who tended to be on the passive and dependent side. Here again we see a case where over the long haul, a person is likely to look back at something he failed to do. And from this standpoint, regrets for acts of omission tend to be much more intense.

> Many people don't regret an actual loss as much as their own lack of initiative and unwillingness to take a stand that led to it. They are most upset that they allowed the unfortunate event to ever happen. This lack of decisiveness or assertiveness boils down to a breakdown between me and what is important to me.

Are there consolations?

Regrets are reduced when there are some consolations.

A case in point involved a woman, Janet, who had gotten married, and later realized that she never loved the person that she married. She'd married him because he seemed to have a secure job, seemed very responsible, and most importantly, this would enable her to leave the home where she had a very difficult relationship with her mother. The mother was very argumentative and easily angered, and Janet felt that she could no longer live with her. When Richard came along, it looked as if this was her way out.

After a dozen years she realized that was not enough to base a marriage on. They were not well suited for each other. He was a very conscientious and organized guy who was very concerned about having everything in its place and in the right order. She had a much looser, more spontaneous way of dealing with things. As a result, they argued bitterly over all aspects of their lives, including the children they had.

Eventually, they got to the point where they realized that they should get divorced.

Looking back on the situation, Janet didn't have any regrets. Why? Because she felt that she had developed a close and wonderful relationship with her children during the course of the marriage. Had she not married, she would probably have stayed in her unhappy situation with her mother much longer, and she might never had had children.

In the case I mentioned earlier, the young woman who had an accident that led to multiple fractures and other health problems, she, too talked about all of the consolations of her situation. For example, as a result of her accident, she didn't have to work. She was on full disability and as it turned out, her family needed her around the house. Her grandfather had suffered several strokes, and needed constant care. Being home all day, she was able to take care of him, as well as do other helpful things. With these consolations in mind, her regrets were not nearly as bad as if these mitigating factors were not there.

There is less regret for the completed

Completed tasks tend to yield less regret than uncompleted ones.

If you complete a task, you know all of the details and circumstances involved. If what you did here turns out to be regrettable, at least you know the full course of what happened. There is only one scenario that the mind has to deal with.

On the other hand, if you don't get a chance to complete something, such as Amy who wasn't able to finish veterinary college, you never really have a chance to see what it would have been like. Thus there is much more potential for fantasizing alternatives, and imagining different outcomes.

ANXIOUS PEOPLE AND REGRET

People who are subject to anxiety react to regrets in a quite different way. People who are anxious are generally more inclined to look into the future. They are usually more concerned with any possible threats in their lives, and establishing their own security, doing whatever they have to do to ensure that they don't suffer any setbacks or losses, or that things don't come unglued. Since they are always looking toward the future, they tend not to be as concerned with the past. They are less inclined to examine their lives, and less inclined, one would think, to feel regret. However, they do suffer from one form of regret, and that is the feeling that if they only somehow had armed or equipped themselves better, they would have been that much more able to make themselves secure.

Anxious types are notorious for being obsessed with planning and anticipation. They are constantly looking at their lives from the standpoint of what could go wrong, how they could avoid it, and what steps they must take to prevent problems from arising. Because of this, and their general cautiousness, typically their regrets have to do with those aspects of their lives that have resulted in problems that interfere with their ability to defend themselves against potential threats and be more prepared for future events.

So their regrets tend to lie in the area of omissions, failures to act, to protect themselves, to develop their skills, to get the necessary training, to pursue a certain lover, etc.

In many cases, anxiety is at the core of people's tendency not to do something. Under the pressure to act, people often become frozen by their anxieties, their confidence slips, and at the time, they are unable to do what they feel is the right thing. Later on, when their anxiety is down, and they are feeling more confident, they may look back on the action and feel that they did the wrong thing. But interestingly enough, when these people are put back in the situation, they often make the same decision that they did earlier.

For example, one of my clients grew up with her sister, and they had a very abusive mother. The client regretted not having stood up for her younger sister, who was often picked on and mistreated by the mother. At the time, my client was so afraid of her mother that she didn't know what to do. Looking back, she wasn't sure that she would have done anything different, because she remembered how intensely she was intimidated by her mother at the time. Her inability to manage her anxiety was a big factor in the development of this regret.

LACK OF ANXIETY LEADING TO REGRET

In some cases it is the lack of anxiety that is the heart of regret. In one case, a Vietnam veteran recalled how when he was younger, he always did daredevil things. One day, for example, he climbed up on a water tower and walked across the top from one end to the other, as all of his friends looked on in amazement.

This lack of fear made him decide to join the Army, so that he could go into combat. He wanted to see action, to be in a position where he could make a difference. He had no anxiety about putting himself in harm's way. As a result, he ended up in some of the bloodiest battles of the war and was severely injured. This injury cost him dearly. Not only did it take a toll on his health, his ability to work, and his ability to lead the life he wanted to lead, but the chronic pain affected his personality. He became irritable, depressed, and easily frustrated. He felt that he was not treated fairly by the Army and the veterans' services, and this led to a lot of bitterness. In addition, he developed PTSD, and this further complicated his situation.

Here we see a case where the lack of anxiety, a tendency to be too bold, leads a person to make decisions that ultimately turn out to be regrettable.

REGRET FOR WAITING TOO LONG

Many people put off matters they end up regretting. During the time of life from say the thirties to the sixties, people often put things off: having babies, going back to school, getting into or starting a new business—waiting till a better time or opportunity.

By the time these people reach their sixties their options shrink, and at that point they may not have the ability to do many of these things. So now regret becomes a real problem. For women this usually hits earlier—they may put off having children until it's difficult, expensive, unlikely, or impossible. Then regret really sets in.

> It's often a good idea to anticipate regret—to be mindful of the pitfalls of regret long before it occurs. You want to beware of forestalling things so long that you put yourself in a bind when you're older.
>
> At some point the ease of putting things off now has a big price tag.

REGRET FOR NOT ACTING FAST ENOUGH

One of the characteristics common to people who have regrets is the feeling that they didn't act fast enough. This is often seen in people who have been traumatized.

They were, for whatever reason, caught up in assessing the situation, and before they had a chance to fully assess it, the other person or thing did something dastardly to them or something else awful happened. They just did not act fast enough.

Our brains are much more inclined to action than reflection, and psychologists tend to encourage people to act rather than respond passively to things. Animals are very inclined to active responses—they see food and go after it, or something threatening them and run off. There isn't much passivity, or "let's wait and see." The idea of taking time to think about something is mainly human.

The rape victim discussed in Chapter Seven was embarrassed that she didn't act fast enough. When she first got a glimpse of the man on the commons late that night, there was something about him that made her uncomfortable. But she was too concerned for his feelings, how he might feel if she ran off right then or shouted for help. Now she was angry at herself for not acting fast enough, not considering her own needs first.

Criminals take advantage of this. They know that most people are concerned with being polite and helpful and not offending anyone. So they approach someone and ask for some change, or a cigarette, or for help finding their dropped contact lens, and when the person reaches into their pocket, or is searching for the lens, is when they strike. They take advantage of people's tendency to want to be nice.

Once victimized like this, people tend to overreact afterward.

This is what happens to many soldiers back from wartime service. The number of vets who claim to act first and think later is very great. They all seem to have learned from combat that being slow, not taking decisive action immediately, is a mistake. Police officers, too, often talk about the need to take immediate control of a situation and assess who is dangerous, and neutralize that person or persons as quickly as possible.

The more time you waste in such a situation, the more likely you are to have problems.

However this idea of jumping into action can go too far. With regret there can be an impulsivity that follows. People who have been traumatized often have a hypervigilant response to situations. They have a rationale for this: "Better to be judged by twelve than carried by six." Better to be a little on the impulsive side, assume the worst about the other person, than be on the passive side, and assume the best about the other person, who might attack you or whatever.

But the courts have a tendency to penalize people who jump to conclusions and act impulsively.

TREATMENTS FOR REGRET

In some respects desensitization is not as effective with regrets as it is in some other areas. In the case of regrets, as time goes by, despite the fact that a person may have spent a good deal of time thinking about the regrets in his life—what they should have done, could have done, or what they didn't do—over time those regrets may in fact become more severe. With time also comes a drop in the potential for a person to change course. As people get older they have fewer possibilities for turning around their regrettable acts and so over time their sense of regret may in fact get worse. The desensitizing effect of thinking about their regrets over and over is canceled out by the increase in these feelings because of the difficulty of changing things now.

Exposure Therapy can be effective with regrets, especially if the act happened not long before the person started to experience a sense of regret. Essentially what the person should do is revisit the act and work it through in his imagination, imagining ways in which he could have handled the situation that he thinks might have been more effective, and examine the regrettable act in terms of the factors that may have accounted for it. The more he does so, the more he desensitizes those feelings.

When treating regret, the hardest part is getting over the anger at yourself for not pursuing an opportunity. We can easily attack numerous parts of our personality for being responsible for this—e.g., I wasn't assertive enough, I was too self-absorbed, I was too impulsive, I overrated my intelligence and judgment, etc. This leaves a lot of things to desensitize. At some point, you may want to try to compensate for the loss by making changes in your personality to provide a gain for yourself. Or, you may want to desensitize your fears of doing something that would correct the problem—such as go back to school or change careers. Every career incorporates aspects of other fields—for example if you are a teacher who regrets not going into medicine, you could get further education if necessary to teach biology, teach medical students, do research on medical problems, teach first aid, or teach EMS. Women who don't have children can adopt, try foster care, work in a daycare center, work for organizations that aid children, and so on. Use Exposure Therapy to enable yourself to take the risks associated with changes like these. You can use the process to help forget or extinguish regrets, but it doesn't work well when the emotion involves a lot of anger at oneself, as is often the case with regrets. So as an alternative, use desensitization to extinguish the anxieties and fears that prevent you from taking corrective action.

In the process of confronting these thoughts you also calm the mind, because the mind sees you in an aggressive, dynamic state, and that is different from the fearful, intimidated state that it sees when you are doing everything you can to avoid thinking about something because it is so horrible or threatening. The mind is aware of how you handle problems and if you handle them by attacking them it creates a certain peace and confidence in the brain. But if you handle them by running away, you scare the brain by communicating your sense of fearfulness and lack of confidence, which undermines your brain's confidence in you.

GAINING INSIGHT

Taking a close look at your regrets can help you gain insight into them, which may also help to reduce them.

In one case a woman named Maureen regretted the fact that she had not dealt more effectively with the situation when her son ran off with a lover at the age of seventeen. The lover turned out to be a gay man who was very controlling and dominant. Maureen felt that she herself should have taken more control over the situation. But as she began to gain more insight into it, she realized that her son had done this voluntarily, and partly because he felt ashamed and embarrassed about being gay. Running off with this man enabled him to avoid that shame, and also to avoid facing his parents over this issue. The reason that he ran off and that he later had difficulty coming back was largely the fact that he was having trouble dealing with his sexuality. It had nothing to do with how his parents had raised him or the way that the mother had handled the situation. As Maureen learned more about homosexuality, she stopped blaming herself for her son being gay, and this insight reduced her regret as well.

For another example, when I first worked in hospitals I saw psychiatrists treating thirty or forty people in day, or in rounds even more, going from one bed to the next pretty quickly, and all of the patients seemed a little better afterwards. There was nothing comparable to this in the work I was doing. It must be great to have that experience, I thought, to be able to get in and out fast, and yet help so many people. I was downright envious of this, and almost regretted not being a psychiatrist. As I learned more, I finally realized that psychiatrists were basically accomplishing what they did by modifying the patients' medications. And there were a lot of down sides to the medications given. When I got successes in therapy, I could credit myself, because I did it on my own.

A BETTER LIFE MEANS LESS REGRETS

As noted in the case of Amy earlier, the quality of one's life in the present is a big factor in how regretful a person is likely to be.

In the case of the man who married Janet, when they got divorced he regretted having married her, as well as the waste of time he experienced as a result of his relationship with her. But when he found another woman, someone he could be happy with, when he developed a new lifestyle and started spending more time with his children and having fun with them, he found that he regretted his first marriage less and less. By improving the quality of our lives we can often reduce our regrets dramatically.

CLOSING DOWN THE POSSIBILITIES

One of my clients had a lot of regrets over the fact that a lover earlier in her life had broken up with her—she felt that if she had been with him she would have had a good life. They probably would have had terrific children, and she imagined that he would have been very successful and an excellent husband as well. She was sure she could never find anyone else nearly as good.

As it turned out, she got a chance to revisit their relationship when he got in touch with her again several years later and wanted to resume their relationship. So she got to see what might have happened. At that point, he was not very successful, was a heavy drinker, and had gotten involved with a number of what seemed to be rather shady associates. He was not the person she had been fantasizing about and after spending some time with him again she realized that it was good that she had never married him. She closed down the possibilities and scenarios her mind was dealing with by reestablishing a relationship with him long enough to examine whether all of her thoughts and images of him were, in fact, accurate.

It is often effective to reduce the number of options and scenarios that the mind has to deal with. When you learn more about a situation you may well find that there were other factors involved that do not fit the scenarios, images, and fantasies that your mind has been processing.

GUILT

Guilt is a secondary emotion in that it is composed of varying degrees of one or more of the primary emotions, coupled with the individual's own unique perspective on the circumstances that provoked this feeling. For example, people who feel guilty often report that they are fearful of being discredited, depressed by the harm they have done, and angry with themselves. Moreover, they usually have strong negative moral opinions about their behavior and towards themselves. The strength and proportions of each of these factors varies with the individual.

For one example, a Gulf War veteran confided in me that while on guard one day he noticed enemy activity in a nearby gully. Rather than organizing a patrol to investigate, which was standard operating procedure, he called in a helicopter to scout the area. When the dispatched helicopter approached the area, heavy fire from the ground nearby caused it to crash, killing all aboard. He and a small group of other men were sent to recover the bodies from the helicopter. He was also asked to report to the families of the deceased about the incident. Upon his return to the States, he never discussed the incident, but it festered within him.

Years later, he volunteered for an inpatient rehab program for veterans suffering from PTSD. The vets met for group therapy sessions, during which they discussed intimate details of their involvements in the war. Nevertheless, even here, he refused to disclose his sense of guilt, although he desperately wanted to.

> Typically, the avoidance and escape behaviors used by people who suffer from anxiety are easy to identify, such as those used by people who have simple phobias. Ones that are more difficult to spot are those that are often associated with guilt or shame. For example, a soldier who was traumatized by his injuries during a battle may also suffer from guilt associated

Guilt is a very complex emotional/cognitive process that is poorly understood, in large part because those who suffer from it are extremely reluctant to disclose it. Because they typically harbor anger towards themselves for their own behavior, they often derive a form of satisfaction from the harm to themselves that their guilt causes, as if they were settling the score by punishing themselves. Thus it is often necessary to carefully examine the intricate web of conflicting emotions to understand the psychological dynamics of guilt.

Guilt is not a pure emotion—it is often a mixture of fear of being found out, a little regret, shame, and disappointment or disgust with oneself, for example. Treating guilt starts with breaking it down into its components and then analyzing their interaction and synergistic effects on one another. This is how the veteran mentioned above was treated.

WHY SELF-HELP IS IDEAL FOR DEALING WITH GUILT

The advantage you have when dealing with guilt is that you know exactly what happened—what you did, when and how you did it, and even why you did it. You have all of the insight already that you could possibly ask for. How many areas of psychology can one say that about?

> Trying to analyze and deal with regret can be very frustrating. You manage to get over one aspect of it, only to have it replaced by another. Whereas you know what the root of guilt is, and you are less likely to follow false leads and dead ends.

You hear people undergoing therapy say, "I can't wait for the big insight!" Or hear therapists say, "We're getting close to a real breakthrough." In the case of guilt, you know all of this already, have the ultimate insight.

This is why self-help is fine—a therapist is not really needed here.

Desensitization, as described in earlier chapters, gets to the heart of treatment.

In the case of guilt, self-treatment can also help you see how intractable and difficult things can be at times, even when you do have insight.

THE FEAR ELEMENT OF GUILT

When I treat a client for guilt, the first step, which is often the most difficult, is to establish rapport with the person so that he will be willing to disclose his guilt. One of the advantages of a self-help approach is that this step, which is not only laborious but often fruitless, can be bypassed. Many people who suffer from guilt are very reluctant to examine their own guilt, since it can be very painful. A person's refusal to reveal and discuss his behavior and emotions also acts to preserve his guilt. This has the same effect as avoiding any feared object—it perpetuates its fear-arousing properties. For example, if a person was afraid to fly and therefore avoided going on planes, his avoidance would perpetuate his fear of flying. Overcoming the person's avoidance is a necessary step in overcoming his fear.

Another obstacle for people who suffer from guilt is that they are not necessarily interested in recovering. They often indicate that they are ambivalent about overcoming their guilt, since they feel that they deserve to feel angry at themselves. This is another consideration in favor of a self-help approach, since the person may be willing to read about the nature and cause of guilt, as well as how others have helped themselves.

People who suffer from severe guilt may harm themselves if left untreated. Some people—especially those in a position to be administering justice, such as police, judges, and prosecutors—feel compelled to punish themselves if they feel guilty about something. And when punishing themselves they tend to be very harsh, because they are aware that they violated their own standards and principles.

Clients in therapy do not readily discuss feeling guilty, nor is this a topic that is routinely addressed in therapy. Many people fail to see how psychotherapy can help relieve guilt and therefore do not bring it up. Assuming that a person is finally willing to discuss his or her guilt, the next step is to examine the person's fears. Most sufferers are afraid of what others, especially family and friends, will say or think about them once they know of their guilt. Many feel they would be held in less esteem and possibly even shunned. This, of course, is often quite true. But there is a vast difference between disclosing your guilt to others and admitting it to yourself.

Many people mistakenly believe that exposure, to be effective, has to involve disclosure. This is not so. Exposure as applied to guilt can be very effective even when one limits it to oneself.

Exposure, as noted earlier, involves summoning up an emotional response in the absence of any real consequences. If one imagines revealing their guilt to friends, and this activates physiological symptoms of anxiety—such as accelerated heartbeat and rapid breathing—then despite the fact that this is being done in imagery rather than reality, it still acts to reduce the anxiety. At first, disclosure to others is probably not advisable because their reaction could well constitute a true negative consequence, which would intensify the person's anxiety.

Many people resist psychotherapy as well as psychiatric medication because they do not feel comfortable with the loss of personal control involved—hence the popularity of herbal remedies and the like.

Exposure, as described here, is completely under the person's control. This means the frequency of use, duration, nature and intensity of the images, as well as when and where the sessions are conducted. This not only facilitates treatment, but fosters greater self-esteem.

The treatment for anxiety described in Chapters Four and Five can be used to treat the anxiety component of guilt.

When people realize that it is not necessary to reveal their guilt to others in order to recover, they are often much more receptive to the process.

THE ANGER IN GUILT

As described earlier, the role of anger in our emotional armory is to goad one to correct injustices. This has enormous social as well as personal value. But when applied to guilt, it often directs the person to punish themselves, as noted above, as their guilt attests that they did something they consider wrong, which adversely impacted others. Therefore, relieving their guilt may undo the self-punishing process that they feel they justly deserve. Often, people must examine their anger to determine whether it is in fact justified, whether it has played a constructive role in their life, and how it has affected others, including those who were the original object of their misdeeds. There are more constructive ways to handle feelings of anger towards oneself than self-sabotage. Moreover, when examined in terms of its effect on others, there are usually more realistic, useful, and effective alternatives, such as somehow compensating those who were harmed—overtly or indirectly, or even anonymously. Or by committing oneself to counterbalancing your guilt with good deeds.

The law and religious principles prescribe remedies for those who are guilt-ridden that may serve as guidelines. The treatments recommended elsewhere in this book for anger can be applied to this component of guilt.

THE DEPRESSION OF GUILT

Guilt generally engenders a diminished view of oneself, which constitutes a loss, which in turn may well trigger a depressive reaction.

Depression may well suit a person who suffers from guilt. Since it acts as a form of self-punishment, it may be consistent with their view that they are not entitled to be happy. And by encouraging passivity, depression is compatible with their perception that there is no way to undo their guilt.

The treatments for depression outlined in Chapters Ten and Eleven can be used for the depressive component of guilt.

> The understanding of how each component of guilt works separately and in combination with the others may be helpful not only for those who treat themselves, but also for those who seek professional treatment, as it will enable them to better assist in the process.

A FEW KEY FACTS ABOUT OUR MENTAL MAKEUP

Here I'd like to explain some very basic things about that awesome assemblage known as the human psyche, things that influence just about every topic in this book. This discussion is admittedly a rather basic overview of the mental processes that underlie our thoughts and emotional responses, how our mind, brain, and circumstances interact to produce our thoughts and feelings.

MIND VERSUS BRAIN

First, the mind is only part of the brain. Psychologists think of the mind as the intellectually based portion of the brain, and the rest of the brain as the part that regulates all of our organs and activities of life and is in control of all of our emotions. In order to live comfortably with your thoughts and feelings, you must be aware of both the mind and the rest of the brain.

In evolution the brain started off in single-cell creatures, and moved up to insects and higher animals, becoming more complex as it evolved.

The human brain relies heavily on past experiences, and when it hits a novel situation, it may have no clue how to deal with it. So as evolution progressed the brain eventually realized it needed to have a tool for problem areas: a mind.

A somewhat simplistic distinction between the mind and brain is that the mind is the intellect and anything related to reasoning; the brain is emotional. When it encounters something the brain brings up the past history of that thing or situation; the mind makes a more analytical analysis. Then the two assessments are put together to reach a conclusion.

The brain is extremely powerful, and has many strong tools at its discretion, such as our predispositions. It also controls our emotions, and is where our basic mental programming is. The mind, on the other hand, for the most part has only logic and objective analysis in its quiver.

Scientists over the years have been able to determine that both intellectual and emotional processes are at work in our heads at almost all times and that it is not possible to completely separate the two. They are designed to work together in tandem, and often do that so seamlessly that we don't distinguish one from the other. This is often a complex interplay and the question as to how a given issue will be resolved is often unclear.

Intellectual people like to use the mind all the time, and are skeptical of the brain, disparage it. But the associations formed by the brain (see following) are more powerful than thinking. Some don't take the brain seriously, but ultimately the brain is stronger than the mind, like a battleship versus a PT boat. This is because the brain controls emotions, the underlying force in many of the mental problems discussed in this volume.

Certain types of people, such as those with the independent trait, are very inclined to go with their minds. They are usually convinced that most decisions should be made logically. When friends come to them and ask how to deal with a situation, they invariably go into some kind of logical analysis.

On the other hand, very anxious or depressed people are more inclined to go with their emotions, what some people call their "gut." They make the decision that will create the least intense emotional reaction. Especially when their emotions are stretched and intensified, as they are likely to be during a major crisis or dilemma, this can cause them to go for the answer that gives the most relief. This usually means staying with the cautious play.

THE POWER OF ASSOCIATION

The emotional part of our mental equipment, what we are calling the brain here, is strongly affected by associations.

Many of you may be familiar with the experiment that Pavlov conducted in the early 1900s. Simply put, he harnessed dogs so that they had to stand still. He then rang a bell and quickly showed the dogs a tempting piece of meat. At first, the dogs did not respond to the bell and only salivated when they saw the food. But after a number of repetitions of this process—the bell followed by the introduction of meat—the dogs started to salivate as soon as they heard the bell. At the start, only the sight of the food had the ability to make the dogs salivate, but after a while the bell acquired that ability. Intellectually, the food made the dogs salivate because they knew they were going to eat. The mind had learned from experience—cause and effect—that food was good and pleasurable to eat. However the brain soon learned that the bell was associated with the food, and the dogs acted accordingly.

For another quick example of the power of association, imagine that you are taking a car ride into the country on a sunny day. The sun is bright, and a hot breeze blows in your open window as you slowly motor down a back road with a friend. Suddenly your car is run off the road by another vehicle. You end up in the hospital for six months with serious injuries and scars.

The accident really had nothing to do with these things, but emotionally you associate it with hot, sunny days, and the countryside. Suddenly you are more comfortable driving in heavy traffic in the city, than on quiet country roads. You may also find that you are reluctant to go driving with that friend, since you associate him, too, with the tragedy. There is no logical link, but a powerful association.

The associations formed by the brain are based on temporal proximity (how close two occurrences are to each other in time), not necessarily real cause and effect, or logical association.

> Our brain and our mind are essentially different things. The interplay between the mind and brain generates a lot of our traits, emotions, and psychological reactions.
>
> In this book you have seen how these two parts of our mental makeup function in different situations and circumstances. This should give you a sense of the complexity of how the brain and mind work together to make decisions, how they deal with problems and challenges, and how this interaction contributes to some of the mental problems people experience.

NORMAL MENTAL PROCESSING

Another thing worth mentioning here is how our mind and brain control and orchestrate our thinking.

Our mind is continually processing our experiences and regulating our behavior. Under the best of circumstances, our mind works efficiently and effectively, prioritizing our experiences and concerns, and keeping track of important information while dispelling irrelevant and inconsequential matters. Experiences relevant to our survival normally are given the highest priority, while peripheral concerns are either overlooked or stored for less pressing moments. For example the hiss of an air conditioner is generally ignored, while the hiss of a snake grabs our attention. We quickly forget unimportant details of a story, but keep track of the main events and the lessons to be learned from them.

Our mind prioritizes each of our concerns—health, finances, job security, relationships, etc. Our attention is then drawn to the matter with the highest priority at the moment—say a problem with a new relationship. As our attention is focused on this matter three processes affect its vitality: first, our interest in the issue gradually subsides as fatigue sets in; second, the emotional importance of the issue is progressively reduced by repeated attention. For example, as we think about an unpleasant encounter that we may have had with a new romantic interest, the emotional intensity of our response—perhaps anger—gradually subsides. We also become less sensitive to or threatened by the matter. After a while, the two processes in combination reduce the overall emotional charge associated with the issue sufficiently that our second highest concern now commands our attention. The process continues as our mind moves from our top priorities to progressively lower ones.

In the process, the fatigue associated with the issues we are no longer attending to gradually subsides, allowing those concerns to regain their priority. In this manner, our attention gradually shifts among our concerns until more important matters replace them.

In the process of repeatedly focusing on our concerns, we noted that their priority and thus their ability to command our attention gradually dissipates. The third process at work here has to do with our memory of the material. Repeatedly focusing on material causes it to be transferred from our short-term memory to our long-term bank, where it is essentially stored permanently. How many repetitions are required for this transition varies with the issue. If you repeatedly recall your PIN number it will eventually go into long-term storage, whereas if you simply memorize a temporarily important phone number by repeating it several times, it will remain for a while in short-term storage and then be discarded. Thus, while repetition causes us to permanently store (remember) information, the emotional intensity of the material, which is determined by its relevance to our survival, determines how much attention we pay to it.

The mind prioritizes thoughts by assigning them an emotional charge—ultimately expressed in chemical electrical units. The higher the charge, the more likely our attention will be drawn to a thought. We can also self-direct our attention, as, for example, when we read, watch television, converse, or engage in other activities. And when we think about something, we normally only do so for a certain amount of time, before we exhaust the subject (or our interest in it) and our mind moves on to other things.

Sometimes an issue, such as the death of a loved one, is so emotionally intense—in this case painful—that we refuse to focus on it. This acts to preserve its emotional intensity. If one were to constantly divert their attention from a very painful recollection, its emotional intensity could conceivably last indefinitely. In reality, we almost always pay at least some attention to these issues so that they inevitably recede over a long period of time.

Some people—such as those who insist on maintaining a positive outlook—refuse to process negative experiences or possibilities. This form of avoidance similarly acts to preserve the very thoughts they refuse to attend to.

Intellectualizing, or attempting to process emotional experiences intellectually, is another way of avoiding unpleasant experiences. This is seen in people who attempt to rationalize away the pain of grief ("it was for the best") or hardships ("it's an ill wind that blows no good, and every cloud has a silver lining").

Our normal sequence of mental processing as described above is at the heart of the healing techniques of desensitization and Exposure Therapy discussed in this volume.

A WORD ABOUT THE STATE OF PSYCHOLOGICAL RESEARCH

In the late fifties and early sixties there was a dramatic shift in the treatment of anxiety and to a lesser extent the treatment of depression as well.

Until then, the dominant theories assumed that abnormal anxiety—that is, anxiety that was triggered by seemingly irrational fears such as the fear of leaving home for any reason, fear of heights, or fear of harmless animals such as small dogs and cats—had to be based on some unconscious event, which presumably stemmed from fearful experiences that occurred early in a person's life, say their first few years. Treatment was often based on Freud's theories. Therapists tried to unearth these fears as a means of allowing the individual to see that they were based on events that may have appeared dangerous at the time, such as toilet training. Looking at these fears as an adult, they could realize that they were now unrealistic and irrational.

Around this time scientists began to experiment with desensitization—exposure to a person's fears in actuality or imagery in the supportive presence of a therapist. The success of these methods, at first challenged by the establishment, ultimately gained acceptance by the late seventies and they are now the treatment of choice for the treatment of anxiety. I was in my doctoral program in psychology at the time and published a study as well as a theoretical paper on desensitization. Psychologists had much less success with this treatment with depression. While it seemed to work with grief, it was not obvious how to transfer this to other types of depression.

We are now beginning to have a much better understanding of the nature and course of depression, and we are also beginning to understand how to influence that course. We certainly can do this to a fair degree with the depression involved in grief. And since the grief reaction is so characteristic of depression, we may be on the verge of being able to do this with other types of depression as well.

IS THERE AN OVERALL ANSWER?

Most people who are exposed to psychology end up thinking that there is a global explanation for how we act and think. Freud thought that this was how we dealt with sexual issues involving our parents. Alfred Adler felt it had more to do with our need to win, and to some extent our need for security and power. Harry Stack Sullivan thought the key was our need for interpersonal relationships, and how we dealt with them.

Others, too, are constantly making statements about how people react and go about doing things, why they do the things they do—coming up with psychological explanations.

The brain is very, very complex, so the idea of having a global theory that will give you a means of arriving at an answer for human behavior in any given situation or set of circumstances is unrealistic. A great deal of the brain is developed based on our experiences and circumstances. The brain has separate sections that deal with this, and separate sections that deal with that. It's so compartmentalized that it's almost impossible to come up with one theory that will cover and explain everything. For this reason, psychology has moved away from global theories.

What it attempts to do now is find answers for specific problems, unearth these things more stone by stone rather than by trying to find a Rosetta stone that gives the key to the whole thing. Studies in psychology have examined things such as why some people assert themselves easily, and others have difficulty asserting themselves, and so on.

In this book I have described many of the major stones that have been uncovered and examined to date, to give you the background and knowhow to help you solve psychological problems that come your way, and help you make the decisions in every area of your life that are best for you.

REFERENCES

https://adaa.org/sites/default/files/Damann%205-day%20handout%20patient%20
materials.pdf, pages 7-8.

Ballenger, James C., Davidson, Jonathan, J.R.T. et al. Consensus Statement on
Posttraumatic Stress Disorder From the International Consensus Group on
Depression and Anxiety. *The Journal of Clinical Psychiatry, 61 (Supp. 5)*, 60-65.

Deffenbacher, Jerry L., Suinn, Richard M. *The Counseling Psychologist* 1/1988; Vol. 16,
1: pp 9-30.

Foa, Edna, Maclean, Carmen. The Case of OCD and PTSD. *Annual Review of
Clinical Psychology, Vol. 12*, 2016, 1-28.

Franklin, Martin E., Kratza, Hilary E. et al. Cognitive-Behavioral Therapy for
Pediatric Obsessive-Compulsive Disorder: Empirical Review and Clinical
Recommendations. *Psychiatry Research, Vol. 227* (1) May 30, 2015, 78-92.

Jayasinghe, Nimali, Finklestein, Fox, et al. Systematic Review of the Clinical
Application of Exposure Techniques to Community Dwelling Older Adults
with Anxiety. *Clinical Gerontologist: The Journal of Aging and Mental Health, Vol.
40* (30), May 2017, 141-158.

Kaczkurkin, Antonia, Foa, Edna B. Cognitive-Behavioral Therapy for Anxiety
Disorders: An Update on the Empirical Evidence. *Dialogues in Clinical
Neuroscience*, 2015, Sep; 17 (3), 337-346.

Kaplan, Johanna S., Tolen, David F. Exposure Therapy for Anxiety Disorders.
Psychiatric Times, Vol. 28 (9), Sept. 2011.

Legend, Adam B., Monica, S., McGuire et al. Cognitive Behavior Therapy for Obsessive-Compulsive and Related Disorders. *Psychiatric Clinics of North America, Vol. 37* (3), Sep. 2014, 415-445.

Muller, Katherine L., Schultz, Luke T. "Selling" Exposure Therapy. *Pragmatic Case Studies in Psychotherapy, Vol. 8,* 2012, 288-295.

Ougrini, Dennis. Efficacy of Exposure versus Cognitive Therapy in Anxiety Disorders: Systematic Review and Meta-Analysis. *BMC Psychiatry, Vol. 11,* Dec. 20, 2011, Article 200.

Milkman, Harvey B., Sunderwirth, Stanley G. *Pathways to Pleasure: The Consciousness and Chemistry of Optimal Living.* Lanham, MD: Lexington Books, 1993.

Peterman, Jeremy S., Read, Kendra L. et al. The Art of Exposure: Putting Science into Practice. *Cognitive and Behavioral Practice, Vol. 22* (3), Aug. 2015, 379-392.

Pitting, Andre, Van den Berg, Linda, Vervliet, Braun. *The Key Role of Extinction Learning in Anxiety Disorders: Behavioral Strategies to Enhance Exposure Based Treatment,* Rapid Science Publishers, 2016.

Rutt, Benjamin T., Oehlert, Mary, et al. Effectiveness of Cognitive Processing Therapy and Prolonged Exposure in the Department of Veterans Affairs. *Psychological Reports, Vol. 121* (2), Apr. 2018, 282-302.

Wilson, Terence G., Fear Reduction Methods and the Treatment of Anxiety Disorders. *Annual Review of Behavioral Therapy: Theory and Practice, Vol.10,* 1984, 87-122.

Wolitzky-Taylor, Kate B, Horowitz, Jonathon D. et al. Psychological Approaches in the Treatment of Specific Phobias: A Meta-Analysis. *Clinical Psychology Review, Vol. 28* (6), Jul. 2008, 1021-1037.

INDEX